I0766303

Cover design and illustrations by S Ferrar
ISBN: 9781694212719

From Amazon's Kindle Direct Publishing

Environmental consciousness is important to us. As a manufacture on-demand company, we produce units only as they're ordered, which reduces excess production. Our ink is chlorine-free, and our acid-free interior paper stock is supplied by a Forest Stewardship Council-certified provider. We currently offer a cream paper for black and white book interiors that is made from 30% post-consumer waste recycled material. We also maintain a commitment to recycling waste materials resulting from the printing process and from daily office operations, and we will continue to review our practices to ensure we are doing our part to protect the environment.

# Xafrica

## Cycles of Change

Volume 3

Sandy Dacombe Ferrar

# Introduction

Married to Science

Many years before Science and I became a working unit, I attended one of a plethora of conferences on communicating science—how to bridge the yawning chasm between communicators, who are generally enthusiastic, outgoing and somewhat dramatic, and scientists, who are reserved, cautious and exact. The key-note speaker, an eloquent French diplomat, claimed to have solved the problem by marrying a research scientist. As a self-employed single mother of two young men, I regarded it as a most unhelpful suggestion. Yet here we are.

Two weeks before the big day, Science fell into a pit-trap and lost his memory. As I drove him back the long uncertain route to Lilongwe and medical assistance, I pictured him responding to "Do you take this woman..." with a troubled "Who is she?"

That episode was the last story in Volume 2, and looking back along a vista of some twenty years, I see it as the moment I stopped being an enthusiastic Tourist of Life and recognised myself as an active participant. In short, I grew up at the age of 54. Stepping out of childlike wonder is a sad thing, though unavoidable and probably essential to a balanced life. Within months of our marriage 9/11 rocked the world, and regaining a sense of the goodness of life and the more dubious worth of man-un-kind was difficult. Is it better to be a disillusioned adult than a joyful child?

So this volume, the last in the series, is a collection of writings from November 2000 through to August 2003. They were taxing times, our health deteriorating and work increasing with less time to write; you will find quite a lot about our second year in Malawi, less about year three. There are just nine stories from our three-month camp in Zambia's Kafue National Park, ending, as all things do, with a new beginning.

# November, 2000

## Wonderful Wet
### 1st November

As October closed, the wet season began with a long night of gentle rain. The transformation is astounding. The parchment coloured lawn we have been watering for weeks to no effect is suddenly tinged with green; distant hills have emerged from a cocoon of smoke-laden air and every leaf on every tree looks new. The flame-trees have burst into a blaze of flower and the fragrance of frangipani makes the moist air sensuous.

Lilongwe is bursting with creature activity. The first of the square-marked toads hopped into the kitchen last night—a youngster, delicate-warted, blotched in biscuit and cream and chocolate, a golden-eyed charmer.

Wolf-spiders have been prowling the bedroom for the last few weeks, much to my dismay. Far more athletic than the dozy baboon spiders down south, these nimble creatures have legs as long as an Olympic athlete's—or so it seems to me—and just when you think you can drop a large-mouthed jam-jar over them they sprint off like an eight-legged Marion Jones. Naturally I apply Science to the problem, and he evicts them with only the minimum hilarity and chase.

We've had jerrymunglums too, solifuges, those bustling insects disguised as spiders, with heavy-weight feelers held out front to look like a fifth set of legs. They're pretty sprightly too, scuttling like radio-controlled toys gone wild, ricocheting from obstruction to obstruction, never slowing down or pausing for thought. Shudder-inducing stuff. They are impossible to catch, and a heavily wielded shoe is the only solution to their intrusion. The resultant splatter is really revolting, seeming twice as big as the living creature was, though that is probably enlarged by one's sense of guilt at blatant jerrymunglicide.

But the beauties have visited too. The mosquito-netting that encloses the veranda often confuses butterflies and moths long enough for me to identify them, and on Monday we found an oleander hawk-moth quietly waiting there. It's as long as my thumb and moss-green, the sculpted wings marbled like expensive paper in rose pink with a trace of cream. I don't think I've ever seen anything so beautiful. Butterflies are almost tawdry when compared to the subtle elegance of moths.

And yesterday Violence brought me a little yellow-bellied sunbird. He had collided with the dining room window, and when she went to investigate the small thud, she found him lying dazed outside. I took the tiny creature from her, a quivering bundle of shimmering feathers scarcely bigger than the moth! His thread-like tongue protruded from the little upholstery-needle of his beak. As I turned him over he struggled and nearly escaped, being so small I could almost not close my hand tight enough to hold him without fear of damage. I took him straight outside and before my fingers were fully open he shot away like an enamelled bullet. My pleasure in his fitness outweighed my disappointment at not getting a really good look at his finery close up.

As for Violence, she is standing in for Floret, who is away on maternity leave. Of course they are actually Violet and Florence, our house-maids, but Science will tinker with words, and sometimes the results are too good to waste.

So, the rains have come, Malawi is going green as we watch. Dry fields are transformed to rich earth rows awaiting sprouting food crops, and the sky has lost some of its haze. The air is considerably cooler, and my eyes don't smart as much. The love affair with Africa never palls. Just when you think you've had about enough, the land does something extraordinary, like a hawk-moth or a sunbird, and you're a slave once more.

## Married to Science
### 6th November

One of the questions uppermost in a prospective bride's mind is the problem of the wedding dress. Somehow, having a second shot at being a bride doesn't make it any easier. So I did what I usually do, and referred the problem of what colour to wear to Science. Almost immediately the answer came back and took my breath away.

"Either sunset-on-sandstone or dawn-on-a-dove's-wing," he said. He may be colour blind, but he certainly has Technicolor language. I hadn't heard anything as romantic since the time he invited me to "find out if we can fart in unison." I went with the sunset option, and we chose the time and a venue to match.

The sky was wrapped in cotton-wool clouds, and greying towards evening. A single slash of salmon and gold tinged the west as we set our faces northwards towards the banks of the Lilongwe River. The dry-season veldt, blackened by late fires, breathed a scent of hot earth and sour ash, a counterpoint to the rich rose and green of new brachystegia foliage. Perhaps it would rain.

At the spot we'd chosen the winter grass was still tall and golden, and pale river sand sloped gently beneath tall trees, *Acacia albida*, the stately giants which grace the Zambezi Valley, and the moepel or red milkwood[1], whose deep green glossy leaves shade the temple enclosure of Great Zimbabwe. Behind their dark trunks the river sparkled and gossiped.

The service was a little unconventional. A Roman Catholic choir, the Poor Clares' wedding gift to us, singing in Chichewa and thumping lyrical drums led us down to the congregation seated on hay-bales under a listing apple-ring acacia. Below a tattered hamerkop nest, the Baptist Minister (who was mildly shocked at there being only one ring) startled us both by reading the vows from the Anglican prayer book. Science had specifically said he would rather we did without them, and I hadn't mentioned it to the minister as I felt confident that he would use a Baptist liturgy. There was a pregnant pause while Science studied the minister carefully. The hush seemed endless before he provided the increasingly unexpected conventional response. Heuglin's robin, Kurrichane thrush, several unidentified crickets and a cicada provided cheerful comment, and the bride wept with joy and relief.

The choir, having lead us out again with much drumming, rattling and ululating, ignored the waiting bus and piled into the bar. By the time they were pried away half an hour later, we had to send home for the emergency crates of beer.

The caterers had a fairly torrid time. A wedding in the bush presents some interesting challenges, none insurmountable given a well-equipped kitchen relatively nearby. However their electricity supply was cut off without warning early that morning, and even the water supply failed, since their pump is electric. All the same they produced a well-rounded meal of spit-roasted lamb, and even the elegance of individual strawberry Pavlovas (specially ordered to honour a visiting quasi-Aussie) as a finale. The rain stayed away, ditto the mosquitos, and to our

---

[1] *Mimusops zeyheri*

surprise we didn't run out of booze and no-one fell down the pit-loo, not even Science.

Once the soul-shaking solemnity is over, there is something charmingly lunatic about a wedding. No other animal makes a ritual of pairing in this way, not even those that are reputed to mate for life. True, the bower-bird builds an elaborate structure for his mate, but that's more of a come-on than a consolation, and it's not a social event. Perhaps that's the key. Perhaps it has less to do with the mutual sharing of promises and ideals, but more with the message sent to the social group, "This is a working unit, do not interfere"? I don't know.

Luckily, understanding the underlying reason isn't essential to enjoying the lunacy, and this public act of private union has had the effect of deepening our bond to the wider local society.

For Science and me—both far from home and families—it was as good as it could be. Leaving last, we wandered hand-in-hand up the path beside the river. Candles in brown-paper sand-bags dotted the way, each glowing like miniature doorways in the velvet dark. How blessed we are to live in Africa, and how much more to have found each other.

By the time Science and I returned from a great-family-honeymoon-for-ten, I found that ripples of chatter had given our marriage something of the flavour of a gala event.

For the expat population of Lilongwe it was a deliciously different African experience; for the Malawians it was another hilarious example of the *wazungu* going out of their way to do everything at once—an ecumenical potpourri and solemn picnic, but whaah! What a party!

## Liwonde Luxury
### 13<sup>th</sup> November

What an amazing week has just sped past. Last week at this time we were arriving in Mvuu Lodge—a luxury too larney for us, usually. This was a gift from the manager on the occasion of cementing a permanent commitment between Science and Wordsmithery. It's the sort of place we'd love to become accustomed to, the best of both worlds—ample comfort and bush-bliss.

The luxury I expected. The sheer theatre of wildlife doing remarkable things was an absolute thrill—all the more so for being unexpected. One of the joys was seeing a herd of about thirty elephant frolicking ponderously in the shallows of the River Shire. The river alone is worthy of admiration, broad and strong-flowing, with picturesque backdrops of palms and fever trees and blue mountains. A frieze of elephants in the foreground, slate-grey and water-slick, white tusks and white egrets accentuating the majesty, makes the scene heart-tuggingly lovely. The little ones rolled and splashed, the big ones slurped and slung mud, and the in-betweens wallowed and exuded such a sense of luxurious enjoyment that being an elephant in Liwonde National Park seems like a nice option for the next life—if you believe in that sort of thing.

Our water-safari/boat-game-viewing trip was idyllic, crowned by a herd of nearly sixty sable antelope. Many of them were youngsters, all rich chocolate brown like the females, with the velvet back males in the minority, as they should be. The entire park seemed alive with youngsters: baby impala, all fragile legs and daisy-petal ears; five tiny warthogs as charming as stuffed toys and playful as kittens; miniature hippo, each a tiny replica of its matriarchal blimp. Baby baboons like wizened old men, and two swallow chicks like a pair of china salt-cellars on the mud rim of their nest.

Everything is burgeoning; the smooth sodic sand beneath euphorbia and impala-lily clumps is sifted with a fine haze of new grass, and the elephant-grey mopane trees are veiled in a mist of tiny butterfly leaves. Fragrances compete with the scent of new rain: Acacias advertise their little puff-ball flowers, the 'fried-egg' flower[2] smells like gardenias and the star jasmine didn't get its name for nothing. And then there are the birds!

A brief but momentous thrill was seeing Pel's fishing owl. We had been told where to look for it, and four of us went crashing through the unavoidably noisy underbrush of a borassus palm forest. Naturally I looked for the tubby bundle of orange feathers on low-slung branches near the water, because that where they always sit when photographers take photos of them. Sarah, British born, gently bred and meticulously urban, had no pre-conceptions and consequently found the elusive bird sitting at the top of a palm tree. By the time I'd blundered over to peer up at it, it had flown away. I was not even vaguely amused.

But Science guided us unerringly to the owl's new perch, the topmost branches of a very tall acacia. It glared down at us balefully while we shuffled round with aching necks trying to get a good view of it. We didn't see it very well, but it was clearly obvious to a passing Dickinson's kestrel who expressed his disfavour with a series of dive-bombs. The owl hunched his broad shoulders and sulked, but stayed put. It was a pretty poor view, but it WAS a view, and I forgave Sarah entirely.

Just to end the week-end on a once-in-a-life-time note, we found a cane rat calmly chomping grass-shoots outside our open-air bathroom. I'd never seen one before, and Science had only seen them at night, but here it was in broad daylight doing what cane rats do best. I had no idea they are so large—like a gigantic hamster, or an agouti. I know it's a rat, but it seems unkind to burden it with such

---

[2] *Oncoba spinosa*, also called the Snuff-box tree.

an unlovely name. Porcupines are really rats too—but their name is far more romantic. Why can't a cane rat be an African tailless land-beaver, or a buff-coloured shrub-grubber? Then people wouldn't look at us oddly when we explain that we're late because we've been watching the rare and remarkable under-story shoot-nibbler. [3] Drum up enthusiasm for a cane rat? Are you daft?

We left early Monday morning, but the magic followed us. We went on to the Shire Highlands, to Thyolo, where tea plantations lie like a sensuous garment on the undulating flanks of the hills. Don't for a moment imagine the year is winding down—in the Warm Heart it's revving up!

## Mvuu
### 17th November

Where the Shire River flows out of Lake Malawi and through the smaller Lake Malombe, is Liwonde National Park—an area of fertile flood plain, lowland evergreen thicket, fever-tree forests, and tall mopane woodlands hung with python vines and starred with impala lilies. Perched on a bank of the broad river is a privately run tourist camp called Mvuu. The name was an obvious choice, for in Chichewa mvuu is the name for hippo, and the Shire River is alive with them.

Hippos are perhaps the least charismatic of Africa's animals. Composed of rubberised bulges, they could have been designed—on a bad day—by the fellow who thought up the Michelin man. They are unlovely and unexciting. Especially if you do nothing more than stare from a distance. They are water-wallowing, grass eating, hollow-honking tubs of lard with piggy eyes and huge tusks, and

---

[3] In Ghana they are known as Grasscutters. It's still not graphic enough for *Thryonomys*, it sound sadly domestic.

the only interest seems in trying to decide if they are grey or purplish-pink.

They become infinitely more exciting when you are in a position of not wanting to interact with them, either on water or on land. Then you suddenly become aware of how huge they are, and how much of a closed book. It's impossible to tell, looking at an uncomfortably close hippo, if he or she is alarmed, surprised, excited, startled, or amused by your proximity. The last is doubtful. It's also impossible to tell what it plans to do next. Which is why it helps to have a plan or two of your own to implement.

Hippos are widely touted as being the continent's worst killers. It is said that more people are killed by hippo in one year than by any other animal, including snakes. Yet I have never seen any figures to substantiate this claim, nor heard of any research programme to monitor it. That doesn't mean it's not true, since most deaths at the hands— um, teeth—of a hippo will probably happen in remote rural villages where the tragedy may be great, but the recording skills may not. Certainly there are fewer survivors of hippo attacks than there are of crocodile or shark attacks.

I found hippos suddenly very interesting indeed when I glanced up from my painting and saw one jogging my way at an easy trot. Utterly soundless! After the first timeless moment while I recognised this illogical fact—that this ton of outsized bath-toy was moving swiftly over leaf-littered and twig-bestrewn baked African earth without a single noise—came a second breathless moment when I realised that if I didn't move, the hippo would pass within spitting distance of me. And I don't spit very far.

A number of negatives became apparent. I have no idea of the relative merits of hippo eyesight. I could not tell if the hippo knew I was there. I didn't know if it planned to go past me, round me or over me. And, more importantly, I didn't have a contingency plan. This was not a good time to think one up.

On the positive side, I was not between the hippo and the water, which I'm told is usually fatal. Also, hippos are not noted for their tree climbing skills. Neither am I, but this was no time to examine that too closely. So, as the hippo passed a bush and I was momentarily eclipsed by foliage, I leaped to my feet and scrambled round the back of the nearest climbable object, a stout sterculia tree.

Straining my ears for some trace of a sound through the roar of adrenalin, I quaked behind the smooth pale trunk of the sterculia. Nothing. An eternal silence. Nervously I peered around the trunk, to see a vast purplish rump vanishing through distant shrubbery in undignified but still silent haste. It seems that the hippo had not known I was there until I sprang up and gave it as big a scare as it had given me. Well, maybe not quite; there's a lot less of me to be scared of.

So, when some hours later a pair of hippos came barrelling up a hippo-path from the river, I was considerably calmer. It still took me a good half hour to retrieve my scattered pastels and resurrect my easel, even though I knew they were horrified to find me there.

It really is a sensible thing to have a plan or two in mind when you're alone in the bush, especially when you think you don't need one anymore. And if you imagine I was being unnecessarily fool-hardy spending the day alone sketching in the bush, I hasten to point out that the only other disturbance I had was the arrival of forty-two Seventh Day Adventists on a day trip from Blantyre. I found that more disconcerting than the hippos; at least the hippos went away quickly and didn't ask me questions.

## Email blues
### 22nd November

It's been a long week of nothing very much except computer problems. My machine has been gutted again, and re-stuffed with software, but it's still not behaving properly, and email is not the simple send-and-receive process it should be. So I'm slow getting this off. But writing seems to have been tough going too.

I find it interesting how some stories just write themselves, and others are hugely labour intensive. I've been wrestling with next week's story—and it should have come so easily and naturally. It details something we saw at Liwonde National Park, and it's one of those happenings that stays locked in your mind's eye for years—but it's very vividness makes it hard to translate into words.

But battle or not, it's such a pleasure going over my memories in this way, reliving an experience, sucking the marrow so-to-speak from events. Thinking back through that afternoon I remember the little jacana who was utterly unfazed by the drama unfolding in the water beside him, intent only on snatching up the odd water-bug uncovered by the surge and heave of crocodiles. And the squacco herons that haunt the grassed banks, making noises like rattling crockery. They arrived with a flap of white wings like egrets, gave a few conversational clatters and then the wings were folded away like a conjurer's handkerchief, and the birds vanished. Through binoculars I found them again, cryptically straw coloured, striped and flecked in camouflage. They stood with necks stretched to look ahead, or bunched down while they assumed a cloak-and-dagger conspiratorial gait, freezing periodically, black-tipped beaks fierce as acacia thorns, avian members of the Assassin's Guild.

Across the bank of the little estuary, or lagoon as they call it at Mvuu Wilderness Lodge, a couple of somnolent crocodiles lay in the sun. They seemed determined to be as near as possible to this sandy depression above the water, and Science thinks it's a nesting site. We hoped hatching would happen while we were there, but we had excitement enough without that.

A waterbuck grazed peacefully beside one recumbent croc, no doubt well aware that the croc poses little threat on dry land. Further into the trees, bushbuck as foxy-red as fallen mopane leaves waggled white tails as they browsed silently under the borassus palms. Yes, it's a beautiful place, Liwonde, even when nothing much is happening, and almost impossible to cram into prose when the unexpected explodes in front of your eyes. But I'm working on it.

Meanwhile all around the capital of Lilongwe the landscape is "plotted and pieced" as Hopkins says, a patchwork in sepia and van Dyk brown as the fields lie open to the slow rain and wait for seeds to yawn and stretch. Summer is here—the frangipanis, for so long domes of stark branches decked with terminal posies of blossoms, are suddenly dense with dark glossy leaves while the blossoms fade and fall. The garden is awash with calls of coucals, cuckoos and tropical boubou. The peak and trill of woodland kingfishers starts with dawn, and the unlikely noises of the drongos. Science says they sound like malfunctioning electronic black-birds. The drongos have assumed a new possessive air around the garden and I think they're nesting in one of our trees, but I can't find where.

The blue-headed tree agamas are flourishing fatly. I saw one chasing a little blue wax-bill this afternoon, all along the top of the garden wall. The fiercely bobbing head seemed to state "Push off! These are MY ants!"

It's heading for 10 pm now, and the cheerful froggy conversation in the dambo below the house bodes well for more rain. I think I'll take a book and retire for the night.

## Mvuu 2 - Crocodile picnic
### 24th November

Liwonde National Park is one of my favourite places. The park is just plain lovely to look at, and it has a staggering checklist of some 300 birds, some of them very rare—like Pel's fishing owl—and others, like the brown-breasted barbet and Lilian's lovebird, only found in this small part of Malawi.

Liwonde, like most of Malawi's embattled wildlife areas, lacks both abundance and variety of game. But don't for a moment think this makes it a poor place to visit. You won't see lion or cheetah or wild dog, but that doesn't mean you'll have a boring time. And don't always believe that nothing happens at the hottest time of the day.

Tent number five at Mvuu Camp's private Wilderness Lodge is set above an s-bend of a well-incised channel filled with water hyacinth. This grassed-over declivity is a lagoon from the Shire River, and though it seems hardly more than a lush swamp, patches of open water gleam between the pretty lilac blossoms. If you watch closely you may see a clump of blossom moving steadily down the channel.

We sat on the little balcony after lunch, just a brief pause before an afternoon snooze, as a mark of respect to the designer who managed to place these five thatch-sheltered tents well out of view of each other. Enjoying the feeling of being utterly alone with this serene view, we saw a clump of hyacinth on the move. I did not remark its passage down-river, but it startled me a little by coming back the other way.

"Crocodile," said Science succinctly.

Once told, of course I could see the double bump of nostrils, and further back the wider-set double bump of eyes, streaming with barely a ripple back up the channel. A battle-plated submarine, shoving waterweed.

A few seconds later we noticed a second smaller croc coming to meet it, nose to nose. We watched with interest. There appeared to be a bit of nuzzling going on, a nudging and playful resting of the smaller snout on the still submerged larger one. Mating behaviour? I hoped so, I'd heard of the delicate shimmering belly-dance crocs do, and was longing to see it.

But this was no time for romance. A third croc came up the channel, moving quite fast, and also drew in nose to nose. The jostling grew more intense, and suddenly we saw a churn of muddy water and a flash of white belly plates as a crocodile spun.

"They're feeding," murmured Science with interest.

Here the big croc broke away and lifted its head a little from the water. We glimpsed something pinkly-purple, a smooth bulge of something big in the jagged gin-trap of a mouth, but the mat of hyacinth obscured it as the big croc sank to swim below water, heading upstream. A

growing entourage of three or four crocs followed, and we could see two more coming down-stream to join in the feast.

They met in a tangle of water flowers, and there followed an astounding reptilian feeding frenzy. The first croc, the largest, raised its head clear of the water and at last we could see what it had caught. A new-born hippo. Clamped tightly in the grinning jaws was a little head the size of a football. With a powerful flick of the neck, the croc swung its captive in a whip-lash onto the bank. Still clamped in the jaws, the baobab-coloured body arched through the air and smacked into the mud.

Again the armour-plated body heaved in the water and convulsed, and the little corpse slammed against the bank. The channel seethed with crocs, each snapping at the rubbery carcase and churning up the water with a flashing spin, flinging mud and weeds and water in a hissing arc. At times we could see as many as four pale bellies spinning like turbines, while still more crocs, olive and grey and mud-brown, just hung on. Once in a while a long snout would point upwards and a few convulsive snapping swallows would proclaim success. Then the weeds would just heave gently for a few minutes before another explosive thrashing of tails and twisting bodies.

The flicking action of the main croc was repeated seven or eight times, interspersed with a froth of churning and twisting as the other crocs tore off chunks. Each time the sad little body arched through the air it was a bit more ragged, but there was an awful lot of effort going into very little result as far as we could see. Life is not simple when you don't have a knife.

We think the big croc was trying to shake the head loose, but hippo hide—as every good Afrikaner knows— is the strongest in the world. We sat, eyes glued to binoculars, elbows propped on the balcony railing, shoulders and backs aching from the unaccustomed stillness and tension, and watched with mingled horror and fascination. The feast involved at least eight crocs and, from its slow and quiet beginning to the time the main owner of the meal made off upstream with the remains of its hippo-lunch, must have taken an hour and a half.

As we contemplated a complaint to the Lodge Manager for this example of bad timing—peak game-viewing when we wanted to quietly digest our lunch in the heat of the day—we wondered about the misfortune that accompanies success. It was clear that the only croc that got nothing down its throat was the successful hunter itself. Its mouth was so full of hippo, it had no chance to feed.

We saw a similar thing happen to a hamerkop a few days later. The bird had killed a pair of mating frogs, but even the smaller male was too big to be swallowed. We watched for fifteen minutes as the bird thumped the rubbery meal into the mud again and again, to tear off a bit or maybe to break the bones and make it swallowable. At last, disturbed by someone's approach, the bird stuffed the poor pulped frog half-way down its gullet and flew off a few feet. There he spat it out and gazed at it in apparent despair. Who would have thought that one can be too successful!

## Gorgeous Grey Skies
### 26th November

It's one of those wonderful grey days where the sun has decided not to get up this morning, but to loll in bed instead. Empathy demands that we do the same. However that would be a waste, since this is a glorious break from the heat. I once heard a South African use a most descriptive phrase, she said, "It's so hot the children's milk teeth are melting." It has certainly felt like that the last few weeks.

So this cool grey weather is very welcome. The world is looking vibrantly green and glowing under the slate-blue clouds, and the flying ants find it irresistible. Even the black ants below the veranda are sending out winged cohorts, much to the glee of the blue-headed tree agamas who patrol the area. I think there are at least three, judging by size. We've actually seen one change colour, from cryptic brown and grey to pointillist purple, orange, yellow and azure. Beautiful. This morning there was one below the nearest tree looking fat enough to burst, stuffed to the eyebrows with ants.

The Kurrichane thrush is doing well on them too. While scouting about looking for its nest we found the chick instead, a little teddy-bear of a bird with a startled look on its face. Science addressed him politely.

"Hello, little fellow with your Victorian mutton-chop whiskers and John Bull waistcoat covered in insect gravy stains, where's your home then?"

The youngster looked embarrassed and ignored him. I sympathise; this is hardly the sort of address you would expect from a scientist.

And the drongos have shown us up, too. I knew they had a nest somewhere, but it was most unfair of them to put it virtually within view of our breakfast table without actually telling us. It's been there for so long that the nest is almost empty again. Almost, but not quite. It has three

young drongos just about to take the feathered plunge. This morning they were standing on the rim of the nest, scruffy fledgling feathers all fluffed out and yellow gapes pouted and sulky looking. It must be most uncomfortable having to sit in a rain-soaked nest all day.

We're off to Salima tomorrow, and will spend the week-end looking at the problems facing the Maleri Isles in Lake Malawi, both ecological and tourist-related. Or at least Science will; I'll tag along as observer and appreciative audience.

I'm still wrestling with the bit about the tea-plantation up near Mulanje, it is most reluctant to be written. So the next story relives a brief stay we had at a beach house near Monkey Bay, a wonderfully romantic spot.

## Lake Shore Beach House
### 28th November

Lake Malawi laps to the pale beach in serried whispering ripples and reaches sea-green and wrinkled to the horizon. A pearl-grey sky hangs like an oyster shell over the distant hump-backed hills, whale blue and smudged with smoke of grass fires. At night the fires glow in the bowl of the hills like a volcano and turn the blue-on-blue scene primeval. In the full of the day the horizon vanishes into smoke haze, and the platinum lake blends exactly with the sky so that we swim suspended in a seamless bubble, or gaze from the shore into what seems a cycloramic stage set—*South Pacific*, no doubt, with those pointy hills rising from the water, and fringed with palm trees.

We paddled round the nearest outcrop of rock—a quintessential African koppie of tumbled boulders and elegant trees, baobab and sausage trees, acacia and cassia. Rocks spill into the water with the casual grace of a Japanese painting. Belly to the fibre-glass ski-board, I lay my face to the clear cool water and watched fish dancing and darting below me. The sting of sun behind my knees and on the back of my neck, and silky water on my arms and face, I hang between two worlds.

Fish shimmer and glide between the boulders—electric and powder blue, widow purple and snake-skin chequered, flashed with orange and shot with silver, a tossed handful of precious metal amulets, enamelled and set with stones. Science found a beautiful dead crab. Prussian blue and lilac, she was caught in an abandoned gill net, weighted with pebble-like baked-clay sinkers and floats of *Acacia nigrescens* knobs. Her tucked-under tail plate still held a myriad tiny corpses, each pale baby crab a ghostly copy of herself. Such a blend of beauty and horror, both the crab and the fine-mesh net.

Behind the tossed head of a coconut palm scores of dragonflies danced, face to the breeze. So many they could be classed as a swarm. When the wind picked up they were scattered but reformed again as it died back to a breeze, coasting along in the palm's wind-shadow. I would love to know what they were doing.

Monkeys, sweet-faced and indolent as fairies, lounged in the loops of lianas and watched us eat lunch. Looking as innocent as nuns and charming as children, they have lightning fast reactions and can leap through an opening door and escape with a few stolen bananas before the door has time to close.

One showed its disdain for Science by showering him with a delicate stream of golden urine. It missed him by a fine margin and, as my sister remarked, left him feeling particularly pissed off. Silent as they are in the trees, they are amazingly noisy on the roof. They seem to hurl their insignificant weight at the metal cladding with fierce delight. From inside, the sound effect is rather like a minor hail of tennis balls. "Not so," says my scientific advisor, "more like a minor cavalry charge through a scrap yard."

Lighter footed and less thieving are the small yellow squirrels that live in the huge sausage tree outside the lounge. Shyly they scuttle up and down the thick branches like miniature racers on a test track. For some reason they always seem to be in a hurry; a sudden dash and a tense watchful wait, and then another scurry. These are the little slender-tailed mopane or miombo squirrels, *Paraxerus cepapi*, which feed on marulas and sausage-tree fruit as well as the more traditional nuts. I'm told they will take birds eggs too,  though I've never seen a bird object to them, not even the ever-watchful drongos. For all their apparent shyness, these mostly silent little creatures can be surprisingly vocal. We were drawn outside by a loud insistent "Kwe kwe kwe kwe kwe!" and found two squirrels virtually nose to nose on a boulder beside the back door, hurling verbal insults at each other. Suddenly all shyness was gone, and they seemed almost oblivious of us, absorbed entirely in their staccato repartee.

The bouldered koppie that comes right down to the back of the house is a fragment of Lake Malawi National Park separated from the main body by fifteen to twenty kilometres. It's too far from the Park to be protected, and as the people-pressure increases, so the trees are slowly being whittled away. The approach to the beach house is a narrow road, running between the edge of this fragment of proclaimed reserve and the back of various corporate and private cottages, to this one, right at the end of the sweep of beach. Having never known the place before I can't judge how much tree-cover has been lost, but it's impossible not to notice the soil being taken from the Park. This must be the ultimate in poor-country poaching—stealing the soil from a National Park to make mud bricks.

# December 2000



The most notable happening this week has been the disappearance of the drongos[4]. We must have spotted the fledglings just in time, for it seems they launched themselves onto the unstable air and found it to their liking. It's not just the babies that went, the parents have been missing all week too. Science says the parents are probably taking a week at the lake now that they've got the brats off their hands. Whatever the reason, we've not seen hide nor hair of them—if one can use that term for birds—for a whole week. I miss their aerial ballet and electronic skritches and skreeks.

Of course, the drongo chicks may have spent all last week-end getting to know and trust their flying equipment. We missed that phase of their growing up by going to the lake ourselves, to look at the Maleri Islands. These are within the northernmost limit of the Lake Malawi National Park and are a matter of growing concern. Like most parks it's a problem of encroachment and degradation, and I'll tell you all about that particular blue and gold experience, but it's not going to happen this week as I have finally managed

---

[4] *Dicrurus adsimilis*

to extract the tea-plantation experience from my reluctant brain. It's sketchless though. Since my little lap-top threw a wobbly a week or so ago, I find my scanner won't talk to my printer and that's catastrophic, since the two are supposed to work in tandem. Ah, well. Perhaps they're skittish due to the mating season.

Meanwhile I've found a vital bit of information regarding life in the tropics. For some reason the insects are so much more determined this year than last. I have flies in my kitchen, ants on the veranda, a ravening hoard of cockroaches and a menagerie of millipedes, centipedes, and otherpedes right down to decipedes in their droves (and more of them later). It seems that this is entirely due to our ignorance of an African tradition of mulching the garden with tobacco scrap.

For those who have never seen it, tobacco scrap looks very like a bran breakfast cereal, little brown and gritty twigs with a squeezed-from-a-tube look. Our house had just had the garden mulched with this unpromising-looking layer before we moved in, and I decided that the scraggy appearance didn't warrant a repeat this year. Yes, the garden grew and the lawn thrived, but it would have anyway. Tobacco scrap was obviously used because Malawi grows a lot of tobacco and somebody's got to do something with the waste.

Of course I had forgotten that nicotine is a potent poison. Hence my insectivorous population explosion. This presents me with something of a moral dilemma. Like all reformed smokers, I can't wait for the tobacco industry to go extinct. Now I feel I have to review my attitude that smoking is an unpleasant, antisocial, suicidal activity, and tell all those remnant smokers out there to stick to their rights. Go for it, chaps, light up another, please don't give it up.

Can you imagine what it would cost to mulch an acre of garden if tobacco was grown purely as an insecticide, if scrap was the main product? My already emaciated purse flinches at the thought. And can you imagine the furore environmentalists would kick up about degradation of good agricultural land in the effort to grow this toxin? This is not currently much of an issue, since the tobacco industry is still vastly wealthy, but it will be as soon as the big money fades away.

Oops, I've just lost the juice. It's power-cut time of year. Once the rains start, the electricity supply becomes wildly erratic, and I'm deeply grateful that I can work on a lap-top supported by batteries, or I would no doubt have lost this whole letter as the juice ran out.

Yours in the effort to stay connected.


## Tea Break
### 4th December

I've always wondered about the Japanese tea ceremony. I would love to know if it really is ceremonial, or simply a tradition like English high tea which as far as I can tell is more like early supper. Where high tea smacks of the banal—boiled eggs and buttered bread—the Japanese ceremony has an atmosphere of contemplation and the soft accompaniment of rustling silk. Or so I suppose, having never witnessed either. Even without my exaggerated imaginings, they are dramatically un-alike. I think the remarkable difference between the two might be a function of geography. The Japanese were far more likely to see a tea plantation than most Englishmen. And once you've seen a tea plantation, it's impossible to think of tea in the same old way.

Hovering in the misty heat haze above Malawi's Shire River Valley is the Thyolo Escarpment. Compared to the heat of the valley, the higher ground is wonderfully cool. In fact, it's still pretty warm and with a tropical rainfall that keeps the earth moist, it is ideal tea-growing country.

The little centre of Tyolo is only 40 kilometres out of Blantyre in the Shire Highlands, but it feels like a different country. Here tea plantations, like emerald moss, cling to the contours of the red earth and skim the sensuous flanks of hills. Fringes of trees break the even sweep of green—a palisade of pines, the broad blaze of flat-crowned flame trees, the regular deep green of a line of Golden oak drawn like a gauze screen at the end of a field. Where the ground is too steep or too wet the natural bush has been left, a rich frieze of exuberant forest with palm trees, acacias, wild bananas and tree ferns in robust diversity. The surrounding manicured green monoculture lends this wildness an aura of horticulture, as if planned by some superb landscape architect.

The tea estates are so richly picturesque that one longs to be a painter—the even rows of bushes squared off like a quilted coverlet; the clear pure green of leaves against the raw clay roads sunken between the fields, each track neat as a street, glowing ochre-orange or glistening red. Here and there the smooth dome of a boulder breaks the surface of the tea bushes, and stands proud of the symmetry like a granite rock in a raked gravel garden.

The fields seem designed entirely as a setting for the human figure. A scattering of people moves slowly through the parallel rows, heads bent forward, bodies slanted against the counter-balance of the picking-sack yawning against each supple spine. Harvesting and pruning are synonymous, for as each bush is stripped of the topmost leaflets, so the height of the bush is determined; it makes those neatly trimmed rows of compact tea hedges a superb example of an inverted browse-line. The leaves are taken at a comfortable height for man—or woman—to reach, so the fields stay roughly the height of a table-top. How well the human figure shows above a table-top! The pickers move with dignity and grace and somehow one feels that they are not there for the sake of the tea. Oh no. The tea is there simply as a setting for them. Above them are Turner-esque skies full of majestic clouds: steam white, lilac and slate grey against Wedgewood and cobalt.

Satemwa Tea Estate is just one of many in the Shire Highlands, and like many others has a bungalow or two reserved for visitors. We drove through the rolling green swell of tea hedges, past neat sheds and stores, whitewashed and gleaming in the rich sunlight, past staff housing set in pretty little gardens and the main estate offices under a canopy of flame trees. Driving round tractors and trailers and past tarpaulined picking stations, we headed still farther uphill, glimpsing the roofs and chimneys of the tea drying sheds and packaging factory.

The road dips through a cloistered groin of wild forest, submarine green and tinkling with water, swings round above the bank of a farm dam, and enters a thick screen of stately old tees. Chiwane Bungalow sprawls graciously on a grassy knoll, surrounded by a rumbustious garden and shaded by huge trees. Beyond are wrap-around views of lush and falling land under tall skies, and Mount Mulanje a purple patch in the clouds.

The garden is an English country joy. I felt as if I was walking through the jig-saw puzzles we used to do as children—riots of flowers and butterflies dancing in the ornamental shrubbery. The whole place smells like England—the scent of moist earth and mushrooms. I sat in the cool blue shadows on the broad veranda and soaked in the view.

"Do you hear that?" said Science in the stillness. I listened carefully to the distant hiss of a breeze through leaves and the indistinct murmur of doves and coucals, and heard nothing at all.

"That," said my Scientific Advisor with satisfaction, "Is the sound of tea growing."

There is something very special about tea. It doesn't deserve to be ground to powder and put in convenient little bags. It is essentially a slow and graceful product of generous serenity and beauty. I bought a half pound of tea produced on the estate to bring home and savour as it deserves. I'll do that... as soon as I've invested in a proper fat-bellied tea pot... and a strainer...

In the meantime, how 'bout a swift mug of cha?

# The Silly Season
## 8th December

The festive season in Malawi is interesting. By the end of next week more than half the white population of Lilongwe will have gone away. They are never very evident anyway, so I wonder if the native Lilongweans will notice. And I wonder what the Malawian interpretation is of the term "a white Christmas"?

Great excitement in Lilongwe—a famous French artist is exhibiting his work here this week. Not only that, but he delivered a lecture on his theory of art. It's a problematic time of year for such an occasion, since so many people are away, and most of those remaining have other end-of-year functions to attend. So a scant handful of art-enthusiasts turned up for the lecture.

The moment I laid eyes on M. Jean Trousselle I knew he was really Father Christmas. The press photographs of him show a man who could be mistaken for an Indian mystic. The gentleman appearing in M. Trousselle's place was very decidedly Santa. It's impossible to hide those twinkling eyes. But I'll say this for him, he swotted up his stuff pretty well. I don't speak French, so I could only intuit what was being said while I waited for the English translation—just as one does in a movie with subtitles—and he was very convincing. It helps that M. Trousselle's thesis on 'Time as a perspective in art' is utterly fascinating, of course. It was one of those talks where you wish you had had the notes to swot up before-hand, so that you would understand enough to ask questions when they are called for. About the only thing I really wanted to ask was, "Could you say that again, a little more slowly, please?" In fact, thank goodness we had bite sized portions through the one-paragraph-at-a-time translator, or I wouldn't even have had a chance to discover how fascinating it was.

The works themselves were equally stimulating, and equally challenging. The art-starved of Lilongwe soaked it up like thirsty sponges. We soaked up the beer too, of course, supplied by courtesy of the French Embassy. A wonderful evening, all in all. And for my Zambian readers, you'll be pleased to hear Fr. Christmmmm...ah.... M. Trousselle is exhibiting next in Lusaka.

The question you'll be asking is WHY should Santa assume the disguise of an international artist? Well, the answer is obvious when you look at him. The poor lad is on crutches! (And I thought that e-mail I got with a photo of Santa plastered over the nose of a Boeing 747 was just a fancy Airways paint job!) The poor chap is out of action, and during his busy season, too. So, being a dead ringer for the renowned French artist/philosopher/mathematician, they agreed to trade places. Very noble of the artist to take on such a mammoth task, but then you need to have a grasp of the mathematical possibilities of time and space to do Santa's job, so I suppose he's well qualified. I wonder what his reindeer-handling capabilities are?

My drongos are back! Alone, without the kids, and going through a torrid time. They seem to bicker constantly. Their behaviour upset the red-billed wood hoopoes who chased them all over the garden. Perhaps they'll settle down and have a second bash at domestic bliss before the summer is over. Still plenty time for that.

We're off to Mangochi for a meeting tomorrow, and then on to Lengwe National Park to look at proposed new sites for the offices. I'm delighted. It's not that I get a huge thrill out of possible building sites, but any excuse to visit Lengwe is to be embraced. I'll tell you about it when we get back.

Next you can read about the Maleri Islands—I'm going to have a stab at scanning a sketch for you, but don't hold your breath, my little coven of machines is still not playing speaks.

Till next week then, have fun—it's about all you can do at this time of year anyway.

## Maleri Isles
### 11th December

Maleri, Nankumba, Nakatenga. Even the names breathe enchantment, and so they should. These are the names of three small islands in Lake Malawi, and the islands themselves are bewitching.

Looking at them across the beaten pewter of the lake, they remind me of Sodilo Hills in Botswana—three unexceptional hills, but rising from the flat expanse around them they have a sense of dramatic significance. These islands seem to hover, a deeper blue above the pale horizon. It seems that the lake has withdrawn and left them to float— a little more solid than the air, more weightless than the lake. Behind them the Nankumba Peninsula is veiled in haze, discreetly focussing our attention on these three small islands, the northern-most limit of the Lake Malawi National Park.

If they have a mystical grandeur from afar, they have a deeper enchantment close to. They are disarmingly beautiful. Rising from clear corrugated water, a tumble of smooth boulders consolidates into rising miombo woodlands, hung with lianas and alive with birds. In the dappled shade a riot of ferns and creepers compete with the grass. Here and there is a glimpse of the pale face of a white lily, or a flash of scarlet shows a clump of haemanthus in flower. Paradise flycatchers [5] dart through the foliage flirting their elegant tails; canaries and weavers compete to out-yellow each other; kingfishers keep an eye on the water and wagtails bob and curtsy on the rocks.

We slipped over the side of the boat and plunged into the gentle coolth of turquoise water. Rounded boulders

---

[5] *Terpsiphone viridis*

coated with algae met our feet, where a welter of cichlid fish shimmied and sped. The wonderful dilemma is whether one should watch the birds or watch the fish! Perched on a boulder, up to your chin in water, you can do both and spend a very comfortable few hours like that.

These cichlids are the reason for Lake Malawi National Park. It was the first National Park ever proclaimed specifically to protect fresh-water fish, and these multi-hued little fish are unique. The lake, like the land, is scattered with separate outcrops of rock and, being far apart, each outcrop has developed a variation on the cichlid theme. It's estimated that there could be over a thousand different species of these endemic cichlids in Lake Malawi, only five hundred of which have been scientifically described. These little fish breed in the shallows and feed off algae on the rocks inshore.

Lost in wonder at the flash and gleam of underwater colour, we were so content and still that an otter broke the surface a few feet away and glided in to shore. He levered his lean, wet length from the water and vanished between the dry rocks. A young water monitor raised his yellow snake-like throat to peer at us and a pair of fish-eagles sat side-by-side in the branches of a huge rock fig. It was a royal morning, golden and blue and emerald.

This should be a perfect ecotourism experience. Hippos don't like the rocky shore-line, and crocodiles, though said to be around, have not actually been seen here in years. It's a unique experience. For those who love a sense of solitude and unspoilt wilderness, this is it.

Or it should be. Unfortunately the Maleri Islands are gradually being consumed. As the outer edge of the Lake Malawi National Park, which has neither boat nor fuel to patrol the islands, they are being colonised by fishermen. The second largest island, Nankumba, has one side almost denuded of tree cover. Deeply incised footpaths show where firewood and logs for dug-out canoes have been hauled to the beach. Squat stone-built squares mark fish-smoking sites, and the oily glint of black plastic shows where shelters have been erected.

The droves of pretty coloured thumb-length cichlids, *mbuna* as they are called locally, are in danger too. Since the bigger fish fetch a good price, the fishermen eat the mbuna themselves (two handfuls will make bit of relish to go with the staple, nsima) or use them to bait the long lines used for more profitable fishing. Each of these lines has between 500 and 2000 hooks. Tens of thousands of mbuna are taken every day in an area where fishing is illegal. Fine-meshed nets are depleting the shallows of these jewel-like fish, and the lake, world renowned for its huge diversity of fish fauna, almost all of which is not found anywhere else in the world, is growing poorer by the day.

It's interesting, if sad, to notice that countries that proudly proclaim (and enforce) a fish conservation policy have only done so after their fishing industries have come close to ruin. It seems mankind is unable to value what he has until it has vanished.

## Farewell 2000
### 15th December

So strange to realise this will be my last news-letter this year. We spent so much time and mental effort in looking ahead to Y2K, either tentative or disparaging, and here we are walking out the other end without, it seems, a backward glance. Bye, bye, Y2K.... yet, according to some, THIS New Year will signal the start of the new millennium. Seems that it's not the actual event that matters, but the symbolic figures that we dream up to identify it. Which makes me even more convinced that maths is not a logical thing at all, but a matter of escaping reality.

Enough! Funny how events like Christmas, New Year, certain birthdays or anniversaries make me all introspective and philosophical. Let's stick to a few actualities!

Our trip to Lengwe was wonderful. Actually, that's not entirely true. Our STAY in Lengwe was wonderful, the trip was... well, I suppose 'full of wonder' is pretty accurate. The only thing unjarringly, in fact glowingly, memorable about taking the route from the eastern side of Lake Malawi down through Zomba was a fellow named Leo Houdini Parker.

Mr Houdini Parker was a huge chameleon (hence the first name Leo) who happened to be strolling across the fossil relic of a road as we bounced past. He was so striking that we came to a juddering halt and cautiously reversed back to take another look. He was more than striking. He was positively staggering. About 22 centimetres long in the body, and with a tail at least that long again, maybe longer. He was bright green, striped light and dark, and amazingly vivid.

Science stopped and picked him up to move him out the road, but once he had the chameleon in his hands, he got a bemused look on his face and instead brought him to me. Leo barely gave me a look, he just struck out over my shoulder into the car. Within minutes he had disappeared among the camping equipment. Hence the name Houdini.

He travelled with us to Lengwe, where we fished him out from the tangle of tarpaulins. He'd gone a very light chartreuse, and I thought he might be suffering from heat-exhaustion. His wide mouth was open, showing an amazing deep purple interior. We splashed him with a bit of water and watched him turn lime and lemon, and his natty black polka-dots re-appeared. He had the most perfectly scalloped spinal frill, and ear-flaps that extended over his shoulders. But the most dramatic aspect of him, apart from his typically gun-turret eyes, was that he wore what looked like a Pitot tube on his nose (hence the name Parker).

Science and I discussed this at length on the trip. We both agreed that it couldn't be a Pitot tube, since chameleons are not exactly noted for their air-speed. I think it's a telescopic sight. Any self-respecting chameleon must need one, especially if you're as big as Mr Parker and your tongue extends almost twice your body length. Essential equipment, to my mind. Science, however, failed to find my explanation satisfying. He brought his trained mind to bear on the problem, and finally declared what the protrusion is there for. According to Science, it houses the return spring for his tongue. As many have discovered, you can't argue with Science.

Whatever it was, it gave his face a most lugubrious look utterly at odds with his whimsical tail. This was, in Science's eyes, his most impressive feature. Longer than his body and decked with scallops down to its tapering tip, this elegant prehensile appendage was kept coiled in a tight, perfect spiral. It formed a flat, beautifully decorated disc about five centimetres across. Spectacular.

Anyway, once Leo got his breath back, he spotted a bunch of leaves over Science's head, and took off like a ... well, like a really determined chameleon. We last saw him painstakingly inching his stealthy way into deeper foliage where he promptly vanished. Good. I hope he stays away from roads and has a wonderful New Year.[6]

And that's roughly my wish for you too—I hope you manage to find some lush green place far from bustle and danger, where you can slack out and wait for your meals to come to you while you fit into your environment seamlessly. I wish you the human equivalent of plenty of fat juicy flies, the odd passing grasshopper, and glorious, colourful serenity.

I'm going to be slacking off myself, for three whole wonderful weeks! So this is the last letter you'll get from me this year, which brings me back to where I started...

---

[6] That, unfortunately, was unlikely. Sometime later I told our friend John Wilson about this chameleon, and asked why a predominantly arboreal creature occasionally takes inexplicably long and dangerous walks. He explained apologetically that it's usually the females that go walkabout. Looking for the right place to lay their eggs. So much for our supposed rescue. Sorry, Leonie! Her Latin name is *Trioceros melleri*, commonly called the giant one horned chameleon.

# Hippocraptic Oath
## 18th December

*At this time of the year we all seem to feel the seasons shift, even here in Africa. In response, our hearts turn towards those things that are reassuringly permanent, perhaps eternal. It's a time for drawing closer together and reaffirming those things we know to be true, like friendship, family and love; a time for sharing memories, traditions, old stories and familiar songs. Here's my version of an old African folk tale to share around your end-of-year fire, outdoors under southern stars, or indoors snug against the northern frost.*

Long, long ago, when the earth was still so new that even swamp mud smelled fresh, the Great Creator called upon all the animals, each to select his or her living place. The animals surged around, and each called out clearly what his or her preference was, and the Great Creator took Great Pleasure in meeting these needs.

It was a huge task, and it took all day and well into the night to see that every animal was comfortably established in a niche of its own in this beautiful new world. At last the job was done, and the Great Creator stood up and stretched, and began to prepare for bed.

Just then there was the sound of heavy shambling footsteps and a deep voice called, "AAAAH! Uh... uh.. uh.. uh.. uh...!" The Great Creator looked up in surprise.

"Hello, Hippo," said the Creator, "You are very late! Where have you been?"

"Uhhhh...uh," puffed Hippo, "Well my legs are a little short, and...er...it's an awfully big world and a long way to come. I did try to hurry, your Huge Creativeness," Hippo tried to stifle a huge yawn, and looked embarrassed.

The Great Creator smiled and said, "Of course. Well, I'm pleased to see you, late or not. Have you thought about where you would like to live?"

Hippo grunted happily and said "Mm, mm, mm....yes, indeed. In the rivers please."

A look of Great Consternation crossed the Great Creator's brow. "In the rivers?"

"Aaaah... Yes, please," nodded hippo.

"Oh, dear. I'm afraid I can't do that Hippo," said the Great Creator sadly. "You see, I've put the turtles in there, and crabs, and frogs, and otters, and water mongooses, and crocodiles, not to mention all the snails and insects and smaller creatures, and the water birds. And of course, the fish. Sorry, Hippo, I'm afraid you're too late. The rivers are full."

Hippo was aghast. He stood with his jaw slack for several minutes. Then he looked up again and began to explain why it was that he so badly needed to be in the rivers. He told the Great Creator about how hot the sun was on his bald skin, how heavy his tubby body was to lumber over the veldt, how short his stubby legs were, and how much he needed the help of the rivers to cool him in the heat of the day, and to carry all his weight around. "So you see, Your Majestic Creativeness, why I need to be in the rivers."

The Great Creator shook the Greatly Creative head and said gently "I'm sorry, Hippo, but it's not just that the rivers are full. It's the fish I worry about. With that huge mouth of yours you will scoop them all up in no time and, before we know where we are, all the freshwater fish will have gone extinct."

Hippo gave a huge grin. "Is that all that's worrying your Creative Hugeness! Well, that's easy!" And he brought his great mouth close to the Great Creative ear and whispered hoarsely.

The Great Creator gave Great Laugh and said, "Well done, my Hippo. So be it! You do as you say, and I'll let you live in the rivers by day, and you can come out at night to browse on the sweet grass, but don't forget your promise!"

So from that day to this, Hippo spends his days in the rivers and his nights browsing the sweet grass, and he keeps his promise to the Great Creator. You can see this for

yourself, for everywhere the hippo goes he carefully scatters his dung with his paddle shaped tail. Every time he does that, Hippo is saying
"Look, God, no fish-bones!"

*I've often thought that if by any chance we do get another shot at life, I'd like to try being a hippo. But I suppose the reality is that if we manage to keep faith with the Great Creator as well as Hippo has, our lives would be just as full of ease and contentment.*

*Best wishes and rich blessing to you and yours at this time.*

## Wet Season Wanderings
### 8th January

Any gardener will tell you that you can't have a beautiful garden without considerable muck. It's a fact of botany.

The tropics are the same. All this lush growth, the wonderful diversity of orchids and ferns and flowers and trees—and butterflies and moths and birds—requires vast quantities of muck. That means it doesn't happen in a way that is convenient to tourists.

This makes travel in the tropics in the wet something of an ordeal. The rain buckets down, the dirt roads turn to slush or treacle or both, vegetation grows a centimetre a second, and insects multiply ecstatically to distribute the increased load of pollen. So the moment the rain stops washing you down, the insects settle. It seems to me that even those *goggas* that don't require a blood meal will take an experimental bite just to see if you're edible. In no time legs and arms and neck are interestingly blotchy with varying sizes of munch-marks, which vary in intensity of itch.

There is of course a battery of creams, lotions, unguents and sprays available to keep little nippers at bay, but applying the stuff might not spring to mind when you're intent on extracting your diesel 4x4 (don't try it in anything else) from a hollow filled with muck the texture of cake frosting.

Camping becomes a little more challenging too. We have a system of erecting a tarpaulin over the site to keep the rain off, a tarpaulin under our feet to keep the mud out, and a little veranda tarp over the tent entrance to facilitate a dry retirement at the end of a soggy day. However, putting the front of this tent-porch under the larger site-tarp was not a good idea, since the pond of rain-water that accumulated in it came cascading into Science's lap as we sat down to dinner. As it didn't happen to me it was hilarious, but it meant that the mud-excluding under-tarp was awash with water. And in the tropics water turns into mud as you look at it. It might not be impossible to stay clean and dry camping in the wet season, but it is very unlikely.

Nevertheless, there are advantages. For instance washing up after dinner is a breeze. Just sling the dirty dishes under the nearest bush. (That in itself is a wonderfully freeing action, especially for those of us who were brought up under a strict no-littering regime.) Next morning a brief foray into the shrubbery reveals them, brimming with the rain water in which they have soaked all night. A quick swill and they're spotless. Which is more than can be said for your feet, but you can't have everything.

Cooking is a bit of a challenge too, since firewood will be anything from damp to dripping. If you have been clever, you will be equipped with a gas-cooker. The usual camping cookers have a single ring. That's fine if you don't mind one-pot suppers. If, however, you prefer to cook your rice or potatoes or pasta and vegetables separately, you have to get cunning. This is when you discover that sleeping bags are vital kitchen equipment. They're perfect for wrapping up pots to keep warm while you get on with part two of the meal. You might discover rice grains in your toes on retiring, or get cheese sauce in the small of your back, but in the general gritty mud-soaked damp you probably won't notice. And it's worth it. It's far easier to sleep in a damp bed when you're well fed.

So why do it at all, you ask?

Simply because it's the most beautiful and fascinating time of the year. The explosion of insect life draws the birds out to feast on them, and since it's a time of plenty it's the right time to have a family—a flurry of courtship and nesting and breeding is going on all around, usually very noisily. It's a time of feast for the whole spectrum of wildlife, and if you plan your trip for the start of the rainy season, the vegetation is not too thick to obscure your view too much. The world seems full of beautiful babies: wide-eyed knobbly-kneed little warthogs; creamy roan antelope calves, perky-horned and high stepping; Bambi-esque reedbuck babies; hesitant little zebra ponies..... Sit quietly and watch for a few minutes and something will come into view, usually accompanied by its babies.

And when the birds and the beasts are conserving energy somewhere out of sight, there is the whole rampant display of vigorous greenery to delight in. The riot of colour is not exclusive to flowers—we found a sedge with a chrome yellow head, and several seed pods in shades of crimson or scarlet, and simple foliage in tints from copper to lilac to puce. Butterflies, and moths too, are wildly colourful. Science found a furry charcoal-grey moth, the hind wings washed with bougainvillea pink and set with sulphur eyes. I found the tattered remnants of a huge ochre moth dangling from a grass stalk like an antique silk banner, huge pink eye marks still just visible. Both these moths seemed near death, yet both flew valiantly away.

The sheer force of burgeoning life is astounding. I saw a mushroom that had forced its fragile white umbrella up through a tarred road surface. To some it's disheartening how quickly things decay in the tropics. To me it's deeply reassuring. Once man has stopped his stupid plunder of the earth and done himself in entirely, this part of Africa will return to the wilderness it should be. All it needs is to be left alone—and, of course, the rain and vast quantities of muck.

## Komani's wedding
### 15th January

"Well, it's not a wedding, exactly," said Komani, "It's more like an engagement. But it's a bit complicated." Komani, compact and dapper, and Memory, his tall and elegant betrothed, belong to different churches, different tribal areas, and different cultures. Complicated is putting it mildly. It was even more complicated for us, since it was all in Chichewa.

We arrived in the early afternoon, to find Komani's little garden crammed with people. One car had been allowed in; three people, swathed in several layers of chitenge cloth, sat in the vehicle, and around it the crush was almost unbearable. Obscuring the little business called 'Fanny Hair Dressing Saloon' that forms the western boundary of his yard was a lean-to shelter, hung with paper streamers, tinsel and balloons, with chairs set under it. Here the guests of honour were ranged, and we were waved to seats among the privileged.

Once ensconced, we had time to look around for Komani. In front of us to the left was a band of two electric guitars, a keyboard and a drummer. And to the right, a plump two-seater sofa, resplendent with hand-embroidered antimacassars, overlooked a coffee table ablaze with a dazzling display of artificial flowers. On either side of the sofa two upholstered dining chairs were set. A pair of immobile forms occupied this nest of luxury, also shrouded in several metres of cloth. These, we assumed, were Komani and Memory.

We were wrong. A couple of winnowing baskets were brought forward, and with joyful dancing and singing the crowd surged around, each guest tossing a handful of small bank-notes into the baskets. When the MC decided the baskets were full enough, someone approached the first shrouded figure and removed a draped cloth. A sigh of mock disappointment ran through the crowd: Ahhh! Not Komani! It is only his attendant best man, and the baskets came out again for another round of exuberant dancing and collecting.

Komani was the second draped figure, greeted with sheer delight by the guests, and then the three occupants of the parked car were similarly unveiled, and the car finally removed, leaving the dance area clear. The third and final swathed shape of course was Memory. Shrill ululations of joy accompanied her as she walked to join Komani on the sofa, her modesty shown in downcast eyes, her sense of the importance of the occasion by her serious expression. Her attendant bridesmaid fussed over her, touching up her hair, smoothing her clothes as she walked.

To us it seemed that vast quantities of money were expended in these formalities, but this was only the start. Every new step of the ceremony meant more cash from the guests, and the guests were delighting in parting with it. Two cashiers were stationed at a table to the side of the dancing area, changing fifty and one hundred *kwacha* notes into ones, fives and tens, and counting up the collected money, ready to swap it out again for bigger notes. Money floated in the air and tumbled round shuffling feet. Some dancers tossed them over the shoulder dismissively, some trickled them mock-casually from their fingers as they moved, others took great delight in pointedly placing a huge showy wodge of notes proudly in the baskets.

Malawi is not a wealthy country. The kwacha itself is not strong. There are between 80 and 90 Malawian kwachas to the US dollar at the moment[7]. So tossing a five kwatcha note to the winds may not seem to be throwing away a fortune. But many Malawians earn less than a thousand kwacha a month. A handful of one kwacha notes flicked abroad to the clicking of fingers is an impressive statement

---

[7] At the time of writing; the exchange rate in 2019 is 0,0014 USD to one MKW.

of generosity. As importantly, it's patently a wonderful experience for the guests. The expressions of blissful abandonment on their faces was a delight. I have certainly never been to a mzungu wedding where the guests had as much fun. It also explains why the small one kwacha notes always look so utterly revolting.

Some of the sections of ceremony were similar to our western traditions; there was an exchange of rings, but worn on the middle finger of the left hand. A ceremonial cake—also unveiled at a price—was formally cut and shared, Memory feeding a piece to Komani with her fingers, and he responding in the same way. The first kiss was given with mouths full of sweet cake—more intimate than our chaste western peck.

But there was also a Traditional Dressing ceremony, Memory being swept away by a retinue and returned in elaborate finery. A roast chicken was shared between the uncle and the brother of the bride, the symbolism of which escaped us, and the fragments distributed among the dignitaries. After a formal introduction of the couple to the community by their parents, came a section of speech-making by whoever had enough money to command the floor. This caused great hilarity and mirth.

Finally the total of accumulated wealth was announced, and the formal proceedings closed with a prayer. After that, I think the dancing probably went on into the night, but Science and I excused ourselves and went home into a pink and lilac sunset.

It wasn't 'exactly' a wedding—Komani assures us that happy event is still to come—but as a start to a life firmly bound together it was admirable. We may have missed some of the symbolism and all of the repartee, but the main message was wonderfully clear. The community is joyous about the union, and hugely supportive.

All in all, compared to western engagement parties or wedding receptions it was low on catering and high on attendance, involvement and joy. Instead of crippling the couple with cost, it set them up with a useful nest egg, and every single member of the community has had a share in providing it—they have all invested in this union. I may not have understood it, but it made very good sense to me.

## Mounting a mole hill
### 22nd January

Don't ask me where the last week went, but it's my guess it was eaten by termites. If you take your eye off anything here for a few minutes it's crusted over with a brittle shell of dry red mud while a million pale jaws snip it up and cart it off to the great recycling machine in the earth. However, I do know where yesterday went. We left most of it in tatters clinging to a fragment of rock on top of Nkhoma Mountain.

Our very good friends Arild and Martha, the idiosyncratic Norwegians who introduced us to reconstituted mutton biltong as a Christmas tradition, invited us to join them on an excursion to Nkhoma Mission, a brief jaunt of a few hours just outside Lilongwe. They had done it several times, and Arild, an outdoors-man used to cross-country-skiing across fjords and tripping nimbly up glaciers, was happy to show Science the route to the top of

Nkhoma Mountain while Martha introduced me to the terracotta delights of the market below the mission station.

The men, we thought, had decided to walk up the boulder strewn, acacia graced western side, over the twin-peaked top and down the eastern slope to meet us for lunch at the Mission. We thought. As Martha patiently pointed out to a very badly scraped and shredded Arild six hours later,

"There are two things here, Arild. There is what you said, and there is what we understood."

Science and Arild, however, thought that they had told us they would go back to where we set them down on the western side if they failed to reach us by cell phone. The only thing we universally agreed on was the time. One o'clock. While Martha and I waited with mounting anxiety on the mission side, Science and Arild cheerfully had a major clash of wills with the mountain which didn't wish to be climbed. During this Arild discovered a helpful fist of rock which, together with the aid of a tenacious trouser button, managed to prevent him from surrendering to gravity and speedily meeting the hard foot of the hill.

Shaken but not stirred, the two men acknowledged that there could be an easier route, and proceeded to the topmost beacon without further ado, and then back down to their agreed meeting place. Which didn't happen to be ours.

Hours of deep mutual anxiety ensued while we sat on either side of the hill. By 3.30 Martha was organising and dispatching rescue missions in the form of a lad on a motor-scooter, two gentlemen in a pick-up truck, and a couple of youths who said they could cross the mountain in an hour and a half if they ran. Meanwhile I had made the acquaintance of two delightful inhabitants of Nkhoma, the Reverend Msina and Sister Henrietta. I will tell you all about Sr. Henrietta later, since she deserves a space all to herself.

Father Msina is the priest in charge of Nkhoma parish, and he assured us of whatever assistance we might require. I could see him mentally assembling a prayer group preparatory to that eventuality. He also promised to give us an answer to the mystery of the mental differences between men and women. But only on our next visit.

On the western front, Science and Arild stuck to the survival dictum of not leaving the agreed meeting place by leaving a note there and wandering off up the road. Convinced we had been car-jacked, they sensibly bought some mangoes and hired a passing bicycle. Arild elected to ride it round the mountain to the Mission while Science sat by the roadside in case we should happen past. Perhaps at gun-point.

The Malawian owner of the elderly bike found he couldn't bear to be parted from it and suddenly leapt onto the rickety wire carrier over the rear wheel as Arild took off. So the sunburned, blond and bloodied Norsman, trailing shreds of tattered tee-shirt and with remnant shorts flapping in the breeze, eventually wobbled into the mission market with the owner of the bike perched precariously behind him. He was discovered by the rescue squad in the blue pick-up and delivered, red-faced and breathing heavily, to Martha and I.

It took a few minutes for me to realise that if Arild looked as bad as that but had still made it back to us, it didn't necessarily mean that Science was in a worse state. It was a tense few minutes. But a half hour of calm discussion—

while we loaded the car and reshuffled our newly aquired Nkhoma-market beer-storage pots—saw us on the road to collect Science and make our relieved and content way home.

Arild has at least one broken toe and severe laceration to his fingertips, chest and elbows, and he'll be bruised and sore all over for several days. Nevertheless, both he and Science agree that that is what one goes scrabbling up mountains for. I can see the logic in that. Science has often told me that he's there to rescue me from difficulties. However, it seems he's there to get everyone into difficulties from which he can rescue them. That's how he knows he's alive. Utterly scientific.

Anyway, we're off to Kasungu to see Birgitt, she and Science have a workshop till Wednesday, then we're off to Blantyre for another meeting. My computer is still u/s, but I'll be in touch somehow through Science's lap-top.

Stay well, and I hope your week is not too lively.


## Stone the Crows
### 23rd January

I wonder why? Why should we do that as a demonstration of surprise or disgust? I can understand the injunction, but not the association. The urge to stone a few crows must be felt somewhere in the world almost every second of every day, since crows are ubiquitous and universally pushy. But why is it used as an expression of surprise?

Perhaps less odd is the amount of times crows crop up in our figures of speech—eat crow, crow's nest, as the crow flies, crow's feet, to have a crow to pluck, and of course, stone them... and those spring to mind with no effort at thought. It seems that our language has adopted crows more than any other wild bird. They have worked their way into myth and legend throughout all cultures.

That's understandable, perhaps, since crows and humans have co-existed since time immemorial.

Scavenging crows value humans as part of their survival strategy. In fact, pied crows are so seldom seen in really wild country that the occasional ornithologist has wondered about the origins of the bird.

Certainly pied crows are a sure-fire indication of a community without an efficient waste-disposal policy. In Malawi they were proclaimed a protected species by the late President Banda. Not a bad move, since they are probably more efficient than rats at removing unwanted debris, and far healthier to have around. It doesn't make them any easier to live with, though.

The thing that gets me about pied crows is their apparent arrogance. They are unmistakably intelligent—I just wish they were not so sure that they can outsmart us. But they probably can, mostly because we don't expect them to be clever at all.

For instance I was told a story about a group of pied crows in Sri Lanka. A couple of little girls eating lunch under the trees were pestered by a group of crows. At length they agreed that the birds were far too annoying, so they left their plates and ran at their tormentors to chase them off. As they put the group to flight a second group of crows came in behind the lasses and swept the food off the plates with their wings. That's the fascinating part. The girls ran back—too late of course, the food was spoilt and in disgust they took their empty plates back inside. And that left all the crows free to enjoy all the food. I'm staggered by the cunning. Had the second group just pecked at the plates I would have thought that opportunistic but fairly smart. The deliberate sweeping of the food off the plates shows an ability to reason and act in concert that demands respect. So much for the term "bird brain".

For birds that have been our closest wild neighbour for as long as we can remember, we know surprisingly little about them. Take the term "as the crow flies", meaning the direct distance between one place and another, absolutely straight. How often have you seen a crow fly dead straight? Of all the birds I've watched, crows are the most acrobatic of aviators. They appear to derive a real sense of pleasure from flying. They seem to play with the wind and each other, weaving, sweeping, tumbling in tight barrel rolls and dramatic stall turns. They swoop and glide and hang on the lip of the breeze like paragliders. And often their hoarse cawing sounds to me like shouts of sheer exhilaration, like a bunch of rowdy street kids.

That's another thing we don't seem to know about them. Are they social birds, or solitary? They seem to spend an equal amount of time being both. I have had a solitary crow stalking round my garden, using my bird-bath to soften up its trophies—a lump of hardened maize porridge, the unravelling corpse of a lizard, a road-flattened and sun-dried frog. I have read that crows often wash their food, but this fellow was far more intent on making lunch chewable than on hygiene. When I remarked on this interesting fact to my Scientific Advisor, he pointed out that it was probably an elderly crow with uncomfortable dentures. So much for my valuable observations.

But while my crow appears to spend a good half of his time disputing the ownership of the bird-bath with me, he is simply not here for the other half. Where does he go? Every second or third day I hear an accumulated cawing overhead, and glance up to see fifty or more crows crowding the sky, like a great social convention, a corvid symposium. They are all heading in the same direction. Why? Where are they off to? Is there a reason for these great events or is it simply fun to fly with a big group of friends?

Some crows roost several hundred together in tall trees, others settle down two by two. Though they seem to have skirmishes with other birds that could threaten their livelihood, such as eagles, vultures and other birds of prey, they don't pick on each other. Yet they must have some internal competition—for mates, for food, for nesting sites. What are they? Why don't we know, when we have been living cheek by beak with them for so long?

Perhaps this is another example of how the closer we get to something, the less we see it. With luck someone will pop out of the woodwork and tell me these things have been studied and known for decades and the blindness is my own. It's a healthy thing to eat a bit of crow now and then.

## Out on a Limb
### 26th January

Our trip to Kasungu National Park was good. Birgitt of the blond tresses, the development worker stationed in the park, gave us her spare bedroom for the duration of our stay, and while she and Science reviewed her project with representatives of the Department of National Parks, I had the run of her little thatched cottage. Set in a thicket of silver-leaf *terminalia* trees, it faces down a grassy track towards a lush dambo and a gushing stream—not seen from this distance, but heard as a fluctuating susurration as the breeze rises or dies.

The area around the lozenge-shaped brick building has been cleared of tall grass and Birgitt has tried to grow vegetables, with a singular lack of success. Where others wrestle with pests such as slugs and snails eating their lettuce and tomatoes, Birgitt has to ward off elephants. It's been an unequal battle and she has all but given up, resorting to growing sprouts indoors on her kitchen window-sill. We were not privileged enough to meet her garden pests, but we saw ample trace of them.

Our early morning bicycle rides took us over rain dampened sand roads, wet green grass-heads whipping our shoulders and strands of spider-threads trailing from chins and foreheads. We found a single lion's heavy pug-marks dimpled by the dawn-fall, and a scattering of the deep double clefts of a duiker. Hippo tracks in the damp clay, instead of their usual four-petaled flower pattern, left triple scoops for each foot, the toenails scouring circular hollows as big as the bowl of a soup-spoon.

A scattered pile of elephant dung had sprouted a haze of fragile toadstools, each translucent parasol as delicate as spider-web. Science leaned on his handlebars and blew. Even from that distance the wind of his breath set then dancing, shimmying and juddering like a forest of tiny tethered balloons. A tortoise—"Short stride and wide wheel-base," says Science—left a twin trace of tracks along the edge of the road, and a wildcat had stepped between the rain puddles neatly, back foot almost exactly where the front paw had been.

Sitting quietly on Birgitt's front step is no less rewarding. On either side in the bush is the triple beat of purring wings as a hidden pair of feathered duellists dispute the territory. Flappet lark perhaps[8], or Ayre's cisticola[9]? Without a glimpse of the birds I can't tell. A dragonfly jinks above the rough lawn and a pair of bronze mannikins[10] edge along grass stems like daring acrobats.

There is a remarkable press around the birdbath just at lunch-time. I can't imagine why, but just between one o'clock and two, birds jostle and shove to get a chance at the water which they ignore for the rest of the day. A family of six dapper pied wagtails balance their elegant tails and their bobbing white breasts as they flirt their wings in chilly anticipation of the water. A shimmering coppery sunbird[11] flits nervously down, hesitates, then thinks the better of it. A pair of black-eyed bulbuls elbow their way past a russet and slate-blue paradise flycatcher, and shout as they splash.

---

[8] *Mirafra rufocinnamomea*
[9] *Cisticola ayresii*
[10] *Lonchura cucullata*
[11] *Cinnyris cupreus*

A scattering of little blue waxbills forage and gossip around the edge, and a scarlet-chested sunbird[12] finds a moment of splendid solitude for a quick dip on the sunlit far side. Obviously all these birds have never been informed that bush tradition has it that nothing happens in the heat of the afternoon.

The visit to Kasungu was not without its sadness, but you can read about that in the next story.

## The Quadruped Nun
### 29th January

I first caught sight of Sister Henrietta at the market below Nkhoma Mission. She was looking intently at a display of roots and powders laid out on a frayed remnant of fertiliser bag. She hesitated a little, sniffed at a piece of bark and moved a few paces forward. She seemed both out of place and entirely at her ease, unperturbed by the constant press of people around her. Such serenity is often found in those of Holy Orders.

From her brown habit and white wimple I guessed her to be a Franciscan, a Poor Clare. As I bent forward to glimpse her sweet face, the herbalist reached out a thin hand and scooped her up. Without a wriggle the neat little brown and white figure was deposited in a tattered plastic bag and the mouth firmly closed with a knot. The herbalist smiled at me and said, "Twenty kwacha."

I blinked at her. That's roughly 50 American cents. I looked at her display of natural cures and saw among them two fragments of hedgehog skin. "What are these used for?" I asked.

A young man beside me relayed my question to the herbalist, who spoke very little English. She replied quietly

---

<sup>12</sup> *Chalcomitra senegalensis*

and at length, with many unintelligible gesticulations. The young man laughed awkwardly, shuffled his feet and said to me, "It's hard to understand. It's for children." Oh? His embarrassment made me guess fertility rather than childhood illnesses, and I refrained from asking more, but fumbled out two limp and dusty ten kwacha notes and took possession of the ominously still plastic bag.

I bought a small basket for five kwacha less, and decanted the Quadruped Nun into it. She gazed up at me without surprise or alarm. We looked at each other for a long time before she got bored and tucked her shiny black nose between her pious paws and her eyelids drooped.

I called her Sister Henrietta, since that seemed the right name for a hedgehog born around Nkhoma Mission, and so obviously a little sister of St Francis. I would release her in Kasungu National Park in the next day or two, but in the interim, she must be fed. Since I was quite sure she would know better than I what she wished to eat, I found a quiet patch of untroubled bush and set her down.

Her tameness troubled me. My previous acquaintance with hedgehogs had been brief and thorny, and I'd hardly had time to see those boot-button eyes and the black suede muzzle before being shut out by a barrage of bristles. Sister Henrietta was serenity itself. Her bristles lay obediently down her back, and she would tolerate a gentle tickle under her velvety ear. She would let me breath down on her while I watched her surprisingly blond eyelashes give a slow wink. There was nothing hurried or fearful about her.

She ambled through the grass stems, stopping periodically to listen or sniff. She sneezed a few times, found a patch of sun and went to sleep. That was all. I put her back in her basket, and later put out a little dish of milk for her which she enjoyed. But it was plain that releasing her to the wild might not be in her best interests.

Once home in Lilongwe, Science and I found that she adored millipedes, each glossy chocolate-brown shongalolo would provide a good few minutes of emphatic crunching

and whiffling, and a few odd sneezes. And we took her to Kasungu with us anyway, since when we introduced her to our faithful watchdog, Bagheera, Sr Henrietta greeted her with the same unconcern as she displayed to humans. Releasing her in our snake pasture might lead to a fatal misunderstanding, since dogs are known to be the chief enemy of hedgehogs.

Perhaps I should have known better, but it's so hard to tell with wild creatures that you've only just met. We had no way of knowing how long she had been in captivity. But by the time we got to Kasungu her sneeze was more frequent and full of mucus. I watched her sink over the next two days. Why should a nocturnal animal sunbathe? It never occurred to me that she was so ill.

We found her juicy cockroaches and fat horse flies, and she dutifully ate them, but declined the grasshoppers and stick insects. She drank diluted milk and traced patterns over the veranda floor in despised egg yolk which she trotted through briskly. Her trotting was delightful. Perhaps that's why I didn't know she was ill. Her nap-attacks would be interspersed with prolonged jogging sprees. She would circuit the veranda like a little clockwork toy, indeed a miniature pig, bristles juddering gently as those neat feet twinkled to a blur under her fringe of white petticoat.

I looked her up in Jonathan Kingdon's East African Mammals, and he describes that wonderful curling mechanism. It seems hedgehogs have narrow chests and wide hips (ever noticed how women touch their toes more easily than men?) and an elastic band of muscle that loops along the edge of the bristles, over the neck and just above the little stumpy tail. It works like the drawstring of a pouch. Just tighten it up and tuck the six unprickly bits inside. Easy. Instant impersonation of an armed cricket ball. The muscle is called *orbiciularis panniculi*—the beastie becomes like an orb (or orbicular) when it panics. Kingdon confirms that the skin and spines are used as a fertility charm. That explains those sad mud-coloured fragments on the healer's mat.

By the fourth day her illness was very clear. Her nose bubbled with each breath and she felt cold to my touch. I wore her against my chest to keep her warm, in a sling of silk scarf. Hedgehogs are not a comfortable fashion accessory, but her laboured breathing and wet sneezes were more painful to me. I felt so big and clumsy and useless. She died soon after midday. I suppose that's the lowest ebb for a nocturnal spirit.

So I have let her go in Kasungu, but not the way I would have wished. And once again I've been taught the hard lesson that it's not enough to care. You can lavish as much love as you like, but if you don't know what you're doing, you will be doing harm. Wild animals are a joyful gift to the world, not to us personally. We are never entitled to interfere.

I don't think I had much of a choice with Sister Henrietta. I either had to take her with me or leave her to her fate in a smelly airless plastic bag. But I wish I had just set her down in the veld and walked away. I would still be able to think of her serene perfection trotting though the tall grass stems instead of the cold, motionless ball in the damp earth of Kasungu.

## The depth of the wet
### 5ᵗʰ February

Another grey and sultry day. This is not so much the height of the rainy season as the depth. Outside Lilongwe entire villages are slowly drowning in a rising tide of leafy crops— their circular thatched roofs are just visible above tasselled heads of maize, some filmed with a straggle of creeper, yellow flowered like pumpkin. Tobacco plants spread their broad leaves in the soggy heat, and already there are yellowing bunches tied like bundles of scarves in the shade of eves. Exotic cassias are breaking into egg-yellow flowers, and sensitive mzungu eyes and noses are steaming with pollen induced hay-fever.

Even within Lilongwe—once described by a visiting landscape architect as "not so much an urban area with patches of open space, but open space with patches of urban area"—the maize harvest looks to be a winner this year. Between the houses and down along the seep-lines private patches of farming are flourishing. It makes bike riding a little more of a heart-stopping challenge for us.

The footpaths we cycle along have become runnels of erosion and collection points for bits of rubble brought down by the rains. A perilous plunge down an incline under an arch of emerald maize leaves leads you blindly into a mini donga of jagged half bricks and masonry, or a tyre-grabbing patch of rain-soft sand or gluey mud. Even the flat stretches require huge confidence or profound faith, since sight and sound are obscured by towering crops. Hurtling along could bring you smack into the back of a silent pedestrian balancing branches of firewood on her head, or an equally precipitous cyclist coming the other way.

Going along the tarred roads is less terrifying, but demands far greater effort, something at which I do not excel. However, Science and I have solved that problem. Since we agree that I need exercise more than he does, but he needs more exercise than I do (that's absolutely true, not just clever) we've developed a way to meet both our needs. It involves a piece of inner tubing, a length of rope and a cleat.

The rope is linked to my bike-frame below the handlebars with the cleat, and the other end is tied to the inner-tube, looped around Science's waist. Ta-daah! Four-wheel-drive cycling! In this admittedly absurd-looking manner I now sail up hills which normally would give me a cramp just to view. And for the first time in our joint cycling career, I can hear Science actually panting! Besides providing him with more exercise, and me with exercise I'm prepared to indulge in more, it provides all of Lilongwe with endless entertainment. Fellow cyclists have wobbled off the road watching us pass, motorists have stalled in fascination and pedestrians barely contain their incredulous chatter or howls of mirth until we are out of earshot. I really don't care.

These stress-free linked-tours of the suburbs of Lilongwe give us time and opportunity to drink in the really pretty rural aspects of the supposed city, the wonderfully wooded gardens, the soft graceful hedges, the tall sculptural summer clouds in the Wedgewood sky, the sudden vistas of distant hills. It's a lovely place, and best enjoyed through stately progressions like this. We are very lucky to live in such lovely surrounds.

The rains have hatched creatures of mystery that haunt my dreams. There is one that chews metal roof sheets. At least that's what it sounds like. It may even be the same creature that strangles cats in the combretum tree outside our window. I have seldom heard such a blood chilling sound. We think it's probably a bird, but the gargling, hissing, scratchy call sounded very like a romantic tom-cat being assisted into the next world. It gave two long choking cries, paused, gave another two short coughing protestations and then lapsed back into unhelpful silence, leaving me saucer-eyed at midnight, peering at the tree with a torch. It remains a mystery.

However, this week's story is utterly unmysterious. That doesn't make it uninteresting. It deals with the problem of parks paying their way and stems from a riveting report in the prestigious journal *Science*.

Till next week then, if your life seems too much like up-hill work you can always cadge a tow from someone, but be braced for ridicule.

Yours free-wheelingly.

## Making Parks Pay
### 5 February

My Scientific Advisor handed me an email print-out and said "Read that!" In the subject box was the heading *Guess what? Parks work* from David Kaimowitz, economist at the Centre for International Forest Research.

I like this man Kaimowitz. He has an easy unpretentious way of writing that makes assimilating facts a pleasure. His article offers a potted overview of a report published by the journal *Science* first thing this year[13] which shows unequivocally that protected areas in developing countries actually do protect biodiversity, despite huge people-pressure and chronic underfunding.

Kaimowitz picks out the point that policing seems to be the most effective factor in tropical conservation. The report itself states that the 15 most effective parks (from a sample of 93 in 22 countries) had an average of 3 guards per 100 km$^2$—these places are hardly crawling with what used to be called 'game rangers' in the bad old days. Also the average budget of these parks per hectare per annum is around US $1.18. It seems a little goes a long way in the wild.

"Over 80% of the parks have as much natural vegetative cover today as they did when they were first established. A large percentage actually have more", writes a suitably impressed Kaimowitz.

He also highlights the fact that the authors of the report from Conservation International and the University of British Columbia found "...no correlation between park effectiveness and the number of staff involved in development efforts and environmental education, or the level of community participation in park management." That's staggering, considering how much time, effort and foreign funding is currently being ploughed into exactly

---

[13]*Effectiveness of Parks in Protecting Tropical Biodiversity*; Bruner, Gulliston et al; *Science Vol 291*, 5 Jan 2001

those areas in southern Africa today, where Community Based Natural Resource Management or CBNRM is the fashionable drive. An equally arresting title for his piece could have been "Guess what? CBNRM doesn't work".

Kaimowitz passes swiftly over the fact that simply having clearly demarcated boundaries and a presence on the ground does not stop hunting. I was surprised by the obvious lack of a "why not?" in his article, but two days later I was handed yet another email by Science (my advisor, not the magazine), again from David Kaimowitz. This one is called 'Hunting for tonight's dinner' and supplies the lack.

From a report by the Wildlife Conservation Society come the frightening figures of 'bush-meat', and they are really eye-widening.

"Total catches from hunting in the Congo Basin exceeds over one million tons of wild meat each year," states Kaimowitz soberly, a major proportion of which comes from large hoofed animals and monkeys. Bye-bye bongos and bonobos. I won't dwell on all the grim details, and the depressing findings like: "In many African... countries people actually consume more wild meat as their income rises...", if you want the whole story you can get it from www.worldbank.org/biodiversity. It's called *Hunting of Wildlife in Tropical Forests: Implications for Biodiversity and Forest peoples*, but I do want to look at an oddness thrown up by these two articles.

In the first, and stated far more clearly in the original *Science* journal report, is the fact that if parks don't work, aid agencies will stop throwing money at them. So it's vital to prove that in fact funding a conservation area is a very worthwhile thing to do with foreign aid.

In the second it's obvious that no matter how clearly demarcated, policed or enforced by penalties illegal hunting is, it doesn't stop. The cute and cuddlies are going to keep on being served for dinner until there aren't any left. So what does that do for biodiversity? Will it suffer without the huge hoofed fellows or the cheeky primates?

You bet your life it will. In the long term, large herbivores like buffalo and elephant keep grass short enough to be eaten by the smaller chaps like zebra and hartebeest. You lose these if the grass is too long for them, and others too. So the entire landscape changes. And apart from passive changes relating to not being utilised, there are the active changes, like seeds not getting dispersed through the digestive tracts of everything from elephants to apes. The whole ecosystem alters like the patterns of a kaleidoscope.

Let's come to the final irony. The impetus for CBNRM is that parks must become self-sufficient. If a park doesn't pay its way and help support the people who are 'impoverished' by its existence, then it has no right to be there. The grand saviour in this is not 'utilisation' in the form of highly lucrative trophy hunting—now despised by all so-called civilised societies—but eco-tourism. However, people simply will not pay vast sums of money to see vegetable biodiversity. They want the furry beasts to ogle at. An African park that can't offer a tourist a lion to leer at has to lop a few noughts off its overnight rate. Very, very few people pay top-dollar to stare at shrubs and creepers, no matter how diverse.

So, should we be searching for a system of sustainable subsidies? Science (the man) thinks so. "There's a vital post needed in every state conservation department in the developing world—someone who can write project proposals to the large funding agencies, and manage the funds effectively when they come in—an assistance-funding co-ordinator."

Now there's a conservation project worth funding!


## Insect nibbles
### 12 February

Hello from the WHOA. As an abbreviation for the Warm Heart, that's quite descriptive of our emotions towards the weather right now. Leaden skies keep dribbling damp on us, and everything is being urged to grow—including mould on odd things around the house, like leather shoes and wooden chair legs.

The incessant rain has brought quite an exciting stream of insects into the house. Last week a huge click-beetle arrived to enliven our breakfast on the veranda. At a distance I thought he was a giant cockroach, but Science plucked him off the mosquito-netting and brought him to the table for closer inspection. The recumbent form on my side plate seemed a thumb-length, slightly flat-looking Darth Vader, complete with shoulder-width helmet and full-length cape.

"It's a flicker," said Science. As if to prove him right, Darth gave a snappy click and flicked himself over onto his tummy, narrowly missing clouting me in the face. So we put him back on the netting as being a little too lively for that time of the morning. Later we found a second slighter version examining the cake-tins in the kitchen. We heard a series of short dislocated thuds, rather like a black Labrador's friendly tail meeting a cupboard door; but Bags was lying innocently and unsmilingly outside my study. A search discovered this economy version of my D. Vader in an empty cake-tin—each of his/her flicks metallic and amplified.

"You forgot you put him in the cake tin," accused Science, on making the discovery.

"Didn't." I said.

"Must have," retorted Science, "Cos he's still there."

"It's a different one," I said.

"No, it's not," said Science.

We argued it back and forth until I managed to convince my scientific advisor that if I had put the beetle anywhere it would have been in the deep glass salad-bowl so I could watch him, not drop him in an open cake tin and put him back in the cupboard.

Finally an examination of his whiskers proved me right. This shallow imposter had plain straight feelers. Darth had wonderfully complicated fingered antennae, like fronds of fern, like strange symmetrical twigs, like stylised antlers.

Science looked at me askance, as if to imply I was improvising. Luckily the insect book has a photograph of just such an adorned beetle. But to my frustration it doesn't say if the fancy-feathered-feeler beetle is male or female, whether the adults eat or not, nor anything else of much interest. I would dearly love to find an insect book that talks about the life-styles of these creatures, and not just what they are.

The next beetle was a gorgeous scarab-like creature of iridescent enamelled green shot with copper and gold. His broad shoulders were as domed as a 20 karat cabochon emerald, and his bull-like lowered head was crowned with a mock snowplough-cum-cowcatcher. This keeled scoop of flat white edged in black had two inverted tusks above it and terminated in a small but business-like trident. What on earth for? We found him to be a fruit chafer, probably the East African subspecies of *Dicronorrhina*. Thanks very much, but we would have loved an explanation along with the description.

Unfortunately his candy-apple green wing-casings showed three or four tentative puncture marks, which would correspond to an exploratory nibble or two by an inquisitive black Labrador... but Bags was once again innocently lolling at my study door, rolling "Who, me?" eyes at us, so we can't prove a thing. The damage looked superficial, yet the gorgeous creature didn't once try to lever his bulk away on his filmy black transparent wings, and after a day of acting as artist's model, quietly gave up the ghost. "Pepani, madala, pepani" as they say in Chichewa. Sorry for that, old one, sorry for that.

But insects had their revenge on me. Something I annoyed took a chomp at my foot and pole-axed me for two days. We have no idea what it was, but I found myself with a swollen foot and what seemed like a mammoth hang-over. We suspect it was a spider, so I've stopped looking for the culprit, in case I find it. See, spiders and I don't get along. I just happen to know that there is not a spider born that doesn't have an evil agenda. Every spider I've ever seen was looking at me threateningly. Well, maybe that's an exaggeration. There are a few of the delicate pastel coloured rose spiders who mind their own business, and one or two little fuzzy-faced jumping spiders are charming little clowns. But for the rest, they're a bunch of malicious miscreants who are all out to get me. Not people in general. Just me. It's a deeply personal thing.

Till next week then, try not to be anything's breakfast if you can possibly avoid it.

## Anthrop-apologist
### 12ᵗʰ February

After talking to Professor Brian Morris, I find I like humanity a little more. I thought at first he reminded me of Noddy's friend, Big-ears, but that's not true. Big-ears, as far as I remember, was a bit wishy-washy and indecisive. That could never be said of Brian Morris. All the same, if you crammed a red pointy hat onto his shaggy head, it would look like it had always been there.

Partly that's due to his beard, his chunkiness and his crinkly eyes—what a birder would call his 'giss', a General Impression of his Shape and Size. But I like the gnomic inference since Brian *is* something of a guardian of the treasures of the earth. Not the common junk like gold and jewels, but the infinity rarer, deeply precious stuff, like the power that animals have in the lives of humans and why a flying-ant appears in the proverbs of the Chewa.

He bustled out to meet us in shorts and tee-shirt, sandaled feet carefully sidestepping a cricket's burrow in the lawn.

"Hello!" he called, flailing his arms in welcome, "Isn't this glorious?" His wide gesture encompassed the elderly house, the rumbustious garden and the gently drizzling skies. "We must go for a walk!"

I saw brief disappointment in his face as I demurred, followed fleetingly by a rueful self-consciousness when I pointed out that it was not the estate I had come to meet. But he waved us into the house with good humour, his voice booming off the bare walls and curtainless windows.

"Well, this is it! Basic, but everything I need. I'm a bit like Gandhi. All I need, really, is a bunch of bananas and a place to sleep."

Mmm. Somehow I can't picture the Mahatma exuding such boyish enthusiasm. Professor of Anthropology at London University's Goldsmith College, Brian fizzes with the enthusiasm of an amateur.

"I'm not an anthropologist," he confides, "I'm a naturalist. It's not people I'm interested in. I'm interested in the relationship people have with the world around them."

So every ten years he takes one year of sabbatical and launches out into another field about which he knows nothing. In the 80s it was botany, and he published a book on his study of herbalism in southern Malawi, called *Chewa Medical Botany*.

In the 90s it was animals, and his ethnography *The Power of Animals* followed. This time it's insects. Every surface of every work space is littered with small plastic bags. He holds one up for my inspection. The contents appear to be a dozen or so small dried wasps.

"These are *mfulufute*, flying ants." Brian says. Two slips of paper share the interior with them. One has the local name inscribed on it and the other the common name. A third slip goes into the bag when Brian has identified the insect scientifically. I glance around automatically for the computer.

"Haven't got one," says Brian cheerfully. "This is what I use here." He waves at a pile of foolscap notebooks.

"Into the Journals go all my conversations and translations from Chichewa, all my observations and notes on the insects and their uses."

Page after page of neat script and pencil sketches riffle through his fingers. He picks up another.

"Then there are the Notebooks. Into them go all the information I get second-hand, from reference books, experts, so on. When my year is up, I sell everything except the clothes I'm wearing, and fill my luggage with my notebooks." Then comes the final synthesis back in his study in London, where his computer waits for him.

I watch him as he intently shares what he discovered about flying ants. Their nutritional value, their popularity as a snack with all manner of live creatures, the difficulty in catching them. He was seeking understanding of the local Chewa proverb, which states "The *mfulufute* are coming out. Do not squeeze them at the hole." It's an enigma to mzungus; but in his battle to catch these little critters as they appeared for their nuptial flight, he understood the injunction not to constrict their exit from the nest. With each nervous grab, the winged ant would just disappear back down the hole.

"Patience!" he booms, "That's what it's about. 'Patience will be rewarded' is what the proverb means!"

Perhaps that's a proverb Brian himself put into practice as a young man. He left school at 15 to work in an aluminium foundry outside Birmingham, like his father and his uncle before him. In his early 20s an accident at work damaged his right hand, and he was declared unfit for foundry employment. Perhaps he had no prospects, but he had imagination and a love of wildlife. He began a slow drift around the world, eventually finding his way to Malawi.

Here it seems he found himself. Employment at a tea estate led to a delight in Malawi's epiphytic orchids, the subject of Brian's first book. In his late 20s he enrolled to complete his schooling, and after completing both O and A levels in Malawi he returned to England, with a wife and three daughters, to teach. He's been teaching ever since.

And he has never stopped studying. He believes it is essential in revitalising tired teaching skills. His curiosity is huge and wide ranging; he has never stopped asking questions and writing down his findings. His doctoral theses focussed on hunter-gatherers in India and among his still unpublished books is a biography of Ernest Thompson

Seton, the nineteenth century Canadian naturalist, and an exhaustive work on Pantheism[14]. It's all one to Brian, all to do with the way people fit into their world. He may not be interested in people *per se*, but running as a current through all that he does is the essential core of his work, a profound affection for that frail beast Mankind.

## A future in the past
### 19th February

Hello from the warm, wet heart of Africa.

The sun is shining for what feels like the first time in more than a month. The sky is a pale washed-out blue and ragged with clouds, like an old tattered shirt. The sunlight has a fragile feel, and one has the sense that the plants are greedy for it, stretching up to it as a cat arches its back to the welcome human leg. One can feel the anaemic yellow-green grass deepening to emerald in the sun's rays while bowing to the light, subservient, ingratiating.

It's a deeply feudal country, this beautiful Malawi, with its fiefdoms of tea and tobacco estates. Employees will climb off their bicycles and see you past with doffed hats and bent heads; whole families fall under the protection of a single estate, their entire weal in the hands of the land-baron, any other option unthinkable.

The way the rural ultra-poor dress in layer after layer of ragged garments, all washed to an indistinct sepia in cloudy pond water, also gives a mediaeval feel. There are glimpses of groups of men resting beside a thatched 'tea-room', sleeves tattered like ornamental jagging and loosely

---

[14] Emeritus Professor Brian Morris published *Ernest Thompson Seton, Founder of the Woodcraft Movement* in 2007. His 16th book is a reprint of his 2003 work, *Kropotkin: The Politics of Community* published in 2018.

bound head-cloths like liripipe hats—our speeding four-wheel drive a strange anachronism.

Even the beliefs are a bit mediaeval. Age is venerated, since death comes fast and easily, and one who lives to a ripe age is highly admired. And death is a profound mystery. A person is more respected after death than before. Who knows what powers the freed spirit might wield?

This week's newspapers throw an interesting light on the Malawian attitude to death. Last year five women were mutilated and murdered in a small village in what was called a 'serial' murder. This year—and bear in mind the year is but a month and a half old—five men have been found murdered in the same village. A newspaper report suggested that this was a continuation of the serial killings. As a result the reporters were arrested by the police and charged with inciting undue alarm through 'irresponsible' articles. This is not a serial killing, say the police irritably. These are just ordinary every-day murders. The fact that all the victim's eyes were slashed has nothing to do with any psychotic serial killer. It is just that in this particular area there is the firmly held belief that the victim's eyes capture an image of the killer which can be seen by the police after death.

Welcome to the 21st century.

Now before we all click our tongues in disbelieving horror at this almost 11th century thinking, just stop a moment. Who can tell if such a wayward idea might not be true? The brain is an electronic device that stores information electronically from a plethora of sources. There are people who can delve into the memory of a computer—all fragments of stored electronic impulses—and retrieve amazing stuff lost to us lesser beings. So why should the same not be possible with the brain? I bet someone somewhere has thought of that and is having a scientific bash at it as I write.

In Africa all the edges become blurred and at times it hard to tell where the past and the future are exactly, or which is more real and relevant. Perhaps there is always only now.

So shore up your heart and keep your feet dry.


# The Old Man of the Mugongo Nuts
### 19th February

I heard this story in Zambia. We had made our camp under tall trees where the Zambezi seems so broad and silken, sliding silently by in hushed anticipation of its leap of faith into the rock fracture that is the Victoria Falls.

My scientific advisor found a thick mat of old trampled elephant dung, and picked carefully through the dry straw-coloured relic, harvesting something as raptly as a baboon. He came back to camp with a handful of large nuts. Fatly oval and neatly pitted, they looked like big unshelled almonds, carved from hard wood. Very hard wood. He set about cracking them on a metal plate with a sledge hammer.

"Mugongo nuts," he told me cheerfully. "Seeds from the fruit of the African balsa wood, *Ricinodendron rautanenii* [15] . Absolutely delicious, but very hard work. Luckily elephants tend to swallow them whole, so instead of having to find a tree and pick them, you just gather them up already cleaned of the flesh and ready to crack."

He took another swipe at the nut. The hammer juddered on impact and the nut shot out sideways, not even faintly cracked. Science grunted and retrieved it.

"Very hard work," he repeated thoughtfully. Then he looked up at me and set the hammer down.

"Did I ever tell you about the old man of the mugongo nuts?" he said. And with the gloom of the trees

---

[15] More recently called *Schinziophyton rautanenii*

gathered about our shoulders like a kaross[16], he began to sift the pieces of the story in his memory, and fit them together to share with me.

"It must have happened, oh, somewhere in the late sixties, early seventies," he said, and his eyes moved across the gleam of water to the Zimbabwean side of the river.

"That was Victoria Falls National Park just there, now it's called the Zambezi National Park, but at that time the warden was a chap called John Hatton. John was a good, solid fellow, an ex-policeman who ran the Park by the book. A dedicated, efficient but rather unimaginative man.

"In those days there was very little actual poaching in the Park, but John liked to run a tight ship, and it irked him that his game scouts repeatedly found a single set of human tracks. These were barefoot and enigmatic, and never in a section where poaching was suspected. They were simply there—an unauthorised person wandering around in a National Park. Simply not allowed.

"So John carefully and methodically set about tracking the fellow down. In time his rangers traced him back to a dry sand-veld valley away from the river, where couple of little natural springs well up. Under the trees deep in the surrounding woodland was a heap of broken mugongo shells. A huge heap, a couple of feet deep and spread over a wide area. John reckoned there must have been about a tonne of these cracked shells. Obviously the chap had been living solely on mugongo nuts for about a year or more.

"Well, they finally caught him, of course. He turned out to be an elderly fellow, past middle age, and no one could understand a word he said. Eventually they found a Mozambican who could more or less untangle his dialect. It seemed he had come from Mozambique or thereabouts, maybe even from Malawi. It was all a bit vague. Seems he'd just got it into his head to travel, and he did. By foot, all the way up the Zambezi. And avoiding people, as far as could

---

[16]A rug of stitched animal skins, worn in the old days by African people

be understood, as much as possible. He may have been a bit simple-minded, or maybe he was a natural recluse.

"By the time he got to Vic Falls National Park, he'd had enough of travelling, so he stopped. And there he was, not harming anyone, staying out of the way, minding his own business. Surviving on his wits and mugongo nuts. But he was an illegal immigrant, and he was trespassing in a National Park, so John, being the upright ex-policeman that he was, took the old man along to the local police station to try to figure out what to do with him.

"I don't know if they managed to make the old man understand what was happening, that they were going to send him home as soon as they could find out exactly where he came from, and that the prison cell was just a place to keep him safe and dry and fed..." Science's voice trailed off, and he gazed across the river in silence for a while.

"John was distraught. He said he didn't know if it was the threat of going home, or the babble of people around him, or the horror of being shut into a small cement room after years of wide sky and clean stars, but they found him crumpled on the cold floor the next morning. It seems he clambered onto the top of the metal cupboard and simply dived off head first."

We sat absolutely still in the gathering darkness, listening for the distant hush of breath as the Zambezi tumbled ceaselessly into the night.

## Oh, for the brains of a bird
### 26th February

I'm sure you have no desire to hear me, yet again, complaining of the damp. Besides, we have had almost an entire twenty-four hours this week without the sky weeping down our necks, and the sense of relief makes us all a little manic. Lilongwe was like a termite mound launching its latest crop of flyers—a cheerful bustle with as many people outdoors as possible.

The weather made up for it this morning with a depressingly emphatic dump of 30mm in a few hours before dawn. However, the bird kingdom seems sublimely unaware of anything even vaguely unsatisfactory. I've caught the flash of a paradise flycatcher from the corner of my eye several times, just the teasing flourish of steaming coppery tail feathers like a cheeky fairy. The red-billed wood hoopoes are examining the creviced bark of the acacias in full evening dress, iridescent blue-black satin with pearls on their skirts. Even their bills look lipsticked. They scuttle among the branches and cackle like raunchy dowagers. Shocking behaviour for mid-morning perhaps, but full of an unsuppressed joy.

The series of cuckoos is shifting too. The rains began with the red-chested cuckoo, whom we seldom seem to hear now. Then came the black cuckoo, eternally complaining about his health. Last week we saw a cluster of striped cuckoos, about five of them, teetering at the top of the acacia, throwing themselves through a circling cloud of flying-ants in clumsy sweeps, and noisily shooing other birds away. Now Klaas' cuckoo is taunting us from his hiding place in the thick foliage.

The widowbirds and whydahs are putting on their finery now—Victorian bustle-backed tail-feathers for some, elegant Twenties-style tassel-tailed pinions for others, all of them collecting an admiring hoard of drab females. It's all very festive. I read somewhere that angels can fly because they take themselves lightly[17]. The same could be said of birds, I think.

But the day is closing, and if I don't get this off at once, I will be too late to wish you a happy week-end. One that involves a glimpse of the sun, I hope.

---

[17] Often attributed to comedian Robin Williams, it is a quote from G. K. Chesterton's *Orthodoxy* (1908), Chapter VII: The Eternal Revolution

# March 2001

## Rain is a four letter word
### 3rd March

Hello from the Wet Heart of Africa.

It's pouring down again today with unabated enthusiasm. Anyone would think the rainy season had just begun, it's so full and vigorous. To me the sound of rain on the roof is so soothing that I've overslept. Just as well it's a public holiday—Martyrs' Day.

Banda's martyrs were a half-dozen rowdy political dissidents whom he had managed to provoke to action. That alone is no mean feat, since the Malawian is generally an observer rather than a doer, and can carry the "live and let live" dictum to frustrating extremes. But Banda got these guys going in Nkata Bay, and they so irritated the colonial powers that all six of them were shot. Since Banda's cause needed martyrs, this was a great step in the right direction and not long after he got independence for Malawi.

Banda defended the memory of his martyrs with a passion. Martyrs' Day in Banda's time was fiercely sacred. You were not allowed to go outdoors, let alone travel, and the white community in Malawi still talk of the chaps in Dwangwa who all got deported for holding a beach party on Martyrs' Day. The whole lot of them. Twenty-four hours' notice and out. I wonder where Banda got his decisiveness.

Of course those were the Bad Old Days, and Malawi is not hide-bound by parochial moral laws anymore. And I've got right off the point, which was the rain. It's been a sort of wax-crayon week, really. Emerald green grass, red earth, yellow sun, royal blue sky glimpsed behind huge heaped piles of muscular clouds. All primary stuff, both colours and emotions. Not much subtlety or sophistication, but plenty exuberance and joy.

For the observer, anyway. Sophisticated technology and first world comforts separate us from the primary realities of life. Those majestic towering clouds are not a cause of delight for others. They are a very real threat, and the fall of water is heaviest on the poor. The rural Malawian roof is a shallow-angled thatch, and it seems to absorb as much rain as it throws off. This year sodden roofs are collapsing inward, the support struts thrust up like inside-out umbrellas. Walls of unfired brick or rammed earth are sodden too, and prone to collapse. The maize crop has a black rust-like fungus on the flower-heads, and unless the rains stop, the crop will fail.

Tobacco farmers are anxious. The leaves must be dried, but in this humidity each leaf takes longer and needs a free flow of air around it to prevent mould. Harvesting must continue and there is simply not enough shelter for the drying racks. For more than half of Malawi, rain is a four-lettered word.

Yesterday as I came back from church there was rich golden sunlight. I topped the rise past the "Devine Touch of Grace Hairdressing School and Saloon" and saw the vaguely-cathedral shape of Mt. Nkhoma hanging above the green miombo. In the foreground the Capital City traffic circle was ablaze with scarlet cannas, saffron daisies and purple petunias. The faces of street vendors carried contagious smiles, each an affirmation of the Warm Heart. How can one not be filled with irrepressible delight?

Meanwhile, today the skies are leaden and the rain insistent. Bad news for Malawi. But pity Mozambique when the run-off eventually wends its way into the distended Zambezi in a week or two. You can't take-it-or-leave-it in Africa. Africa is all-or-nothing-country.

## Celebrating Cape Maclear
### 5th March

The first surprise was that the level of Lake Malawi has risen by about a metre. The rocky bases of the islands are low in the water. The rain required to raise the lake by a metre 365 miles long by 52 miles wide boggles the mind. No wonder we all feel a bit waterlogged.

Chugging out to the islands, there are still pale rings on the rocks marking earlier higher waterlines, a sort of limnological Plimsoll line. It looks like the weight of jungly growth has made each island sink a little. In the distance, violet and jacaranda-blue storm skies are overlaid with glowing white clouds trailing veils of diaphanous rain.

We stopped behind Domwe Island in a cove of rock-lined jungle. Domwe is a bastion of piled boulders melting into liana-hung trees: rock-fig, quinine tree, the elegant upheld arms of euphorbia looking oddly cactus-like in the crowded tropical lushness. Above, a scatter of trumpeter hornbills glissade down the humid air to dip and glide into foliage, while below we are cradled in the rocking lap of teal-green water, sweet water the colour of antique glass. Further out the lake deepens to the rich deep shade you might get if an emu's eggshell turned to clear clean liquid.

Close to the islands the water reveals its fish with startling ease. I had been a little disappointed with the fish at Otter Point, but here I was transfixed. I'm not a great swimmer, and I like water that has a solid, unsurprising bottom just below my feet where I can see it. Gazing down into heart-shrinking depths I found I had nothing to fear as long as I stayed absorbed in my sense of sight, and didn't think about it.

Head down over the deep, the outer rim of my goggles revealed my dog-paddling arms giraffe-patterned with refracted sunlight. Far below, a soft blue moonscape of serried rocks faded into pastel shadows, shot through with gleaming fish, satin and shantung and silk in blue and bridal white, peacock and azure, brocaded in silver and velvet black, starred with gold, netted in copper and zebra'd in purple and indigo. A thicket of fish, a storm of tiny glinting bodies, a jewelled rain, a flickering mist-cloud of piscine pulchritude. I hung above them like an eagle, or a god.

My biggest problem is that I can't help smiling at such glorious abundance, and a stretched mouth tends to let the water in. Coughing and spluttering I made my way to a barely submerged rock and perched on it. Here I found Science feeding scraps of stale biscuit to the myriad cichlids, which hovered around him like a nebulous sequined waistcoat. He held in his open hand a few biscuit crumbs, and tiny eager mouths sucked up the fragments like miniature hoovers. One little black molly stayed confidently in his palm as he closed his fingers, and he held his hollowed fist out to me before shifting his thumb. The small black body emerged without panic or undue haste.

Then came the rain. The polished glass surface of the water roughened to slapping peaks, etched with a frosting of falling water. Each fat smacking drop seemed to push a bubble of air under which bounced back to the surface with a tiny pop. With our bodies bobbing in the little bay, we felt like we were swimming in a bowl of green champagne.

Back in the boat to rest tired smiling muscles, we puttered out to Mumbo Island to look over Kayak Africa's newest camp.[18] It's the stuff of dreams. A sensitive blend of rustic and environmental high-tec that leaves one in touch with nature and divorced from the hard facts of survival.

---

[18] Though much changes in Malawi in eighteen years, Kayak Africa is still going strong. Visit their website: https://kayakafrica.co.za/

Picture the lake, blue as a swimming pool; rising from its gently rippled surface is a heaped castle of boulders, crowned with lush jungle. A wooden walk-way leads up from a spit of golden sand and threads its way around boulders and under trees to a scattered colony of raised thatched platforms, each set privately into secret pockets of bush, each with a breath-catching view over the lake. Each platform shelters a tent..... no, I'm not about to go into an advertorial inventory, just believe me, it's extremely comfortable, utterly beautiful and ultimately romantic.

This little "dormitory" island is joined to Mumbo Island by a spit of golden sand, currently knee-deep under water due to the rains. Interestingly the thatch and reed kitchen is on the main island. Science hoiked his shorts up

and demonstrated how supper would be delivered to the dinning glade across the spit. Picture a stork-legged scientist, trousers hitched in one hand, the other balancing an imaginary tray above his head, high-stepping through the waters of paradise. [19] In my minds' eye I saw a moonlit line of five diminutive Malawian waiters following his lead like ducklings.

How can one not celebrate this Africa?

---

[19] Since our time in Malawi, Kayak Africa has installed another wooden-walkway, obliterating the need for high-stepping waiters.

# Glorious Mud
## 11ᵗʰ March

Last Saturday we loaded up our Norse companions and headed out East towards the lake. Our destination was about twenty kilometres short of Senga Bay, a long defunct and wonderfully wild ex-Government-cattle-ranch called Kuti. Through it was sort-of-work for Science, it was pure pleasure for me and our friends from the frozen north.

We trekked out in convoy early, with late-summer mist swaddling the valleys, and the hills rising above it like a watercolour wash. The countryside is looking rampantly verdant with all the rain. We talked of the floods at the southern end of the lake and along the Shire, but here there is an aura of well-being. The white bauhinia flowers are fading and falling[20], and the air is tinged with the tom-cat smell of wild asparagus fern. A sprinkle of huts in tall maize lands have large-leaved loofah vines trailing gracefully over their roofs, ablaze with big sulphur yellow flowers.[21] Glossy goats teeter on rocks or skitter across the road with startled ears and wagging tails. Their milk-white and chocolate-brown kids exude a defenceless innocence and play chicken with the traffic.

Just before Selima we branched off to the left amid rolling maize fields under tall acacia trees. Here the ground alternates between swampy hollows and dry ridges—the pretty miombo and dambo mix that reminds me a little of Zambia.

Kuti Ranch is being turned into a conservation area by a private group, and though most of the game will have

---

[20] *Bauhinia petersiana.*

[21] Also called *Luffa*, this is a genus of the cucumber family. The fruit is cultivated and eaten as a vegetable when small and tender. The mature fruit is left to dry out, the remaining skeleton of fibres houses the seeds, and is well known loofah, providing a small income for vendors.

to be introduced, the current manager has seen quite a lot of wild creatures, some quite surprising. He's seen kudu, bush buck, duiker and reed buck, and at night he's spotted bush-pig rooting in the soft earth, and the cat-like eyes of a genet glowing like little green mirrors. Most surprising of all, he's seen a leopard. Probably sleek with goat's meat, it's remarkable that it has survived this close to Salima.

The men set out on an exploration of the ranch with the manager while Martha and I, left with all the picnic stuff in Science's Land Cruiser, selected a noble tree for our attentions, and composed ourselves for a happy morning's painting. It was perhaps not wise to lay out our day camp in the middle of the road, but we knew we were the only people on Kuti that day, and it is a private road.

By the time a third car had inched itself painfully around our glowering selves we were beginning to consider moving. But a dry-season Gaudy Commodore had settled on Martha's painting like a solid patch of sunlight, and while she tried to photograph it with its wings open, I was having a conversation with a matt-black and knobbly toktokkie beetle.[22] This chunky fellow startled me by emitting a thin scream when I picked him up. So I put him down again, where he sat looking indignantly sullen. Thinking I'd been mistaken I picked him up again, he squealed again; Martha's butterfly flew off and the first car re-appeared coming back the other way.

In the gap between the returning second car and the expected third, Science and Kuti's manager, John Dacombe, appeared at a business-like walk. Marta and I looked at each other and said in unison, not "Where is Arild?" but, "They've got the car stuck in the mud."

Spot on. They had come to fetch the 4x4 to pull it out. About an hour later they were back, mud crusted, sunburned and admitting defeat. Arild announced seriously,

---

[22] A member of the *Tenebrionidae* family, also known as **Darkling beetles**. Toktokkies are a flightless species which make distinct tapping noises.

"I have invented aqua-pedestrianism."

"How so?" said Martha.

"Water in my shoes," muttered Arild.

The third vehicle went off to fetch willing hands to lift the bogged vehicle out, and half-way through our lunch we heard it again.

"Off to fetch MORE people," suggested Martha.

Somehow getting stuck in the mud is a wonderfully fulfilling and entertaining experience on a lazy Saturday, especially when it is actually someone else that's stuck. Martha and I savoured the last of our lunch in total contentment.

There is some talk of bringing a few of Zimbabwe's currently under-employed safari-elephants across to Kuti. It's an exciting idea—imagine swaying across these marshes on elephant back, the backdrop of the Rift escarpment behind you, teal-green Lake Malawi glimpsed through borassus palms ahead. Around you the rich sounds of water-birds, and a frieze of buffalo against the tree-line. Magical![23]

## Kuti
### 12th March

Kuti used to be a Government-run cattle ranch. Set just north of Salima, close to Senga Bay near the southern end of Lake Malawi, the ranch land lies in flat acacia-brachystegia woodland, edging down into swampy ground towards the lake. This tract of land recently changed hands and is now owned by the Game Producers Association of Malawi, known here affectionately as The Hunters and

---

[23] Kuti has been developed considerably since we were there, but alas no elephant rides. https://www.kuti-malawi.org/

Poachers. They obtained Danish funding to start a game breeding project on this land. Now the place is called the Kuti Community Wildlife Ranch.

The road to Salima from Lilongwe is a lovely bit of engineering. It curls and loops over the low swells of the central African plateau before taking on a more energetic feel as it threads a fluid path down the escarpment to the lake. As the road begins to level out towards the lake basin, baobabs raise hippo-coloured arms to the early morning sky and the road is lined with rattan furniture for sale and in the making. Pedestrians and bicycles multiply as we draw near to Salima itself, and the stately winter thorns, (*Acacia* or *Faidherbia albida*) are just coming into leaf. Now they look less like pencil sketches and more like hand-tinted etchings against the bold oil colours of late summer. Science muttered darkly that they should be a nationally protected species, as we turned across the long abandoned railway line towards Kuti Ranch.

We were there in a semi-official capacity. Science had been asked to give advice to the fledgling Game Producers company regarding their land, and he is always happy to look over any unexplored (by him) wild area, and to hand out generous advice to anyone involved in conservation.

"But these are the Hunters and Poachers!" I exclaimed on being told of the visit.

"That's right," came the mild reply, "Hunters often make the world's most effective conservationists. Ethical hunters spend a lot of time on foot in the bush just tracking animals, and they're acute observers. So they get to understand game far better than a lot of people. Consequently when they do go into conservation they understand about conserving habitat rather than species."

"But they're going to kill the animals in the end," I complained. Science looked at me pityingly.

"Tell me something," he asked. "Which would you prefer—to die of slow starvation when your teeth wear out, or to go very quickly?"

Without waiting for an answer he went on.

"You see, as that great Canadian naturalist, Ernest Thompson Seton, said over a century ago, 'The life of a wild animal always has a tragic end.' That's a fact, whether we like it or not. To me, being shot cleanly is less tragic than several other kinds of natural death."

I opened my mouth and waited for words to come, but couldn't find any. Science glanced at me sideways and smiled gently.

"I'll admit that a hunter's involvement in conservation is based purely on self-interest. They protect areas so that their grandchildren will have something to hunt. That's fine by me. It's a darn sight more noble than not noticing creatures are dying out, like 90% of urban humanity. Wildlife in Malawi is in trouble. These guys want to help put that right so they can maybe hunt something in ten or fifteen years' time. Good for them, I say. I'll happily give whatever help I can."

Suitably silenced, I noticed a scatter of rose-coloured blooms of wild ginger among sky-blue dayflowers. A red bishop bird clung to a bulrush like a scarlet fuzzy clip-on toy and a gabar goshawk swung across the track like a grey breeze, his banded tail a broad fan.

The brief tour of Kuti's 3000 hectares was a delight. A lot of it is open miombo woodland, and though many think that utterly dull and monotonous, I adore the wonderful elegance of the brachystegia trees and the dappling of light and shade. Besides, I have it on good authority that if you sit still in miombo woodland in Malawi, you are likely to see up to 100 species of birds. You could see 150 in an hour and a half. At least, that's what our local bird expert expects to see. But since I love looking at the trees and grasses and flowers as much as the birds, I don't mind seeing a little fewer of the latter.

We did see what I thought was a waxbill's nest, about shoulder height in a hostile little thorn sapling. Science bent his head to it and enquired politely,

"Gok, gok, gok?", the almost universal southern African imitation of knuckles on a wooden door. There was an unsurprising lack of response from the nest. In his best Chichewa he asked, "Odi? Odi?" the polite Malawian equivalent of "Is anyone at home?" Still nothing.

"I think the bird's out," I suggested helpfully. Science looked momentarily taken aback.

"It's not a bird," he said. "It's a *Dendromus*—literally 'tree mouse'. This is a climbing mouse's nest."

We examined the scraggy looking bundle of coarse grass and found a small opening in the side. Through this we could see a neater inner nest of fine woven grasses, and not a feather to be seen.

"See?" said Science smugly. "Mouse-house."

Climbing mice are exclusively African and not often

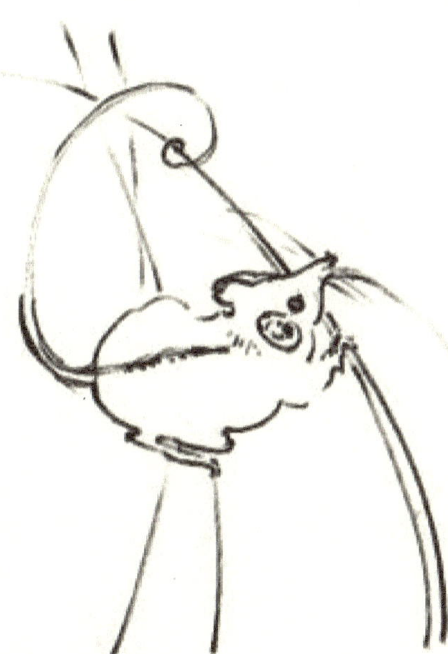

seen. Tiny insectivorous creatures, they have specially adapted feet for clambering, and a semi-prehensile tail to twine round their fragile perches. I have lived in Africa for more than fifty years and I have never seen one.

Suddenly I recognised what Science had been saying about the value of conserving this whole area. Apart from providing a safe breeding ground for valuable game like sable and roan and Lichtenstein's hartebeest— thanks to the hunters—the Kuti Wildlife Ranch will also be a haven for the tiny, unnoticed but equally scarce creatures which could disappear without anyone noticing.

There is one particular part of Kuti that is gorgeous by anyone's standard. The woodland thins to lush long-grass meadow with a distant view of the purple and blue barrier of the Rift Escarpment. This is the view of Africa every tourist wants. Purple mountains behind flat-topped trees amid rich savannah. All it needs are the quietly grazing herds of zebra, wildebeest and impala.

And giraffe! I hear you add. No, not giraffe—there are no giraffe in Malawi, there never have been—but that's another story.

## Solly for Dat
### 18ᵗʰ March

Once again the week has been devoured by termites. I've just managed to wrestle this last fragment back before the week is irrevocably gone.

Assisting the little critters whittle away the week have been some sneaky blood-parasites called *Falcatum Tropicana*—better known as malaria. They began their assault on Science late on Friday night, and by Saturday morning he had a fever.

"I feel fragmented," he muttered, "Fractured in great giraffe cracks from the dermis all the way through my being."

This Scientific description of his state of health was confirmed by an attack of the shivers after his shower, and by the time we got to the clinic for a blood-test he was politely throwing up in the laboratory sink. He has an inbuilt flair for politeness. He is the only person I know who says "May I?" on the point of puke. Luckily the technician was wise enough to say "Yes", since my wildly searching mind failed to come up with a useful alternative.

But we've caught the illness right in its opening phase, and blipped it on the head with the Chinese Cure, as we did over Christmas. By this afternoon (Sunday) his fever was barely there at all, and he insisted on a bicycle ride. I eyed him dubiously, but arguing with Science is a pointless process for a wordsmith. However, once I'd agreed to a gentle local totter through the overgrown jungle of urban corn-fields, I found him strapping his grass-slasher to the cross bar.

"What's that for?" I demanded.

"Just to clear the path of a bit of grass," he replied serenely, "And a bit of *Acacia ataxacantha*."[24]

"Attacks a camper?" I asked blankly.

"And cyclists too if we're not careful," he threw over his shoulder as he and Bags raced for the gate.

"Malaria indeed!" I muttered, puffing in their wake.

It's been a while since there's been enough dry weather to go out on the bikes, and despite my misgivings, it was a beautiful afternoon for a ride. Rich sunshine turned the rampant bush to a glowing Technicolor foreground, with noble clouds heaped majestically on the horizon. There is a shift in the season though. The air is notably cooler on the skin, and high against the sky as it pales to twilight is a pattern of cloud we haven't seen for a while—little cloud-cobble-stones, and wisps of horse-tails. Perhaps the rains are coming to an end at last. How sad for Bags.

Our third-hand-dog had a repressed childhood we think, and the most urban of upbringings. She's of an age with us—grizzled on the muzzle and a faint tinge of blue on her brown eyes. She's deeply, maturely refined, and you know what they say about old dogs. Yet here she is, discovering something new. It's very low-key yet, but she's actually crossing to the other side of the path to splash through a puddle instead of carefully going around it like she used to, and while Science parked his bike in a patch of twelve foot elephant grass and attacked the fiercely thorny acacias that shred our legs as we pass, Bags was actually on the point of playing.

Three times through the same puddle, each time with a bit more speed, the last with muzzle lowered and a delicate shake of the head. It's enchanting to watch this old

---

[24] The fiercely thorny Flame thorn.

girl rediscovering her lost puppy-hood. I hope she won't have forgotten this by the time the rains come next season.

And Science? I think he's in better shape than I am. We've been back for about an hour and I still feel a bit blown. He's chirpy as a cricket and brim full of energy. Which is more than I can say for the week that was. It's been such a useless week that I haven't even managed to get a story down for you. As they so charmingly say in Malawi, "Solly for dat." This comment covers a breadth of circumstances from a mislaid key to a derailed train, "Solly for dat." And they genuinely are, too.

Never mind, I will do better next week. Till then, please stay well and never forget that despite the resilience of Science, the most dangerous creature in Africa (apart from man) is the mosquito.


## Sauce for the Goose
### 25th March

Hello from the Wan Heart of Africa.

No, it's not a spelling mistake, it's me planting my feebleness on broader shoulders. Where Science succumbed to malaria like a dabchick to water, or a kingfisher—splash down, bob up and off again—I have taken to it like a cormorant. I sank swiftly, stayed under longer, and have surfaced feeling water-logged and heavy.

Which reminds me—before we took our relayed plunge into illness, we drove out to Lilongwe's least salubrious bird-watching spot, the water-purification plant. It's not the sort of place one likes to admit to hanging out, but if you yearn to see water-birds, this is the one-stop-shop. Besides, we hadn't been there before, and any funny comment you're thinking up about the link between the sewerage farm and a dose of "bad-air" can just be scrapped, ok? Or I won't tell you what we saw.

It's actually not such a shocking place to be. Once you're there. From the gate to the end-of-the-line overflow pools is a bit hairy, the road winds through all the settling tanks and the air is somewhat rich and hard to breathe, but the combination of stout lungs and a good accelerator will see you through. There is a shielding dump of spoil, thrown up as the pools were dug, between the overflow pools and the smellier working half, so both view and aroma are considerably improved. The pools themselves are boringly rectangular, laid out in stark grassed surroundings with a raised walkway like a tow-path between them. The entire area overlooks a stretch of the Lilongwe River, and the opposite bank has an attractive relic riverine fringe.

Looking at the view of the river seemed so much more interesting than looking at the apparently birdless pools, that we spent some time ignoring the latter altogether. It was only when I happened to notice the distinctive head of a lady pochard peering at us over the crest of the walk-way that we began to take an interest in the pools.

Funny thing about focus. Once it's fixed on something, it seems to draw attention from all sorts of quarters. Suddenly Bags found the water irresistible and a trio of local lads arrived, obviously intent on leaving no tern unstoned. By this time we had discovered a handsome group of southern pochard, a flotilla of dabchick and a pair of redbilled teal, not to mention the flurries of bobbing pied wagtails and scudding drifts of little sandpipers.

Between the attentions of the locals and the distraction of Bags, the birds weren't happy to hang about much, so our visit was relatively brief. To add to our accelerated departure, the lads enlivened their bird-hunting by alternating with a bit of mzungu-baiting, and calls of "Give me money!" followed us around the pools, as they strolled the walk-ways.

Just as the entire afternoon was beginning to seem utterly pointless we saw Hottentot teal! Not one, about a hundred and fifty of them. They sat contentedly on the sloping bank of a pool, neat little blue bills all pointing westward, speckled tummy feathers lowered over their feet. Their eyes are just inside the dark cap that runs from the top of the bill to the nape of the neck, so I couldn't see if they were awake or not, but they seem still enough to be snoozing. A couple of redbilled teal kept them company, looking like outsized cousins.

There was one other remarkable bird there. At first I thought it was a pelican, since it seemed to be floating on the surface, but as it moved towards the bank we saw it was a flamingo. What a daft idea, a flamingo up to its armpits in water! But it had been, and now there it was, all pink legs and snowy tutu, its too-heavy beak propped up on the end of its neck like an elevated waiter's tray. Poor bewildered bird, I wonder what it was up to, all alone among the ankle-high Hottentot teal.

"Who knows?" said Science as we held our breath and headed hastily for the gate.

"Who knows," he resumed after a while. "Maybe it got blown off course. Maybe it still thinks it's an ugly duckling. Maybe it's the only one that hasn't yet been eaten. Who knows?"

I dunno, I expect Science to provide all the answers, just like the rest of the developed world does.

Uplifting stuff this—a visit to the sewerage works retold by a malaria invalid.


# Tall story
## 26th March

The wood carvers of Malawi are well known. Few tourists leave the country without at least one example of the carvers' art among the trophies of their stay. One of the most popular is the enchantingly elegant giraffe.

There are at least two reasons why the giraffe carvings are so popular. The first is that it so neatly symbolises the African experience. It is unlike any other animal on earth; it is, like Africa, astoundingly over-the-top. It's an almost-antelope stretched up tall with a coat pattern as pretty as a jungle-cat, and its size is as impressive as that of elephant or rhino. It's the only huge mammal with hair, and it has an all over military no.1-style haircut, except for its tail tuft. It is enigmatically silent for the most part, is confidingly curious, has the world's longest eyelashes, and has been known to kill a lion with a single kick. How can one possibly resist it?

I've seen tourists go through the most remarkable contortions manoeuvring six-foot carvings of giraffes into aircraft as hand-luggage. These cumbersome curios will take pride of place in their homes and forever remind them of their visit to Malawi. Yet the only giraffes they are likely to see in Malawi are wooden ones. Malawi doesn't have any giraffe, and according to the 1897 journal of the Consul-General to British Central Africa, Sir Harry H Johnston, KCB: "...the existence of giraffe...is still a moot question...up to the present time no European has sighted the animal... nor have any tangible proofs, such as skulls, tails, or skins, been sent back as evidence of its existence."

If there had been any in Malawi, the evidence would certainly have been seen. Giraffe tails make wonderful fly-whisks, a very important part of a chief's regalia, and the length of the hide is invaluable for the very long whips needed to reach across the backs of an entire span of oxen. Yet Sir Harry saw no sign of these in Malawi, while admitting that there were rumours of giraffe in the nearby Luangwa Valley.

Indeed giraffe are found in Luangwa, and if you know your geography, you'll be intrigued by the fact that the Luanguwa Valley converges with Malawi in the north. So why there, and not here?

The reason is obscure. It seems there is only one species of giraffe throughout Africa, though several sub-species have been named, due mainly to the pattern of blotches on the hide, though there is some variation in the bony structures that we call horns. But it would suggest that long, long ago giraffe were found everywhere in sub-

Saharan Africa. Though not tagged as an endangered species, its distribution has become fragmented through human settlement, perhaps the rinderpest, and general over-exploitation.

Yet it's hard to see how giraffes got that far across what must be giraffe-unfriendly terrain. They are remarkably picky when it comes to habitat. They feed on foliage, and like a certain mix of trees to browse off, but they don't like forests. They also don't like open plains, because there are not enough trees. They don't like marshy ground, and neither would you if you walked on stilts, and they don't like deserts because they do drink water now and then. They're not noted for their mountaineering aspirations either. All that seems to make finding the right place for giraffes to flourish surprisingly easy. You know exactly what to look for, and obviously Malawi hasn't got it. Or not enough of it.

But it's actually not that obvious. Zoologist Reay Smithers wrote,

> "In several parts of their range they occur on one side of a river and not on the other (Niger River in West Africa; Lundi River in Zimbabwe, and the Save River in Mozambique). This is understandable where major rivers with permanent water form barriers, for it is known that in captivity a water barrier effectively contains them. But in the last two named examples these rivers, in the dry season, are in parts dry and sandy, yet the giraffes do not cross."

However, the proto-giraffe and his mate wandered the length and breadth of Africa, and left a nucleus of this tribe in each expanse of treed savannah. Each little pocket of giraffes interbred and produced the varieties we see (or think we see) now, the net-patterned Reticulated giraffe to the north of Kenya, Thornicroft's giraffe in Luangwa (whose special marks of variance from the southern giraffe I fail to see), and the Maasai giraffe *Giraffa camelopardalis*

*tippelskirchi* with its wonderfully irregular leaf-patterned blotches. And others.

Then there is the Malawian wooden giraffe, which is—must be—unlike any giraffe anywhere else, since the wood-carvers have never seen one in the flesh. That the carving is recognisable at all is due entirely to the giraffes exaggerated physiognomy, not to artistic skill or keen observation. A giraffe is unmistakable, and that is rare indeed.

The second reason why wooden giraffes are so fabulously popular, and this perhaps the tourists themselves don't know, is that modern living spaces are notoriously small. But a six foot carving of a giraffe takes up only one foot of floor space, and makes a grand statement in a confined area. African ethno-chic worth every ounce of embarrassment on the way home.

## Something squishy
### 31ˢᵗ March

Well, the lurgy won the last round. We went back to our charming local Doctor, a fine-boned Hollander, who patted my hand and told me it's not my fault, that malaria is causing problems all over the country at the moment.

"But don't you worry!" he exclaimed fiercely, planning an assault of two sets of anti-malaria drugs and a hyper dose of antibiotics, "We'll get those little bugs out of your system! We will kill them on the beaches!!"

I sat through the irritation of yet another blood-test unsure of how I felt about my Doctor referring to me as a beach. Science found it so funny that his mirth was infectious, and we sat in the waiting room shaking with suppressed hillaria. We left loaded up to the eyebrows with an arsenal of malarially-deadly muti. End of an interesting week.

We had spent the first half in Kasungu National Park—with another of Science's seemingly endless workshops. The place is absolutely sodden. The rain is still bucketing down, and the earth is so saturated that it all just runs straight off. Small streams are gushing brooks, and the

dambos are wall-to-wall—or at least woodland-to-woodland—water. There is so much water around that the hippos have wandered away from Lifupa Dam on an extended tour of the Park and their big flower-like footprints are found in places that they normally wouldn't go.

Before breakfast on Wednesday morning Science decided to see how the dam-wall was holding up in all this wet. We trundled along squelching mud tracks to the spillway, about two feet deep in rushing water. Science got out, commented scientifically on three sizes of pug-marks in the mud—"Hyena, serval and a weenie ikkle puddy-tat,"—climbed back in and casually drove across what looked to me like a mill-race. He'd clearly forgotten that he told me how he'd lost his footing in this very place at low water, and took an algae-greased super-tube trip down about ten feet of concrete to the river-bed below, giggling helplessly. Unfortunately my memory is less selective than his, and malaria ate my sense of humour.

Of course we crossed without incident. But the sedate progression along the crest of the dam-wall was pulse-provoking. The packed-earth wall stands twenty or thirty feet above the shallow valley, and since we were there to examine possible damage to the base of the wall from the out-flow pipe, I didn't feel all that secure. At times like this there is great comfort to be had from Science being not the least given to the sort of vivid imagination that plagues a wordsmithing story-teller. By the time we got across to the other side, I couldn't wait to leap out, regardless of shoulder-high rain-soaked grass and ankle-deep mud.

The inspection of the blow-hole below the dam showed that the outlet was coping remarkably well with the huge volumes of water, and there was hardly any erosion to speak of. The water boiled and slapped against the drenched bank of the river-bed, spilling over into the grass in sheets and runnels of shimmery wet.

"Look," said Science, "The Shining Path. I've always thought that was an odd name for a bunch of guerrillas."

As we looked we realised that half the shimmer was not from the water alone. Each shallow rivulet was seething with little fish. Tiny fingerlings, about as big as my little finger, flanks flashing silver in the early morning light, wriggling and squirming though grass stems and roots.

"What are they?" I gasped, and Science, always delighted to supply an answer, said knowledgeably, "It's a gillieminkie subspecies."

Just when you know he's taking the Mickey, the wretched man turns out to be quite serious and spot on. "Gillieminkie" is the common name given to the small *barbus* species, which is exactly what these were. The fish seemed intent on working their way back to the main body of water. The serious Scientific suggestion is that they came out into the grass to feed at night, and were now making their way back to the comparative safety of the deep water. What a delight to see a million little fish hurrying home in the pale dawn light!

We made our damp and squishy way back to the car, and Science sighed.

"Soggy from the knees down and grass-seeds in the crotch. This has to be paradise."

Amen to that, I say. If malaria is the price, I'm happy to pay. Almost.

Till next week then, stomp on any mosquitoes you find, please. It won't help, but it will make me feel less resentful.

## Even Taller Story
### 2nd April

With giraffes on our minds for the last few days, Science remembered the incident of the lovelorn creature of Kyle National Park. This hand-reared giraffe had, like so many hand-reared wild animals, developed a personal kink which made him very difficult to live with. He had no fear of people and a passion for their laundry. A wash-line hung with drying sheets and blankets was his ultimate turn on, and the staff at Kyle frequently had to re-wash their bedding after enthusiastic insemination by the fence-breaking reprobate. This giraffe was one kinky puppy.

"It was early in my career with Zimbabwe's Wildlife Department," said Science, crinkling his eyes thoughtfully, "And we had one of our in-house training courses at Kyle. Rangers came from around the country for these sessions, and we were camped out under the msasa trees[25]. Most of the chaps had their tents in a neat little group, military style, the guy-ropes neatly interlaced and ship-shape. I was a bit

---

[25] Msasa is the common Shona name for *Brachystegia spiciformis*, and is used in place of Brechystegia or miombo woodland in which *B speciformis* is the dominant species.

of a loner, and didn't often use a tent in those days, so I was on the other side of a little dry water-course, my camp-bed on a tarpaulin under the stars. Nice, neat little camp, my kit box at the head of the bed, everything stowed away. In case of rain I'd slung a cable between two branches above me, so I could whip up a tarp if needed, and quite contented I stripped down to my usual sleeping gear[26] and went to bed.

"I was just dozing off when this giraffe appeared at the foot of my bed." Science looked deeply offended. "His front feet were right there, at the end of my camp bed. I don't know what he thought he was doing, maybe he was playing with the cable, but he began to swing his head at me. Do you know how big a giraffe's head is?" he demanded.

"A big male's head can weigh up to 40 kilograms. This chap wasn't quite as big as that, but he was as big as a fully grown female. They use their heads as a bludgeon to batter each other." His eyes narrowed.

"I watched this stupid animal swing his head over me a few times, and his head got a bit lower with each swing. But I was more concerned about that pair of giant hooves at the end of my bed. History is too littered with stove-in skulls and the corpses of trampled crocodiles for me to ignore those feet. So I loosened the bed-clothes and reached over my head into my kit-box, carefully feeling for my .45 handgun. As the head came past again, I let off a shot right next to his ear." There was a tense pause as Science lined up his memories.

"It didn't have quite the effect I wanted. The giraffe's head went up, and as it went up, so did a foot. I rolled out of bed as the foot came down in the middle of the camp bed. The weight of it pushed the bed right down, flat against the tarp. Damn thing could have killed me! So I let off another round, this time with enough distance for it to see the flash and know something unhealthy was happening."

Science grinned, and shook his head.

---

[26] i.e.naked

"The only thing that happened was a growl from one of the tents opposite. The Chief Warden's voice, saying 'If you kill that fucking animal I'll have your guts for garters!' And the giraffe was still coming for me. So I ducked off among the trees and round the back behind their tents, giraffe in tow. Then I carefully threaded my way between  all the guy-ropes, and back to bed. For the next half-hour or so there was much cursing and yelling as the giraffe got entangled in the web of ropes, and tents toppled and collapsed." I pictured Science, tip-toeing stark naked through the night followed by a smitten giraffe, and rocking with laughter at the irritable sounds of an entire campsite being savaged and salvaged by moonlight.

The story wasn't quite over. Come daybreak Science's camp-attendant, who rejoiced in the name of Dilly, came waving an empty frying-pan to complain, "That animal won't let me cook". And there the giraffe was, straddling the breakfast fire, looking at Science with love-lorn eyes. He tried a few thwacks on its rump with a steel radio aerial, but gave up at the creature's apparent enjoyment, and eventually, after half an hour or more of failed attempts to dampen its ardour, Science managed to literally drive the beast off by repeatedly reversing a Land Rover against its legs. In time it was rounded up by game-guards on horseback, and herded out of the fenced administrative enclosure and back into the park itself.

Science has no idea what happened to the giraffe in the end. Perhaps it met an amiable young female giraffe and gave up its kinky bent. It is more likely it came to a sticky end, but we don't know. For me, the most hilarious part of the story is that a giraffe found Science as sexy as a wash-line of wet blankets. That must say something for the man.

## Pumpkin Time
8<sup>th</sup> April

Suddenly, it is pumpkin time. The maize plants are looking wilted and withered, and the deep understory of pumpkin leaves is dotted with swelling spheres of speckled green and yellow. Piles of pumpkins wait at road-side stalls for sale, and the local art group is starting restlessly to think of still-life studies.

Today we woke to a sky of pale eggshell blue with not a cloud in it. Not one! And then we noticed that the moss on the top of our garden wall is turning brown. It hasn't rained for two whole days. All week the drizzle has pussy-footed round the house at night, tapping at the foliage and rustling in the reeds. Then on Thursday great thunder-heads built up and growled a bit before dissolving into a weak patter of drops and an ignominious retreat. I think the rain is really over now.

But the aftermath of a long wet season is still being felt. At the local clinic the technician told me that 95 percent of the blood-tests taken are proving malaria positive. The worst for us is that the acclaimed Chinese cure—a wonderfully fast, *Artemisia*-based drug that seems to have no side effects—appears to be insufficient. The problem is one of packaging, I think, since the English instructions imply that you need to open a second package to complete the cure—and by then you're feeling in the pink, so why bother? Then, bingo, in a week or so you're sick as a dog again.

Science and I are taking turns. He'd been feeling a bit off-colour for a few days, and cheerfully poo-poo-ed my suggestion that it's malaria. It caught up with him on Friday and really hit him hard. Within minutes of getting him to the clinic he could hardly stand. The blood test showed 3+. They tell me a count of 4 is about as sick as you can get and maybe survive. He went onto a quinine drip immediately, and to my utter amazement managed to get himself discharged on Saturday. He swears he didn't intimidate the doctor, and I'm so pleased to have him home that I chose to believe him.

But I don't think we're out of the woods yet. We'll both be back to see the doctor in the morning and have another blood test done—it's no fun feeling like your bones are made of boiled spaghetti. Especially when the sun is shining and Schalow's lourie[27] is rattling its teeth in the acacia, and a coucal is sneaking like an assassin across the moss-covered wall. The brown mossed wall.

Winter is definitely on its way; as if in confirmation dusk fell like theatre lighting this evening—swift fade to black. We were startled to find it was only six-thirty. Half-past six in early April, and it's dark. Amazing.

Next week is Easter. Science and I will be taking a bit of time off to recuperate; I hope the Bunny brings you everything you wish for. I bet dentists everywhere concur.


## An Infestation of Aunts
### 9th April


On one of her infrequent trips into Lilongwe, Birgitt received a small parcel from Germany. "Oh, good!" she exclaimed. "It's my aunt poison at last!"

"Sorry?" I asked, startled.

"Aunt poison," repeated Birgitt waving the parcel about. "I have an infestation of aunts in my kitchen in Kasungu."

---

[27] *Tauraco schalowi*

Of course. Why not? And what better way to deal with superfluous aunts than to poison them?

It didn't take me long to realise she meant ants. Birgitt is officially German, but she has quantities of Portuguese in her blood, was brought up in South Africa and Greece and educated in Canada and England. I think the aunts may be Canadian rather than German, but I didn't point out the flaw. I happen to think that having an infestation of aunts is much more interesting that plain old ants, which every other person in Africa has.

Besides, she's right. It's probably the rains that have done it and a higher water-table; aunts have invaded our house at an unprecedented rate this year. Where last year we had one group of constant kitchen-cleaners, this year there are no less than three separate groups.

The original cupboard colony is a society of tiny pale brown ants who are not much of a nuisance at all. I see a pale stream of them in ragged Indian file across the back of the grocery cupboard, but seldom if ever in the food. Occasionally they become revolting by being ground into a paste as you open the honey jar, but they are so small and their numbers are not overwhelming, so we have been content just to let them be.

The next arrivals are the ones I've always called sugar ants—the hordes of little black ones that find jam pots irresistible. And bread, and meat, and fruit, and absolutely anything else. Most annoyingly, they love to hang out in the kettle. We have an entire sink with hot and cold water at their eternal disposal, but they insist on trooping surreptitiously under the kettle lid and appearing as little boiled corpses in our morning tea. Of our three aunt populations, these are the ones I would most like to poison.

The third and latest aunt invaders came two-by-two, like Mutt and Jeff, Laurel and Hardy, Morcombe and Wise, Livingstone and Stanley. These are really big chaps with bodies as long as the first joint of my thumb. Their legs are long and slender and their hugely active feelers are a cause of constant concern to them. After a short explorative meander, each ant will stop and nibble and fuss and clean its feelers. They are also concerned about their abdomens, since they will frequently tuck their tails under and groom themselves much as a dog will.

 These are the comedy aunts. They are nervous, irresolute, and wildly sensitive to vibration. They are also prone to substance abuse. Having tentatively explored for a few days they soon made full acquaintance with the kitchen, and invited all their mates in. Their full focus is on the sugar bowl. That seems to blow them away. They provide Science with the highlight of his tea-making activities in the morning. I hear a few sleepy crockery noises, a pause, then a thud followed by Scientific chortling. He re-appears in the bedroom with two steaming mugs of tea and a wide grin.

I can picture the scene. A sugar bowl full of big, glossy, apparently dozing ants. Science gently picks up the bowl, and thumps it down again. After a second of stunned surprise, the ants boil out, hitting the counter in a starburst—you can almost hear them shout "Every man for himself!" Within seconds they've gone, some rushing straight over the edge of the counter without stopping, and landing on the floor like Wiley E Coyote on a bad day, feet thrashing all the way down.

All except one or two who are still out cold in the sugar, totally immobile. They don't even exude a lazy "Hey, chill out, bro." They are utterly zonked. Science carefully picks them up and escorts them to the door personally. Getting wasted on sugar must be the most harmless addiction around.

We found an unusual ant heap in the garden a few days ago. Quite an impressive affair. A flattish cone of equally sized little stones, like miniature boulders, heaped around the entrance hole. Later I learned that these are not excavated from the ground, but gathered by workers from the surface and deposited there. Extraordinary thing to do! I would love to tell you this is the home of the comedy aunts, but I really don't know.

I found a lot of fascinating stuff about ants when I began taking an interest. Like—they are close relatives to bees and wasps, hence the distinctive narrow waists and why a wingless wasp can masquerade as an ant. That all ants have stings, though many don't use them. And the delicious dramas that unfold as fierce raptors disguise themselves as friends to bluff their way into ant colonies—stories of butterfly larvae being sheltered and nursed by ants, while their caterpillars stuff their little faces with the ant's favourite food.

Then came the ultimate revelation. "Hey, Science," I yelped, thumbing through Skaife's *African Insect Life*, "Listen to this! 'A colony comprises a queen or queens... and a large number of workers, all of whom are sterile females.' Birgitt is right! They really ARE aunts!"

Naturally Science had the last word.

"Indeed, they are," he said, "and maiden ones at that."

## Season of mists
### 23rd April

The early sun is blazing in a colourless sky, pale as paper. Long light striking through the grass-heads in our snake-pasture creates an illusion of mist on the ground and the air is cool as glass against the skin. It's a glorious time of year.

Lilongwe is ablaze with yellow cassia trees and scarlet poinsettias. It seems every garden has two or three of each, even out in the countryside where villages are looking romantic in forests of elephant grass. It's been a great year for creepers, and butter-coloured loofah flowers raise their saucer faces on long stems to nod at passing traffic. Jelly-powder-pink foxgloves, saffron-yellow daisies and a scatter of marshmallow cosmos follow the road; the grass is ripening heavily to gold.

A ruby mist of *Rhynchelytrum*, the fluffy headed red-top grass, tinted the flanks of hills and the blue bowl of the sky was marbled with cirrus as we headed north on Friday. The first sour smell of burning grass pricked our nostrils— a startling foretaste of winter.

Science addressed the Wildlife Society at the Dwangwa Sugar Estate on Friday night, and with his flair for extracting delight from unlikely sources it's always hard to tell where business stops and pleasure begins. We had an entertaining evening and a comfortable night at the country-club, and, wrapped in kikois[28], took our early morning tea out beside the swimming pool, where the pool-light had been on all night. Before breakfast we had rescued two fat beetles, three mole-crickets, a large shabby moth, four big 'brown bombers'—sometimes called sausage ants, they are winged male driver ants[29]—and a huge click-beetle. This last was clasping the bloated corpse of a little frog to its plated chest, hanging on so fiercely we suspected it of carnivorous intent, despite its vegetarian reputation.

And we retrieved the body of an ant-lion adult, bigger than a dragonfly, its broad transparent wings mottled black. As I studied it in the early sunshine, I found it littered with tiny survivors and a few corpses—minute beetles, midges, spiders and winged creatures too small to name. This must have been a veritable life-raft in the Titanic of the night.

After breakfast we were shown the Dwangwa fish sanctuary, wonderfully encouraging stuff. An innovation spearheaded by the Wildlife Society with the full approval of the local chief, it is simply a stretch of lake shore where

---

[28] A Swahili word for a length of cotton cloth generally worn around the waist in lieu of trousers by men, and tied like a towel under the arms by women, popular casual clothing in central and east Africa.
[29] *Dorylus*, the genus name for driver or army ants; in Malawi there are three species and two subspecies.

fishing is banned outright, but it deserves a full story to itself. To see something positive being done raised our spirits considerably after our depressing time at Cape Maclear—you can read all about that in this week's story, which I've called Lake of Tears.

The rest of our week-end was an equal blend of business and delight, a gradual progression southward down the lake and back home, revelling in the early autumn air. The lake is still tinged with cocoa-coloured silt from flood waters, the level is 1.6 metres higher than last year. The *mwera* has begun to blow, sending waves crashing to the beach with a sea-like roar. Out of the wind, golden reed-mats have been dragged into the sun and spread with the pulped flesh of cassava tubers, white and fibrous. It has the most off-putting smell, as if someone had been sick. But the glossy leaved jasmine tree is in bloom, and the fragrance of those flowers keeps one sniffing hopefully.

## Lake of Tears
### 23rd April

It is said that when Livingstone first saw Lake Malawi in all its sparkling beauty, he had a rush of uncharacteristic romanticism and called it 'The Lake of Stars'. It's a very apt name. The water is the colour of the brief African twilight, a deep tantalising jewel shade between turquoise and lapis—rich, translucent and deceptive. Its dimpled surface cups fragments of sunlight in a fractured blaze of tiny flecks, breathtaking as the milky-way. So much beauty makes the heart ache.

Cradle this water in an arm of cinnamon sand backed by green hills and set it with elegant islands of smooth boulders topped with forest, draped with lianas. Scatter the water with millions of jewelled fish, add the odd crocodile and a hippo or two. If you do all this, you will have a close approximation to Lake Malawi National Park. Or rather, Lake Malawi National Park as it once was.

Between the green hills and the cinnamon sand is the enclave village of Chembe at Cape Maclear, home to four thousand souls[30] all subsisting on fast failing fishing and sporadic tourism. The leached-out sandy soil between the beach and the hills is given over to precarious fields of unhappy maize, whose meagre cobs are coveted by hill-dwelling baboons.

Planted in a field right beside the only road through the Park to the lake is a six foot stake bearing the impaled head of a baboon, a banner in the eternal war between man and wildlife. Thieves are treated as they were for centuries in Europe—a satisfaction to the robbed and a warning to the robbers. The people have the right to farm this land, and the baboons have the right to live in the hills. Stopping baboons from raiding the crops is as impossible as stopping the villagers from chopping their firewood from the gradually balding hills.

We shook the sad image of the dead baboon from our eyes, and drove on to the rest camp. A group of villagers met us at the gate, each desperate to sell us something—carvings, boat-rides, fish, marijuana. Beyond the gate, the road curves past run-down buildings, ill-kempt and unattractive, more squalid than the village. These are the Park staff quarters. We pulled into a parking area beside the shell of an abandoned grand homestead, empty window frames peeling green paint and wooden shingles on the gap-toothed roof curling like old bark on a blue-gum tree. Crumbling terraces down to the beach are edged with rocks, half bricks and fragments of broken masonry. Dappled sunlight glints on broken bottles, swept neatly off the paths to lie ignored between tangled tree-roots. In a row between

---

[30] At the time of writing.

the terraces and the staff quarters are six metal-roofed rondavels.[31] These are the tourist accommodation.

When we arrived the Park had been without diesel for three weeks. No fuel for patrol boats, if they had any, no fuel for the generator, no lights, no fridges and no pumps working, so no water. No water, for three weeks. Why? Because there has been no money from the Ministry of Tourism and National Parks for more than a month, and fuel is expensive.

Nevertheless we gritted our teeth, hired a bungalow and sent one lucky sales-man to fetch his boat for a bit of refreshing fish-watching off Otter Point. A message came back an hour later that the man with the key to the boat shed was in the village and a bicycle had been dispatched to find him. Sunset arrived as the boat did. Too late to fish-watch we told him, come back tomorrow morning. We set out our camping table and began supper, with a little cooling breeze coming off the lake. As the breeze faltered, we became aware of the smell of death. No dead rats in the ceilings—no ceilings. At last Science asked the night-watchman, who was very helpful.

"That's the hippo," he said.

"Hippo?" We gaped at him.

"Yes, the hippo. The hunter shot a hippo that was worrying the village last week."

"And the carcass is still here?"

"Of course. We told him he could keep the meat here," came the reply, while he waved vaguely towards the smoke stained staff house right behind the tourist accommodation. Why not? The space was available, and the aroma is the scent of survival. The butchered hippo represents a wealth of valuable protein to the hunter, the villagers, Park staff themselves. It simply doesn't occur to anyone that it could possibly be offensive to a tourist.

---

[31] A circular one-roomed building, traditionally thatched.

We crawled onto our limp sponge-matrasses on sagging spring and steel frame beds, and draped the skimpy mosquito nets over our heads. Not wise to open a window since there are no fly-screens, and the late hippo may impinge even more with windows wide. Science and I lay sleepless, agonising over all this squalor and unused potential.

The big puzzle for Malawi is why tourism here is so slow. What is wrong with the smell of hippo meat? Why should a rogue baboon's head upset squeamish white people? The paths are neat and swept, what is wrong with the broken masonry and bottle shards? Why don't people come and spend their money here, when they have so much money and we have so little?

We drove back dispirited and unhappy. As a parting shot the elderly and unrepaired dirt road brought us literally to our knees. Gingerly manoeuvring around the rim of a pot hole and avoiding the ubiquitous pedestrians, we ran our right wheels over a solid concrete culvert hidden in the lush grass. Our solid 4x4 gently toppled over into the dust.

"She lay down like a tired elephant," Science said to friends later, and that's exactly how it was. We were bruised, dusty, and shaken, but at that slow pace no permanent damage was done. To us. However, the vehicle stayed behind when our unwillingly extended stay at Cape Maclear came to an end. With luck and help from friends, and the wonderful natural warmth and concern of Malawians, we got home safely, but still burdened with something close to guilt. We can drive away from the awkward place, but the problem stays. How do you make what should be Malawi's most attractive tourist destination workable? Can it be done? We don't know.

## So-long, April!
### 30th April

Despite the early day laying its cool cheek on my shoulder, it's still warm in the Heart. The sun has shifted closer to the horizon, and breakfast is taken with the glare full in our eyes. Honey-coloured sunlight coats the deep green leaves of the combretum trees and a red-necked francolin[32] is gloating loudly in the ripening grasses near the stream.

After almost two years here, there are still bird calls I can't identify. This morning well before dawn a diligent little feathered beastie started chipping away at his territory, carving a space out with his short sharp voice "chip..... chip... chip.. chip. chip chip chipchip", a sound almost like a ping-pong ball bouncing to a stop. Another little avian tease calls "See—saw—see! See—saw—see!" and I just can't see at all. Most frustrating.

Other singers are less secretive. This morning a line of six or eight children came threading down the footpath between our garden wall and the stream. Young voices rose and fell, meeting and blending and separating again like a plaited garland of wild flowers—a little ragged, but joyfully unselfconscious. Autumn stings the eyes like wood smoke.

It's been a fearful month. Full of illness, mishap and frenetic activity. I'm not sad to see the back of it. I'm more than ready to welcome in May, its three simple letters seem symbolic of a slowing down of the seasons.

Somehow in the last week there has been no time for a story to filter down from my brain to my fingers, and I stand before you empty handed. I need to write about fish conservation in Malawi and that story is brewing but it's not ready to be poured out yet. Perhaps a little later in the week.

---

32 Now called Spurfowl, *Pternistis afar*.

## Writer's block
### 7th May

There are times when one sails through life like a summer breeze, and times when even the simplest or best loved tasks are unfathomably difficult to achieve. For the last week or so I've been wading through three feet of mental mud with leaden legs and flailing arms. Partly, I think, it's a bout of people-poisoning brought on by over-exposure to too many new acquaintances, and partly it's due to gazing inward for too long instead of outward.

Anyway, there is no problem that can't be solved by the application of Science. Um... well... perhaps I should say I have no problem that defeats Science. For any length of time, anyhow. After weathering a week of gathering gloom, he loaded me into the car on Saturday and we drove out to Dzalanyama Forest Reserve for a bit of remedial camping in the bushes.

It's more than a year since we visited Dzalanyama. The spine of hills curves against the Mozambique border, and gurgling peat-dark water spills off their flanks to feed the Likuni, the Lilongwe, and the Namitete Rivers as they wind their way to the lake. The woodland is thinning a little now as the autumn msasas slowly lose their leaves, but it's still deep green and lush.

The grass is at the peak of its glory. Tall and lion-coloured at a distance, close-to it's a tangle of textures and  shades, rich and beautiful seed-heads hung with shimmering fibres and filaments, a riot of shaded greens, tints of gold between ginger and cream, lilacs from rose to grey. As seed-heads ripen, the leaves wither to elegant ringlets and scroll down from each stem like an Elizabethan flourish. How can one doubt a Creator when faced with the perfection of grass?

So much more rewarding to watch the dancing flicker of a campfire than the hollow shifting shapes on a telly. Conversation spirals gently with the pale smoke as it climbs into the black lace canopy on bars of moon-shadow.

We slept under a mosquito net bathed in moonlight, lulled by the litany of a distant nightjar. Somewhere between moon-down and dawn a thick-tailed galago [33] called, and I dreamed I was gathering hand-made treasures in a rich exotic market.

Sunrise, and a prelude played by three doves woke us, a peremptory turtle dove, a red-eyed dove's more discursive sentence and the tender sobbing of the emerald spotted wood dove. In no time, it seemed, day was in full blaze, and a little brown bird was expressing her annoyance at the lost morning, "tsk, tsk, tsk, tsk tsk!!!" Indeed, too soon over. But refreshing for all its brevity—and I've knuckled down with a will today, barely moving from the baleful

---

[33] *Otolemur crassicaudatus,* also called the greater bush-baby because of it's brief, repeated wailing cries in the night.

cyclops of my computer. It's been a wrangle, but I've wrestled the fish conservation story into submission, hopefully not too tied up in heavy looping prose.

Here's to inspiration, where-ever you may find it.

# Kettle of Fish
## 8th May

There is something miraculous about fishing. Something mysteriously wonderful about dangling a line into another element, and pulling into our own a live and wriggling creature. Miracle and mystery have their roots in the real world, though they seem not subject to the laws of nature. Water is colourless, but what lurks within it is mostly obscured from view. The few tantalising glimpses we get simply heighten the air of mystery and stimulate our imaginations. We see monsters in the deep, strange otherworldly beasts that fill this vast substance with spine-tingling menace.

Like children we constantly fidget and tamper with the fearful waters to prove ourselves all-grown-up. But we can't see what's going on down there. Let down your nets, and behold, a multitude of fishes, great shimmering heaps of natural silver and gold! Magical and inexhaustible, the oceans seem. Seem, because we can't see.

We assume that there will always be as much left in the water as we take out of it. A nineteenth century proverb states "There are as good fish in the sea as ever came out of it." That may have been so in the nineteenth century, but it's patently not so in the twenty-first.

Today's fishermen know this, even in Lake Malawi. Today's catches, by weight or size of fish, are smaller than ever before. The fishermen shrug, and use a finer fishing net. There are more mouths to feed; nothing can be done.

Conservationists periodically suggest reverting to traditional fishing methods to safeguard fish populations.

Nice thought. Obviously one can't catch as much fish with a fishing basket and a spear as one can with a seine net. However, contrast the ideal with this anecdote sent me by a friend in the USA. He writes:

"A small native American tribe in Washington State had been trying to earn some income for tribal collective coffers by offering up ecotourism experiences... and having a real tough time of it, until they got permission from the International Whaling Commission to reinstate their traditional whale hunts. Now 'ecotourists' are showing up by the droves who want to experience this piece of traditional packaged culture."

Great idea, and so far, so good. But there is a sting in the tail, as he ends by saying:

"Interesting that high-speed boats, radar tracking, and automatic rifles with injection-tube ammunition are all considered part of the 'traditional' hunt by the Commission."

Malawi, like the rest of Africa prior to the arrival of literate invaders, does not have a written history, and there is no record of fishing methods used before that time. But certainly the Victorian Missionaries would have been quick to introduce the locals to the labour saving devices of steel hooks and factory-made lines and nets. After all, there is a saying that goes "If you give a man a fish, you help him for one day. If you teach him how to fish, you have helped him for ever." Or words to that effect.

Unfortunately, mankind has a penchant for exploiting the environment to the limit of the technology available. Making fishing easier just means we'll run out of fish faster, even at Cape Maclear, the site of the first National Park ever proclaimed to protect freshwater fish. Casual observers, like tourists and weekend anglers, are expressing disappointment in the numbers of fish seen or caught today compared to five years ago.

Then there's the conservation tool of re-invoking old fishing taboos. It's thought that traditionally certain months of the year were fishing months and others were not, a sort of genteel sportsman-like observance of the breeding season and the need for nature to replenish herself. What seems more likely is that there were simply far fewer fishermen.

In 1861, Livingstone reported that on his approach to the place he named Cape Maclear, he "met two fishing canoes". Today you are more likely to see forty or fifty. When the first Mission Station was sited there in 1875, the greatest disadvantage was felt to be "...the absence of people in the immediate vicinity." The fishing village of Chembe, now home to four thousand people at Cape Maclear[34], simply did not exist.

The problem of over-fishing in Lake Malawi is the 'tragedy of the commons' all over again: what is communally owned is the responsibility of no-one and each person will exploit it as much as they can.

There is a small ray of hope. Up toward the north, where the Rupashe River flows through the Dwangwa Sugar Estate and into the lake, a group of concerned Malawians have proclaimed a Fish Sanctuary. With the assistance of local tribal authorities, they have declared a ban on all fishing along the coast of the lake for a distance of ten kilometres. Reed beds are left undisturbed, inlets and gullies are monitored for nets and traps, and periodic boat patrols keep fishing canoes at bay. It's early days yet, and poaching is a problem still, but it seems to be working. There have been reports of fish not seen in 16 years appearing in the river—after only a year of not very strictly enforced conservation.

This seems to tell us three things: firstly it seems to say that the old fashioned, currently very unfashionable, painfully politically incorrect method of what I call Enforced Exclusion Conservation (pronounced "eek!") is the only thing that actually works. Secondly, that like every other fishery in the world, Lake Malawi has to come to the very brink of depletion before conservation measures are seriously applied and studiously enforced.

---

[34] At the time of writing, i.e. 2001

But thirdly, and more importantly, it shows that given half a chance nature WILL replenish itself, and there is hope for the future.

## Bleating about the Bush
14th May

Good morning from the Rapidly Cooling Heart of Africa. We were woken before dawn by yet another heavy branch falling. It's obviously general knowledge now that this place possesses a mad mzungu woman who screams and threatens to call the police when people chop wood. So the use of almost silent saws on moonlit mornings has become the norm.

It's enough to make me weep. The beautiful wooded stream below our house is steadily being denuded and there is absolutely nothing I can do about it. Gradually these tall and graceful trees become lopped and deformed until at last the sad amputated trunk is felled and dragged off.

No, it's not legal. But unless one has money to buy the right to fell fire-wood in the municipal wood-lots, what can a poor man do? As the weather gets cooler, the rate of attrition will rise. Families need the wood for warmth and cooking. Nothing can be done. So there'll be a typical Malawian shrug of the shoulders and probably a bit of amusement at this strange woman who is more concerned about trees than people.

Nothing can be done. That sense of resignation that is so ubiquitous in Malawi is the one thing that I really hate about this country. Malaria? A shrug, and the comment, "The disease is with us." AIDS? Nobody dies of AIDS in Malawi! They die of pneumonia and consumption and poverty and unspecified illnesses, but not AIDS. We're running out of fish? As long as we have food today, why worry about tomorrow? Tomorrow we may be dead of unspecified diseases, but today we will eat. If Malawi is a treeless desert in ten years' time that's not our problem; don't tell us our children will suffer—there will be no children if we don't cook their food today.

It's a very interesting problem, this lack of self-determination inherent in Malawians. There are many cultural groups who actively promote the idea of living one day at a time—Buddhists, psychologists, Alcoholics Anonymous to name just a few. Christianity emphasises it too, by insisting we consider the lilies and believe that what we need will be provided. So what's wrong with truly living from hand to mouth, from day to day? Either there is a flaw somewhere or Malawians have actually perfected the art of living.

To my mind, the philosophies leave out one vital component. Yes, take each day as it comes; yes, consider the lilies; yes, have faith... but for heaven sake get involved! Julia Cameron puts it beautifully in her book *The Artist's Way*. She says, "...pray to catch the bus, then run as fast as you can."

Malawi's beauty still tugs the heart strings. It seems just the other day that I noticed the delicate delight of lace poinsettias in full bloom, and here they are again, lighting up town gardens. The huge daisy bushes are rampant in the wild, sulphur yellow starry heads towering through the elephant grass and lining dusty roads. Pink fields of fluffy red-top grass have replaced the aging gold of reaped crops. The leaves are gradually thinning on the trees, as the trees themselves are being thinned...

And for all my despair about the people, it's the people who make this the Warm Heart—both the Malawians and the mzungus.

God speed your heels as you go for the bus.

# Howard's Beginning
## 15th May

A remarkable thing about Malawi is that one meets such extraordinary people. They seem to arrive as if brought by some irresistible current. These are people who have peered into the full glare of the African sun with scrinched-up eyes and liked the view, despite glimpses of themselves in the shadow. People who are prepared to be flexible about life, but are uncompromisingly themselves. People who don't need to make a way in the world, for they have found where they want to be. Among them I have met the first white baby ever born in Mongu, a tiny village on the banks of the Zambezi; the plain-clothes nuns; the un-Happy Valley child; and the man who took his late mother to lunch. I will perhaps tell you about each of them, but this story is about a man with a mid-life crisis.

Mid-life crises are not uncommon. What is a little unusual is that Howard, a very urban electronics engineer, saw it coming. Even more surprising is that he discussed it with his wife. So they sat down and wrote out lists of their hobbies, passtimes and favourite amusements, and then compared notes. Quilting for her and rugby for him; Bible Study for her, electronics for him... but in the end they found it... yachting.

Yachting. Let me tell you, there is nothing small about Howard. He's one of those people you don't really see, because he makes such an impact. His gestures are expansive, his voice is energetic, his body is always active. It's hard to describe Howard, because he leaves a powerful impression. His wife, on the other hand, is a little lady. She's petite and finely drawn, close cropped dark curly hair and a neat smile. She's the still centre of the storm that is Howard, the buoy he ties up to, his anchor. His Danforth anchor.

So Danforth Yachting was started. With characteristic velocity, Howard set things in motion. However, velocity means nothing in Malawi. He found a lovely little bay as the site for his Lake Malawi marina within a month or two, and spent three to four years trying to locate the owners (who happened to be a pair of Government Departments) to effect permission, settle a price and pay for it. It was a circular path which lead nowhere. After four years, says Howard, his love affair with that little bay "died of old age and apathy."

He and Michelle were losing heart when it occurred to them that they should concentrate on the boat rather than the base. The great boat hunt began. That took five years. But unlike the land problem, this was time well spent. They refined their ideas and honed their thinking as they searched, and finally agreed on their dream boat. She's a thirty-seven foot ocean going catamaran, almost complete at the time of writing, and her sea trials start next month. She sleeps eight passengers in absolute luxury and has a crew of two. She'll be in operation by July this year, and is already under charter for one full month in 2002. As I said, there's nothing small about Howard.

He gives a slight shake of the head and says cheerfully "It'll take one year to get established and eighteen months to perfect, but still..." and he grins. The atmosphere of excitement completes the sentence for him: it will be demanding, draining, nerve-wracking and wild, exhilarating fun!

In the meantime, a corporate holiday cottage came up for sale at Cape Maclear, and Howard bought it as their land base. It's being revamped into a luxury four-suite lodge equipped with everything from air-conditioning to mountain bikes. Howard and Michelle glance at each other and smile.

"We've got two kids at school," admits Howard, "and this is not exactly an early retirement plan..." Michelle chips in, "But it is something we'd love to do." That's reason enough for them. In the next month they will have sold up their successful but hum-drum businesses in Lilongwe, moved their entire household to Cape Maclear, and will be awaiting the arrival by road of their catamaran "Mufasa". The problems of import duty and surtax charges are still hovering. Malawi has a 100% import tax on new goods, which the Department of Finance is prepared to waive. However, the Malawi Revenue Authority runs Customs and Excise, and they are not bound by Finance's promises.

Howard shrugs. He has a firm of accountants working on it. Neither is he concerned about the brand new, state-of-the-art telephone system installed at Cape Maclear just before Christmas last year. It got hit by lightning one week later and there is no-one in the country qualified enough to repair it. "I'll use cell phones," he says. Nor by the state of the road, which suffered serious wash-aways this last wet season. "Our guests can fly in to Club Mac and we'll fetch them by boat."

For Howard and Michelle, no problem is so big that it can't be surmounted by thinking bigger. It will be almost ten years from the time Howard recognised his mid-life crisis to the day Danforth Yachting takes to the waters of Lake Malawi. That's a long time for any crisis. Like I said, there's nothing small about Howard.

# Plain-clothes Nuns
## 21st May

To a non-Catholic, the dictates of the Vatican are a little obscure. I'm told that "kicking the habit" was a papal decision sometime back, but so what? A uniform can't make that much difference to anyone's life.

I met Doris almost by accident. Certainly it was through a misunderstanding. A German friend of mine phoned me to ask if I knew what an anagram was. Pha! Ask a wordsmith such a question! The more I explained the simplicity of an anagram, the more bewildered my friend became. Eventually she said,

"Well, whatever. There is a workshop about that this weekend. Are you interested?" Of course I'm interested. Anything to do with words is my business, so to speak.

While I mulled briefly over how anyone could stretch the subject of anagrams to fill a weekend, she volunteered to fax me the details. "Beginners Enneagram Course," read the fax, "Lead by Doris Gastonguay." As my friend had said—well, whatever.

Doris proved to be a diminutive lady of inscrutable age. She wore a sensible haircut, a practical skirt, tennis shoes on her tiny feet, and a supreme air of knowing exactly what comes next. I think Doris has always known what comes next. I have occasionally seen her at a loss for a word, but never at a complete loss. "Call me Dot," she said.

The weekend was almost over before it dawned on me that Dot is actually Sister Doris, a Missionary Sister of Our Lady of Africa. A veritable madonna in mufti. So too is Antonine, built like a lion and silent as a mouse, and dark-headed Ursula of the wide smile and large voice who follows Formula 1 and admires champion driver Michael Schumacher.

I felt shocked. I tried to scan back over the weekend, in case I'd said anything that might offend. These are the fragile flowers of the cloister, not built to withstand the coarseness of everyday life! And perhaps I was a little scandalised too—how can a nun be a motor-racing fanatic?! A plain-clothes nun sounds like a contradiction in terms.

But that's the whole point, it seems, of kicking the Habit. Dot is an American of French-Canadian descent, and has spent most of her life in Africa in a role that comes pretty close to human-resource management. She is a career-guidance professional for the entire Catholic clergy of Malawi—and anyone else who needs her help—she is an itinerant spiritual director.

"It's not a job one can do," she points out, "Unless you really understand people and the world they live in. How can you advise a young man to become a celibate if you don't understand the strength of the drive to procreate, and his particular personality?" There are many ways, it seems, of serving both mankind and a higher power, and no way of guessing how people can best serve unless they themselves are fully understood. Hence her familiarity with the enneagram, a system of personality analysis through nine basic types. Dot needs to be completely in this world, if not of it.

Ursula, too. German-born and still in close contact with her family, she understands her sister's divorce and her nephew's bitterness. She specialises in assistance to the terminally ill.

"It's all about love," she says. "People ask how I can spend day after day with people who are dying, and sometimes all night too. But if I can help them come to terms with themselves, and even more importantly, come to terms with a family that has probably abandoned them— then it's worth every minute spent at their bedside."

Somehow people expect this kind of selfless devotion from a figure in a veil and wimple, and the sacrifice is not really valued. But coming from an ordinary looking woman, the impact of such kindness is profound. We know a nun is not of this world; she has no understanding of human nature, especially the aspects we're not so proud of. She's not like us; she's closer to the angels and further from sin. Of course she can forgive and love and accept, because she doesn't understand.

One of my fellow beginners on the weekend course remarked, "I'm so glad I've had the opportunity to discover that nuns are just women like us. I was schooled at a Convent, and we knew the nuns were clockwork. We pictured them being packed into a cupboard at night and taken out and wound up again in the morning."

We all roared with laughter, but it's quite true. Women laugh and shout and weep and get their feelings hurt—nuns, we think, are way above all that. I would not, perhaps, be as impressed with Dot's more than forty years of devotion to work in dusty, fly-blown, poorest Africa if she wore a plain-coloured frock and a veil. I certainly would not have seen the fragile female frame inside those garments, nor the diamond-like personality that animates it.

## Early morning missive
## 22<sup>nd</sup> May

Dawn has laid her oriental fingers on our curtains, and outside I've found a watercolour world of soft misty blues and fading greens. The fork-tailed drongo has fluffed his breast-feathers out to cover his toes and is uttering chilly little hiccups of protest.

Now, just in case you're getting the idea that winter has us in her icy grasp, let me point out that I'm still wearing sandals and early morning protection against frost-bite consists of a long-sleeved tee-shirt. Hardly arctic stuff, but a shock when we spent the week-end near the lake and got mobbed by mosquitoes. The little critters are building resistance to the drug war, so let's hope the relative cold will cause a mass mortality on their side for a change.

We went on an extended bird-watch over towards the lake. Science had a bit of work to do on the gradually developing Kuti Community Game Ranch, so we took our camping stuff and simply wandered into the bushes and stayed over. The grass is still way up over our ears, so the view is a little less than one would like. But between the trees are glimpses of the Rift escarpment growing gradually cloud coloured as it gathers fragments of smoky mist around its shoulders.

There were only four points of excitement. The first was a flock of black egrets doing their umbrella dance in the shallow water of a dambo. Elegant sooty silhouettes with tasselled crests and bright yellow feet, they stand thigh deep in water and cup their wings over their heads like a cape. This cuts out the bright reflection of the sky and they can see fishes inspecting the tempting yellow of their toes. To see twenty-five or thirty of them curtsying and popping open their sinister black capes was like watching a convention of magicians.

The second was a very strange coloured bishop bird. Science though he was a fire-crowned bishop who had been laundered once too often. He certainly wasn't a golden bishop, but almost half-way in between. To me he looked like an apricot bishop. "Hah," says Science, "Hanky-panky among the clergy!"

The third was a beautiful lily-pond, picture perfect with delicate blue water lilies and starred with tiny yellow water-buttercups. Wading unconcernedly among them, a lesser jacana[35], one of our rarer birds in South Africa, strutted and preened. We hoped to see pygmy goose, but ran out of time.

The fourth thrill I missed altogether. Science put up a serval cat as he went to inspect a water-tower. It was little more than a rustle in the grass and a flying bound of compact fur with pointy ears and a bushy tail. But it's pleasure enough to know these rangy-legged cats are still around. To temper the delight was a brief encounter with the dreaded buffalo bean—but more of that some other time.

## The man who took his mother to lunch
28th May

Out of the way places have out-of-the-way people who inhabit them. Malawi is no different. This little story gives a glimpse of a distant place in a distant time, and a man for whom those distances were more real than the norms of urban society. I find it a touching tale; but others, more

---

[35] *Microparra capensis*

closely linked, may be offended, so names and places have been changed.

Gerald's old house is perched high above the milky ribbon of the Great Rift Valley. It seems to have sprouted like a toadstool from the damp earth where granite boulders pile up between the broad trunks of miombo forest trees. On two sides a broad veranda is roofed in corrugated iron dark as mushroom gills. A huge jacaranda tree leans wearily on the rusting roof of the lean-to kitchen behind it, and a narrow bricked path threads through a thicket laced with runaway bougainvillea to the "new" house just beyond a bulge of the hill.

The two houses seem diametrically opposed. Under the huge trees the old house is crammed with elderly furniture of dark wood and sagging cushions. Dim paintings in heavy frames deepen the gloom, and the windows are hung with fragile relics of curtains like military colours laid to rest. Dust accumulates on little tables, scattered journals and fly-blown books. Tarnished silver candlesticks gleam dully beneath heavy layers of candle wax. The carpets may have been Persian, but now are uniformly dust-coloured in the gloom.

The "new" house was built to accommodate officers in the last world war, perhaps a decade or two after the old house. It is utterly empty. It stands in the sun with a view out over the lake, a pale smudge of smoky blue below. The wooden floors are swept and clean, the deserted bathroom gleams with white tiles and light-coloured vinyl flooring. A steep path from the kitchen door winds up through strange beds of Australian plants, mostly varieties of bottle-brush. The path is hedged with an exuberance of delinquent lace poinsettia, and over it loom the huge forest trees, hung with Spanish moss and tree-orchids.

Gerald himself was an elderly pensioner when his mother decided to spend some time with him. She was probably well into her nineties by then. Since she and Gerald had never enjoyed a particularly warm relationship, it suited them both to have Mother live in the new house while Gerald stayed in the old. They met for meals in the old house and continued their almost entirely separate lives in a state of distant neutrality. A retainer, almost as old as Gerald, saw to their needs. There they lived in this neighbour-less seclusion, hardly speaking to each other, for many months.

A little village sprawls on the slopes below the houses, and the nearest town is two hours away over an appalling road. Beyond that, a slightly better tar road stretches for another three hours before reaching the nearest major city. Gerald saved his elderly little car the trip as much as possible, but once a month he would make an exception. Old friends of his lived on the road to the city, and, with the absence of a telephone, he had a regular lunch date with these friends, set for every third Sunday of the month.

It so happened that Gerald's mother died gently in her sleep on the night of the third Saturday one month. It had been her wish to be cremated rather than interred. Gerald was perhaps not demonstrably fond of his mother, but he was obedient to the last. Burying her in the vegetable garden was simply not an option.

So he and the retainer loaded Mother into Gerald's not very ample vehicle, and off he set for the city, where a large Indian population ensured the existence of a crematorium. It's a very tiring trip in an old car over bad roads, especially for an elderly man. And Gerald, like most elderly people, was a creature of habit. It was the third Sunday of the month, and he would be virtually passing their door, so stopping off for lunch with his friends was the obvious thing to do.

Both the trip and lunch were uneventful. However, when Gerald stood to take his leave, his friends were a little surprised. "But, Gerald," they protested, "Why go so soon? You always stay on for tea. What's the rush?"

"Well," said Gerald uncomfortably, "You don't understand. I have to go. I have my Mother in the car..."

"For heaven sake!" chorused the friends, "Bring her in!" Gerald hesitated awkwardly, "Well, you *really* don't understand..."

## Slugged!
### 3rd June

Hello from the Worm Heart of Africa.

This was the week of the Sulf Slug, even in Malawi. We had diligently deleted the suspect file, and followed it into the recycle bin to deliver the coup de grâce. The big job was lining up all the emails sent after we got the slimy little creature, and passing on the bad news. Luckily for me (and quite a few of you!) I had problems with the local server and couldn't get the warnings sent before lunch.

Lunch itself brought the revelation. A colleague of Science's listened to our litany of relief and frustration, and quietly nodded. "Ummm." he agreed, "I did that too. And a few minutes later I got a call from Germany to say it was a hoax. The file is one that allows Windows to cope with more than eight digits in the file-names."

We should have seen it coming. I remember getting a message forwarded from a friend almost a year ago, saying something like, "I am a third-world hacker and this is a virus. Since our technology is a little under-developed, please go to your hard drive and delete as many files as you feel will inconvenience you. Your cooperation is greatly appreciated." Hilarious. The sulf-slug hoax uses the same principle, but much more cleverly. Seldom have I been so grateful to Malawi.net for temporary congestion, or I would have helped to spread the confusion.

These periodic breakdowns in infrastructure have a decided charm of their own. My personal favourite is the early-evening power failure. After about ten minutes of almost silent blackness, you can hear generators starting up around the block. We don't have anything that fancy, so we just fish out the gas burner, light up the candles and settle down to sit it out. Far from being an inconvenience, it's almost a treat. Science and I find a book that we're both keen to read and take it in turns to read aloud to each other.

When last were you read to? I think for most of us that hasn't happened since childhood. To snuggle down on a sofa, sipping a steaming cup of tea while candle-light shrinks the room to a warm cocoon of gentle light, and your unencumbered mind can dance with the spoken word. This is a rediscovery of magic.

I feel very sorry for anyone who has such a reliable power supply that they never experience this richly simple pleasure. Generators are probably responsible for the emotional impoverishment of half of the more affluent areas of Lilongwe.

However, help is at hand! Also by email came a glorious suggestion for assisting Bush to see the error of his energy ideas. A rolling global blackout! I think it's a brilliant idea. It aims to suggest that if there's a power-supply problem, the answer is to use less power. The date is set for mid-summer's night in the northern hemisphere—June 21—and the suggestion is that we shut off all electrical appliances between 7 and 10 pm. Three hours of magic—and almost an entire month in which to plan for it. Candlelight and barbeques, live music and paraffin lamps, moonlit picnics and poetry readings. Bliss!

I don't see why the States should have all that fun by themselves, I think we should all join in and have a blackout roll gently right across the globe—to our individual pleasure.

Mind you, we won't be at home on the 21st anyway. Down in this neck of the woods we have a chance to glimpse the total eclipse of the sun on that day, so we'll be as south as we can get without falling into Mozambique, in wonderfully wild Mwabve Wildlife Reserve—camping in midwinter. I can't think why I'm looking forward to it so much!

## The Gooseberry who turned into a swan
### 4th June

There is something innately charismatic about east and central Africa, and the denizens of the region accrue a special fascination. Somehow Kenya has a higher gloss than most. The sun-drenched days of Karen Blixen's Africa and the gin-soaked nights of Happy Valley dissolution, gone for almost half a century, still rivet the imagination.

I met the only child of those Happy Valley days over a cup of tea on a Malawian veranda, and found she has inherited all that charisma, and added some of her own.

"Come and meet Juanita Carberry," my friend urged.

"Who?" I echoed blankly.

"You know!" she retorted, disbelieving of my ignorance, "The daughter of June Carberry, the woman so involved in the Lord Erroll murder. Remember the film *White Mischief*? Well, Juanita was a child when all that happened."

Carberry? I thought—oh, yes, June Carberry, wife of John Carberry, the rich fellow who lent his aeroplane to Beryl Markham, the woman who was the first to do a solo flight the other way round the world. She wrote a book about it, published in 1942, *West with the Night*. Beryl was thought to be having an affair with Blixen's boyfriend just before he flew into a mountain.

John Carberry himself was somehow not quite of either world, a sinister shadow on the furthest fringe of Blixen's brighter view and a dark malicious presence at the White Highlands' flings. Born an Irish lord, he sloughed off the title together with any noble instincts that he may have had. He sold the family castle from underneath his mother and headed for Kenya where his third wife contributed greatly to the free flow of gin and jollies that led to Lord Erroll's death.

Children had no place in that society, and Juanita must have been the single eternal gooseberry at those parties. Meeting her should be fascinating.

Whatever I had expected, it wasn't a lady-sailor. A real Merchant Navy sailor, not just week-end yachttie. Tough as a rope of chewing tobacco, black polo-necked sleeveless tee-shirt showing sinuous shoulders each with a cluster of tattoos—an elephant, an albatross, an anchor.

Someone said, "The Honourable Juanita Carberry" and she rose and shook my hand, a grip as firm as a hawser. Her shoulder-length hair was held off her angular face with an Alice-band, her clear jawbone framed by big dangley-silver earrings that looked like antique maritime instruments. She wore four or five rings on her long fingers and had an artless, uncompromising way of sitting. I pictured her swilling rum and swapping raucous stories in a smoky tavern while puffing on hand-rolled cigarettes.

Through cheerful tea-cup chatter I realised I was wrong on most counts. Juanita prefers milk to alcohol and always has. Perhaps it's the key to her remarkable looks. She could be in her late 50s. She is 76. Not a smidgen of surplus fat on her, and muscles that look as taut as a forty-something athlete. I mentally scrapped the tavern scene and asked if she remembered Beryl Markham.

"Oooh," she exclaimed with relish, "I hated her! She was a superb horsewoman and used to ride my pony. She could stretch down from the saddle at full gallop and pick a handkerchief off the lawn. That was MY pony! And there she was, doing all these things I couldn't do!"

I doubted that her arms had been long enough at the time, but her possessive jealousy surrounding her pony is understandable. As an unwanted responsibility, the scorned and rejected "brat" terrorised by her sadistic father, the only creatures to accept and return her affection were her pets. Animals have none of the vicious spite of humans.

After the horror of growing up as John Carberry's whipping-boy, Juanita found life beyond his reach blissfully without fear. She secured her distance from him by joining the Merchant Navy at 17. Her eyebrows rose in reminiscence. "I hadn't even touched a dish-towel before I joined the Navy—you can imagine the shock." She nodded a few times, and added, "But it was the making of me!"

It gave her the freedom to explore the world on her own terms. She joined up on ships bound for places like Antarctica or the Amazon, and simply signed herself off on arrival to wander into the unknown interior, unhampered by company, timetables, taboos or too much luggage. Freedom from fear, for Juanita, is almost total freedom.

Almost. She has lived too long with fear to be able to ignore it today. Nightmare memories of her father's demonic cruelty to animals and her own love of them makes her deeply sensitive to their fear, most of it man-induced. Retired from navy-larking and living in a flat in London, her days are filled with campaigning for a better life for animals. When teams of rescue workers were sent out to assist in the Indian earthquake aftermath, Juanita went along to see to the well-being of animals trapped or injured by the same disaster.

So here is the last of the notorious Happy Valley set— a fierce campaigner for, amongst others, the rights of camels in Kenya. Barely into her teens when the Erroll murder took place, she's just published the paperback edition of her account of her life at that time, called *Child of Happy Valley*. The title makes me smile. It sounds like "Son of Superman" and I hope this is a money-spinner for her. She said,

"I really wanted to write about my life in the Navy, but the publishers said there was not enough sex and violence. They told me to write my Happy Valley memoirs and to stop at sixteen."

It's a sad comment on life when there is more sex and violence prior to the age of consent than there is after. But there is no clearer indication of the woman's personal strength of character. I felt honoured to have met the Honourable Juanita. I'm glad she's claimed her title, she suits it. She deserves a less cynical publisher.

## The froggy, froggy dew
11th June

Here we are heading for mid-winter and it is perfect camping weather. How spoiled can you get? It may be a little chilly when the sun goes down, but that just makes the camp fire more of a pleasure, and it has certainly thinned the mosquitoes out.

We spent Saturday night under a monkey-bread tree[36] at Kuti. It's a time of beautiful contrasts; tall Titian-blond grass and deep green foliage still on the trees. 'Travellers joy', the wild white clematis, trails clouds of blossoms over shrubs while the growing load of red dust bronzes the vegetation on either side of the dirt road. Newly prepared loofahs are stacked beside the road for sale, together with fat baobab seedpods, mustard coloured and fuzzy, the white inner pulp prized for its tart flavour.

It's harvesting time for thatching grass. Women carry huge grass bundles more than twice their own size on their heads, their arms raised ballerina-like on either side. The shaggy bundle teeters above them, feathery tips sweeping the ground behind. They seem to have the gentle strength and sure-footedness of ants.

------

[36] *Piliostigma thonningi*

Out at Kuti a minor blizzard of butterflies dance in and out of the cool shade of a tamarind tree. Fresh pegs up the pockmarked purple flank of a baobab tell a story of annual honey harvesting. Under our monkey-bread tree millions of minute puddle-frogs, drab as mud, skitter before our feet like insects. Each about the size of a mosquito, so small and perfect they seem to float on the breeze. Almost impossible to see them when they're still, being exactly the colour of grey clay, some with a delicate cream line down the back, some without.

I twice found Science stalking through the grass like a heron—one step and pause, ear bent towards the ground, then another step...

"What are you looking for?" I asked.

He said, "Just listening to the little fellows; they sound like a tiny veld fire with grass-stems popping."

I watched the mini tidal wave of frog biota move before his feet and was grateful that I'm not a heron or an egret. There are so many froglets one could imagine them auditioning for a future part in The Great Plagues of Egypt, but catching even one is almost impossible. Any self-respecting frog-gobbler would suffer a dreadful sense of failure among all that plenty.

On Sunday afternoon we were taken by boat to Domira Bay, directly north of Kuti, in the hopes of finding a way up the Chitala River that drains the wetlands between Kuti and the lake. With a steady wind making the water choppy, we smacked our diesel-powered way over waves of beaten silver shot with electric blue. Pebble-like clouds cobbled the sky, and the on every side the land is a smudgy purple with the smoke of veld fires. Utterly, exhilaratingly beautiful.

At least l thought so. At my elbow Science growled,

"Worse than the roads! Whole wretched lake needs re-surfacing! You'd think the government would take better care of an asset like this."

It certainly was a bone-jarring experience, but worth it, though we didn't find the mouth of the Chitala River. We did find Chidoola Creek, clear tannin-black water filtering though emerald green reed beds. A wind-blown cloud of white winged terns wheeled and lifted like a chiffon scarf over the reeds, and fishermen in dug-out canoes worked each little inlet and cove with huge hand-made fish-trapping baskets.

We got back after dark, feeling rather emphatically tenderised—wind-flayed and wave pounded. But a wonderful week-end, despite the battering. I find myself struggling to gather my thoughts today, as if fragments had dropped overboard and been lost among the polished facets of the lake.

If you know of any really efficient Lake Re-surfacing Contractors, Science would be delighted.

## Jack in the Beanstalk Country
### 11th June

One of the most remarkable people Malawi has ever known was a diminutive fellow with a handle-bar moustache and a voracious appetite for knowledge. His name was Harry Hamilton Johnston and at the age of 33 he was the first Commissioner and Consul-General of what was then Nyasaland. That was 1891.

Harry Johnston, more recently described as "five foot three inches of demonic energy and ambition", burned himself out within five years. Ground down by tropical diseases, he retreated to his home in England where he was awarded a knighthood, the youngest recipient of the honour in the Empire at that time.

Those five years were hardly a stroll in the park. Slavery was rife, and Johnston—a trained artist—was being paid by the British South Africa Company to administer North-Eastern Rhodesia at the same time. Just in case time should weigh heavily on his delicate hands.

One wonders what a Victorian artist knew about warfare. Yet Harry Johnston broke the slave trade on Lake

Nyasa in those five years. That alone demands huge respect. Johnston did more. He established administrative posts in Nyasaland and North-Eastern Rhodesia at the same time. He named this area British Central Africa and—presumably on those long, TV-less tropical nights, working by candle or paraffin lamp—wrote a hugely popular *Report on the First Three Years' Administration of the Eastern Portion...*

This monumental work was reprinted several times, and it's not surprising. He was a very knowledgeable man with a lively imagination and a flair for descriptive writing. This lends a charming, typically Victorian, flavour to his writing and his *British Central Africa*, first published in 1897, was still being reprinted in 1969.

Lavishly illustrated with his impeccable paintings, drawings and etchings, this to me is about as thorough as a single book can get. It covers botany, geography, history, zoology, the people and their languages, and includes appendices detailing things from "present administration", "an analysis of Nyasaland Coal", "diseases of the natives" and "vocabularies" to lists including all known plants, butterflies, "land shells and mollusca", and much more. A staggering weight of research. I wonder if Harry Hamilton Johnston was an insomniac. Perhaps his journals and paintings were a therapy and counterweight to thumping recalcitrant Arab slave traders and treacherous colluding chieftains.

It's when I'm faced with work of this nature that I'm delighted not to be scientifically trained. I'm free to frankly admire how much this man achieved in one book without wanting to disregard it for his humour and his delicious flights of fancy. He often refers to aspects of what is today Malawi as "Jack-in-the-Beanstalk's country", at one point going on to elaborate by adding, "... a little section of land upraised and quite apart from the rest of Tropical Africa with a climate and flora of its own..." I like to think of him as Jack, amazed and thrilled by this new wonderland, a diminutive, wide-eyed stranger documenting sights no-one had recorded before.

Like Jack, Harry found there were unpleasant aspects to his Beanstalk country. In Harry's case it wasn't a giant at all. Unperturbed by marauding chiefs, murderous slavers and fierce beasts, Harry Hamilton found a truly Victorian foe. It was "malicious vegetation".

Malicious vegetation, forsooth! Among them he mentions a little plant that gives off "the most noxious smell of bad drains" when stepped on. (He's right, I've smelled it myself but never found the actual culprit.) Foul smelling arum lilies and euphorbias with toxic latex offend him equally, as did "...an atrocious pest, the 'Spanish needle'..." which I guess to be today's black-jack[37]. But he saves the worst of his spleen for the buffalo bean.

It's obvious the poor little fellow had personal experience of this, since it impressed him sufficiently to do a detailed botanical drawing of the offender, which he calls the *Mucuna* bean[38]. It's a notorious vine found throughout the tropical regions. Pretty bunches of flowers, rather like a creamy version of wisteria, give way to fat pods, covered by a coating of equally pretty golden fur. That's where the problem lies.

These fine golden hairs fly off at the least nudge or slightest puff of wind, and irritate the skin. Even clothes hung out to dry can be coated with the hairs, and the unsuspecting recipient of clean, fresh laundry be set ablaze by them. Seasoned hunters have been known to tear their clothes off and plunge into the nearest mud-wallow to ease the fiery itch, or risk crocodile infested rivers rather than endure for a moment longer. I picture Harry H Johnston's outrage at this cowardly "cow itch" as he calls it. Could nature not have provided him with an adversary he could come to grips with? How can a man who has halted the entire slave trade of a region be brought so low by minute fragile filaments from one "malicious" vine!

---

[37] *Bidens pilosa*
[38] The velvet bean *Mucuna pruriens* is a recommended crop plant and green fertiliser in Malawi.

Despite the frequent bouts of malaria and black-water that broke his health, and the spectacular amount of work he blazed through in five short years, I would not be at all surprised if it was this betrayal by a beanstalk that finally routed Johnston from the Africa he so loved.

## Mice time
### 18th June

Winter burning has begun in earnest now. Last night the old maize patch between our gate and the dambo was fired. Supper was eaten to the accompaniment of the erratic pop and crackle of exploding grass-stalks as we watched our curtains catch the shifting orange glow—a sort of 'aurora tropicalis'.

It's so much an accepted part of life in Africa that it's forgotten almost as soon as noticed. The smell of burning would drift in and out with the changing breeze and we'd glance at each other uneasily for a second or two, wondering if we'd left something on the stove. Early this morning the smoke still hung like a heavy mist over the dambo.

The days are bright and brittle. The distant sun is business-like but uninvolved, as if it has other things on its mind. It seems so much colder than last year, and the air is dry, dry, dry. It's hard to believe this was the wettest year in a long time—moisture seems to be sucked right out of our very skins and our hair is full of static electricity.

It's mice-time too. Beside the road opportunistic vendors stand with mice-kebabs held up to tempt the passing trade, and the sticks are longer than ever. It must have been a bumper year for mice. Usually there are six or eight mice to a skewer; this year there are fifteen to twenty per stick Those sad little silhouettes with scribbled tails always make me think of Roald Dahl—perhaps because of his delight in the macabre, perhaps it's the memory of Quentin Blake's gloriously bizarre illustrations.

Tomorrow we're off to view what we can of the total eclipse. Though we'll be a little outside the path, we will teeter on the edge of Malawi in the hopes of catching a second or two of the total obliteration of the globe of day. Perhaps that's what is preoccupying the sun at the moment. Fancy being upstaged by that pipsqueak, the moon!

I don't know which I'm looking forward to more, the actual eclipse, or having a second chance to see Mwabve, the smallest and most distant of Malawi's protected areas.


# Environmental Manglement
## 18ᵗʰ June

Man has a wonderful capacity for improvement. And one of our greatest problems is our absolute certainty that we can improve anything.

Take as an example the old story of the pans in Hwange National Park in Zimbabwe. These natural pans, ephemeral by nature, would fill every year with the rains— a wonderful resource for both the wildlife and the tourists who pay to watch them. So the park management decided to improve the pans by deepening them. Eons of experience in making dams tells us that the bigger the basin, the more water it holds. If the pans held more water, they would last longer, the wildlife would stay in one place longer and so would the tourists. The ultimate all-win situation—a non-fail option.

Except for one small factor. No-one realised that these particular pans were in effect shallow clay-lined depressions in sandy ground, rather like the saucer of a tea-cup perched on a bed of sugar. Trying to increase the capacity of the saucer by scraping a hole in the bottom of it simply lets all the contents out into the absorbent sugar. Ooops.

Of course it's not their fault, and our understanding of the mechanics of perched water tables has come a long way through that very experience. Failure is a great teacher.

Here's a more recent example from Sri Lanka, where wild elephants live a tenuous life of shrinking habitats and the usual encroachment by man. It was noticed that a particular rock-lined watering hole was under considerable pressure from elephants. Hardly a water-hole, really. It was so over-utilised, it was little more than a mud wallow. International funds were donated to scour out this watering point so that the water would be deeper and cleaner, a better resource for the poor old elephants.

Considerable thought went into the delicate task of clearing away the mud-overload and re-establishing the natural pool as it must have been years before elephant attentions reduced it to slush. At last, there was this sparking pool, utterly environmentally friendly and looking completely untouched by human hands. The project was a complete success.

There was only one slight problem. The elephants never came back to it. After a while it began to dawn on the local management that what the elephants had liked about the place was the mud.

You can imagine, in the light of these examples, my reaction on hearing that the Global Environmental Facility is keen to fund a Lake Malawi Environmental Management Project. Exactly. A detectable shrinking of the lower gut region.

Lake Malawi is a tad larger than a pan or a water-hole. It's the 'calendar' lake in miles, 365 miles long and 52 miles wide. And it's deep enough to have a thermocline at 120 metres and an out-of-reach benthic ecosystem and all that marine-type nomenclature that goes with huge bodies of water.

But, as a famous tennis star once said, it's too soon to panic. The plan is being drawn up by Malawian ecologists with the assistance of an entire battery of international environmental scientists, a brace of whom joined us for dinner last week.

Naturally we mulled over the various threads that form the warp and the weft of the Lake's rich tapestry. The project envisaged is staggering, it's proportions almost too wide to grasp. Aspects as varied as silt build-up through catchment degradation and bad farming practices, over-fishing in the shallower waters and fish-breeding areas, and the increase of nutrients in the lake are just a few of the areas that need to be addressed.

"The chemical composition of the lake is changing," we were told. There is a steady increase in levels of phosphorus—far more than could be caused by run-off from increased cultivation in the catchment areas.

"It's increasing, we think, through biomass burning. Phosphorus is carried in the smoke of grass fires, is absorbed by atmospheric moisture and is washed into the lake through rain."

They went on to explain that this enriches the lake water and feeds blue-green algae, which in turn will stifle the micro-organisms that fish feed on.

"Of course," came the disarming disclaimer, "We don't know if that change would necessarily be a bad thing. But it would be a change." I admire that honesty, but it does nothing to unclamp my lower gut. The aim is to manage a system that no-one really understands fully. This is another way of trying to fix something that we are not quite sure is broken yet.

## Midwinter maunder
### 25th June

The jaunt to the lower Shire valley was as splendid as I had expected, with a couple of bonuses thrown in for good measure. Chief among these was far too brief a look at a conservation area put aside by Sucoma, the Sugar Corporation of Malawi.

Begun some eighteen years ago by one of the estate's hunting enthusiasts, Nyala Park was initially referred to as the "nyala feeding paddock". A section of the estate was fenced off, and a few nyala borrowed from Lengwe National Park which is just a stone's throw away. The animals then on loan are now in the process of being returned to the Department of National Parks and Wildlife, having had sufficient time to thrive and multiply.

I imagined that Nyala Park would be a small echo of Lengwe, but it's not at all. It lies closer to the Shire River and has a very different feel to it altogether. It's most attractive feature is a glorious forest of fever trees. These elegant acacias have a distinctive yellow-green bark that seems to trap and hold the light, and an avenue of fever trees seen in slanting late afternoon sunlight is a sight long remembered.

In the scant two decades of its existence Nyala Park has shown how resilient indigenous bush can be, if left to its own devices. There are occasional exotic plants to be glimpsed—the odd prickly-pear, a foreign cassia or two, an occasional relic blue-gum—but on the whole, it gives a great boost to the spirit to think that it is possible to regain such apparent wilderness in a relatively short space of time.

Nyala Park also contains the only giraffes in Malawi. Trans-located from Zimbabwe, I think, the original group has grown to ten with the youngest a mere week or so old. We saw all ten of them, delicately dappled in the shade of the fever-trees—how tall those trees are to dwarf giraffes so! They looked surprisingly small to me—but then I'm more used to seeing giraffes peering over the flat crowns of rather stunted dry-land savannah trees.

Then on to Mwabve Wildlife Reserve and the almost-total eclipse. It was great fun, but not an earth-shattering experience for us. I've since been told that some astronomer somewhere likens a 98% eclipse to going to hear Pavarotti and having to listen from outside the concert hall. I'm sure he's right; friends who made the journey to Lusaka to see the full Monty are still radiant about it.

We might have rather missed the point, but that didn't dim our enjoyment and we came home full of quiet contentment, to the delight of finding a barn owl snoozing in the branches above our veranda. It was ramrod straight in its regal array, like a caricature of Queen Elizabeth the First—even to the ginger widow's peak—white-faced and slit eyed, ornately ruffed and fur-bordered in ermine, the body tapering as tightly as a laced bodice. It stood on the branch, immobile as a portrait while all the garden's birds hurled raucous abuse. One can only feel humble in the face of such noble restraint.

I was glad of that example later, on finding that while rescuing my e-mails from an incoming virus we managed to wipe all my document files. White-faced and slit-eyed myself, I buttoned my narrow beak and worked at emulation. Such regal disdain is not as easy as the owl made it look.

## Eclipse eclipsed
### 25th June

We travelled to Mwabve Wildlife Reserve with a sense of growing expectation. Dropping down from Blantyre to the Shire River through bands of winter smoke, the road snakes through eucalyptus plantations, bamboo thickets and scattered villages to level out on the broad Shire flood plain. The river itself lies along the reed beds and sandbanks like a huge green python, its muscular strength masked by deceptive lethargy

The road, so much improved since our first trip to the lower Shire Valley, crosses the river at Nsanje Village and bowls straight as an arrow through kilometres of towering sugar cane. Areas of indigenous forest remain— Lengwe National Park, the Wildlife Reserves of Majete and Mwabve, and the sugar estate's own Nyala Park—but for the rest, the billiard-table of cane stretches into the hazy distance, bounded by the blue escarpment.

Among the cane fields baobab trees lift their podgy arms to the blue enamel bowl of the sky. It may just have been more economical to leave the arboreal monoliths there than to root them out, but whatever the reason, I'm grateful. The trees give scale and interest to the boredom of the cane, and somehow link the distant hills to the here and now.

It's less than three hours to Mwabve from Blantyre. The most southern of Malawi's protected areas and the smallest of the reserves, it is a little gem. Some areas are naturally imbued with an additional sense of grace, and Mwabve has it. As the dusty track dips to cross the threshold stream, the glimpsed vista of elegant forest tugs at the heart.

The little park is looking glorious. The grass is rather rank, missing the weight of large herbivores, but the trees are spaced enough to provide tantalising vistas of sunlit glades backed by rising ground or tumbled boulders. There seems as much vegetation hanging from the trees as growing from the ground; lianas and creepers loop and spill over branches in swags, and wonderful spiked cucumbers glisten orange against rough fissured bark. A bright yellow weaver picks through a festoon of leaves and a group of white helmet-shrikes skim low through the undergrowth.

The weather was perfect—the winter solstice, and us in cotton shirts. A sky dotted with formless puffy clouds and the mildest of breezes. The evening just cool enough to demand long sleeves and inhibit the still present mosquitoes. A mid-winter moonless night, a cobweb of stars entangled in the balding branches overhead. Our campfire creating an orange dome of light in the cavernous dark. Picked out in chiaroscuro our folding camp chairs, the bole of a tree, the pale cone of our suspended mosquito net as the ghostly substitute for a tent. A scops owl[39] burped gently in the dark.

---

[39] *Otus senegalensis*. The name scops comes from the Latin scopae, which roughly means broom and refers to the brush of feathers the owl has around its beak.

We had intended to visit a hill southwest of Mwabve, reputed to overlook the Zambezi valley. From that vantage point we hoped to catch a second or two of total eclipse, but on investigation found the distance between the parking area and the hill too great for my short foot, so we retreated to the reserve to search for a suitable dwala as a view point.

It was not the high ground that attracted us in the end, but the bed of the Mwabve River itself. A pale sweep of rinsed river sand cradled the spill of clear water, a shallow wash network of ankle-deep rivulets flanked by steep rocky sides. Gnarl-rooted fig trees clung to the gorge and above the crown of rocks sterculias and baobabs showed smoke grey between green foliage.

We lay on our backs, bellies to the sun and spectacles of cardboard and silver foil on our faces. The shallow stream fed cool sand into my hair as we watched the noon sun munched away by the invisible body of the moon. Gradually the light faded, till even without the specs it seemed as if we wore tinted lenses, and a drop in temperature drove us out of the water and onto the still warm rocks.

Science pointed out that suddenly the birds had become more active. In the mid-afternoon false-twilight there was emphatic avian coming and going, as if settling down for the night. Both red-billed and white helmet-shrike bustled about in the luminous blue light, and bulbuls, thrushes, hornbills and doves made themselves loud in the gloom.

The curved black patch crept up from the lower left of the sun till only a thin sliver of light blazed white-hot above it, then seemed to sink and swivel as the patch rolled past, and gradually the day regained its natural colour. Ah, well... was that all? No matter, the 98% eclipse gave additional interest to a serene afternoon of rinsing our souls in unspoiled solitude.

It was as interesting as the golden-banded foresters, butterflies of sapphire blue and chrysanthemum yellow who danced in the shadow of the trees, or the algae-fringed water-scorpion who stalked river-boatmen in the rippling shallows around our toes.

I doubt if we would have minded if the eclipse hadn't happened at all—except of course we would have had no reason to be there on any ordinary Thursday in mid-winter.

*Post Script 2019*

*One remarkable incident sticks in my mind regarding that experience, and for me it's a facet of the warm heart of Malawians. Three young men from the impoverished settlement beyond Mwabve had attached themselves to us as volunteer guides, for a fee of course, to the spot on the hill which promised the best sighting. We loaded them into our vehicle, and set off. We found the parking area, and they pointed out the hill with excitement, and were about to climb out of the car when I said quietly to Science, "I can't make that distance."*

*There was an immediate stillness in the back seat. Science scanned my face for a few minutes, and then turned to the boys in the back and said,*

*"Sorry, lads. We're not going up. My wife can't walk that far. We'll go back to the camping site."*

*There was an appalled silence from the back seat. I could feel the disappointment of these young men—here was a chance in a lifetime of making a little bit of cash virtually in their own back yard, and it was slipping out of their hands. Out of that heavy seemingly endless stillness, one young man suddenly said,*
*"It's true."*

*Immediately all three of them climbed out the car, closed the doors gently, politely wish us both good bye and left. I was astonished by this, for my own deep disappointment at not being able to do something that was so simple for others, had made me, for the first time, deeply angry and distressed. And these young men had recognised that, without even being able to see my face. I felt their empathy as they greeted me on leaving, a gentleness in their demeanour. I have often thought of those lads, and how profound the moment was for me, this revealing of an almost psychic recognition of truth that fires the warm hearts of Malawi.*

## Wednesday wail
4<sup>th</sup> July

The good news is that winter is definitely retreating. Perhaps the shift of the sun and the marginal change in the daylight hours has thrown me into disarray, but I can't believe it is Wednesday already. The universe conspires against me. I have no other explanation.

It's blustery enough to be August. Despite being shaken by the wind, foliage carries a heavy burden of dust. Even the scarlet poinsettias and purple bougainvillea seem a little tarnished. Periodic fires sweep up the dambo beyond our garden wall, the crackle of leaping flames catapulting ash into the air to be swirled away by the wind. The brick storm-water furrows beside the road (some almost three-feet deep) are being repaired against the coming rainy-season that seems far too far away.

The last of the tobacco crops are trickling into town. Battered lorries laden with huge hessian cubes totter unsteadily to the auction floor. For the last month or two a drive through Kanengo, Lilongwe's industrial area, brought vividly to mind childhood memories of sneaking a sniff at

Grandad's cigarette box. The air has been redolent with the opulent smell of good cigars. Gradually now the all-pervading amber scent of leathery leaves is slowly lifting, being replaced by the less ambiguous smells of dust and burned grass.

Here's a delightful little Malawian tale for you. Like most very poor countries, Malawi has a booming security industry. Since anything that is not actually nailed down or constantly watched will find a new owner in a very short space of time, guards are inevitably in great demand. However, despite the fact that perhaps as much as 25% of the labour force is employed as guards, there is the utterly Malawian acceptance that sleep is inevitable. You may employ a guard to protect your property at night, but to expect him to stay awake for that time is unreasonable.

Sleeping is regarded as an act of God. Nobody in their right mind would sleep during the scary dark hours, it is always against one's will, and leaves one very vulnerable. So to expect a man to keep his eyes open against the irresistible force of nature is to expect the impossible. It's perfectly logical when you think about it. It's just that the expats seem to have these unreasonable expectations of local employees.

A recent visitor told us of his amusement at a local security company who had made the well-known SAS motto their very own by changing the "dare" to "care". He discovered that the rubber stamp maker had run out of space, and the office stamp read, not "Who Cares Wins", but more simply "Who Cares".

To be honest, I've looked for that delightful flaw and have not found it, but the story is too good not to share. And I'm afraid it's the only story you're likely to get out of Malawi this week. I am working on one for you, but for some reason it doesn't want to be written. My muse has lost her tongue. But I'll keep working at it. Mind you, I might just embrace that motto as my own.

## Thuma revisited
### 10th July

The sun is playing peek-a-boo through dense grey cloud, and every time it vanishes, the temperature plummets. It's the frustrating kind of weather that whatever you're wearing is not right. Slough off your sweater in the sun, and you're chilly in no time. Pull on a long-sleeved shirt, and the sun comes out. My personal solution is a tee-shirt and a blanket wrapped round my middle. It's not exactly traditionally Malawian, but it is distinctly African.

I may be resenting the cold, but for the insect world summer is on its way. The ants marched straight back into the kitchen on the 22nd of June and the mosquitos are making a valiant recovery. On the up side, though, the butterflies are magnificent.

We've seen two this week that are new to us—a Golden Piper flitting around our garden like a little independent veld fire, and a Dry-leaf Commodore on the leaf litter in Thuma Forest Reserve.

We paid a brief visit to Thuma at the tail of a glorious long week-end of idling slackly in the bushes near the Lake. We reacquainted ourselves with a place called Safari Beach, but I'll tell you all about that in next week's story. Georg Kloeble is the link between Thuma and Safari Beach—he began the second as part of his fund-raising mechanism to support the first—I wrote it all up in a story called "Baobabs and Bamboo" in 1999.

It's two years since we last saw Thuma, and we were delighted to see so much evidence of elephant activity. Obviously whatever Georg is doing is pleasing them, and the buffalo too. I find it quite odd that these rather cumbersome animals take to the hill country so well. I picture them in rolling grasslands or open parkland rather than this rather steep environment. But I suppose that depends entirely on people-pressure, and there's plenty of that in Malawi.

But the biggest group of herbivores in Thuma, and elsewhere, are the insects. We lay on our backs under an enigmatic baobab and gazed at the shimmering leaf cover above our heads. Each leaf had been reduced to a lace-work tracery of remnant green by a myriad munching mouthparts of caterpillars, leaf-miners, inch-worms, katydids, and others. No wonder there are so many butterflies—there must be millions of caterpillars. The Dry-leaf Commodore, which vanishes into the pale leaf litter on closing its wings and blazes to life in a flash of flame and brown as it flies, specialises in eating the *Plectranthus* species—bushy shade loving herbs and shrubs.

If you close your eyes you can imagine the sound of the leaf-eaters magnified to reach you, like the crackle of a veld-fire or the scuffling murmur from a termitarium. On the other hand, what you hear could well be a veld fire—especially at this time of the year—so it's best not to doze off...

## Drongo
### 9th July

A friend of ours tells the story of how her cat came in one day with a black bird in its mouth. The bird hung limp, eyes closed, bill slightly agape, apparently lifeless.

Scolding the cat gently for its hunter instincts, she reached out a hand to free the little corpse when the bird suddenly opened wild red eyes. It let out an outraged squawk and deftly grabbed the cat by the throat. Naturally the cat was so shocked at this treacherous behaviour that it opened its mouth and let the bird go. The bird, however, hung on. It took some fast footwork to catch the terrified cat and release it. The bird was a drongo.

The Concise Oxford Dictionary says that a drongo is "a black bird of India, Africa, or Australia, of family *Dicruridae*" and adds that in Australian slang it means simpleton. Which just goes to prove that the Aussies are a bit daft, since a drongo is very definitely not half-witted. Slightly mad, perhaps, but not stupid.

The family name *Dicrurus* is from the Greek, meaning "two-tailed", presumably that implies forked, since that—together with the blackness of the bird—is the most obviously distinguishing feature[40]. If you're lucky, you'll get the light at the right angle, and you'll see those dramatic red eyes.

It is a very common bird of the African bush, and it seems to make up for its sombre colouring by flamboyance in every other regard. If there's a drongo around, you are bound to see it. It certainly is one of the most entertaining to watch. Not quite as big as a thrush and a little smaller than a turtle dove, it has the sublime confidence that comes from knowing that, on a size to weight ratio, it is considerably more bloody-minded than other birds.

Its very posture seems to indicate an avian arrogance. Where the ample bosom of the turtle dove proclaims motherly love, and the bowing and scraping thrush embraces industry and humility, the drongo is in a class apart.

"Look at him," said my Scientific Advisor in tones of awe, "That's really a little raptor." The bird clearly thinks so too.

He sat as upright at an eagle, his shoulders squared and neat. His crown feathers were ruffled slightly, making his head look even more solid and hawkish. Around the surprisingly straight bill a neat fan of bristles protruded, and that cleanly v-notched tail hung down like a pennant at

---

[40] However, not all drongos have forked tails; there is also a square-tailed drongo, *Dicrurus ludwigii*. Perhaps the family name refers to two different looking tails, rather than a forked tail.

rest. He seemed a little tubby, but perhaps those tummy feathers were just keeping his toes warm.

In flight, he is remarkable. Swift and dextrous, he can spin, loop and barrel-roll any fighter-pilot into oblivion. Frequently you will see a couple of drongos emulating the Battle of Britain, apparently just for the exhilaration of it. Mind you, the exercise stands them in good stead. Watching a drongo chasing a moth or a butterfly is wonderful—an avian martial arts spectacular.

Adding to the sense of speed and magic are the drongo's flight feathers. The wings look almost transparent in flight, a pale grey blur of elegant movement. I've never seen the wings close up, so I don't know exactly how they look, but the books tell me that the "inner webs of the flight feathers are grey" which gives that translucent look.

The drongo's aggressive nature is well known. In India it's been given the nickname King Crow because of its bullying habit. I think the equally pushy crows deserve what they get. We watched a pair of drongos defending their nest from the attentions of a hungry looking pied crow, and I was fascinated to find how quickly I could recognise the drongos "bandit alert" call.

Which brings us to another fascinating aspect of the tubby black bird. The wildly psychedelic voice. An Australian bird book describes the drongo's song as "strange metallic notes, some like a well strained wire-fence being twanged", while a South Africa book calls it "strident twanging, creaking and rasping sounds like unoiled wagon-wheels". Interesting the inadvertent comment those descriptions make on the age and background of the authors. To my Scientific Advisor, the drongo's voice sounds like "electronic mayhem, like an oriental radio malfunctioning."

The drongo also mimics other birds, and will include electronic versions of the robin, the thrush, the bulbul and even the pearl-spotted owl, in its manic soliloquies. I can understand one butterfly mimicking the colours of a foul-tasting friend, or a harmless beetle dressing up in colours that ape a poisonous distant relative, but what earthly use can it be to copy the songs of other birds?

Several birds do it—the robin is a prize song thief, and so is the fiscal shrike. There must be a good pro-survival reason, or it wouldn't be worth the effort. Certainly a drongo wouldn't do it without some benefit. As I said, he may be a little mad, but he's definitely not stupid.

## Science in Winter
### 17ᵗʰ July

In the allegedly Warm Heart of Africa winter is not giving up without a fight. The sun has lost its courage and huddles behind grey unresponsive clouds and the wind is as restless as a bored child. The cold seems as insidious as the wet was earlier this year. I almost expect to find ice-crystals growing in the dark of our cupboards, just as the pale coating of mould did a few months back.

Most of pale-faced Lilongwe is rosy-nosed and shuffling. There's a dose of the flu doing the rounds and this cold snap adds to a general sense of grievance for those of us who are still here. It's summer over towards the topmost pole, and a good time to take "home leave" for the northern born. It's such an accepted migration that during July and August it feels as if Lilongwe is barely ticking over.

But things are indeed happening. For instance the Department of National Parks and Wildlife has just produced Volume 1, Number 1, of its official newsletter, *The DNPW News-Park*. Crammed full of interesting incident and comment, the fledgling journal provides the occasional wry smile.

For instance, the brief article which breaks the first official word on the reappearance of lions in Liwonde National Park—a rumoured occurrence which has been generating excited speculation throughout Malawi for a month or more—has a headline that leaves the reader in some doubt about the attitude of the Government conservation body to lions in general. It reads LIONS REFUSE TO EXTINCT IN LIWONDE NATIONAL PARK.

The lions may be refusing, but if this bone-jarring cold doesn't stop soon, I might be happy to do an extinct myself. It hasn't affected the birds though. Schalow's louries are still scuttling up and down branches of the thinning combretums like psychedelic pterodactyls.

"Listen to them rattling their teeth," said Science profoundly.

"Teeth?" I asked tentatively, watching the fluid elegance of the birds.

"Can't you hear them?" he said in a slightly flu-muffled voice. "They bark like muted fox terriers."

"How do neutered fox terriers sound?" I asked, riveted by the thought. Science cleared his throat loudly and repeated,

"Muted! With a mute. You know! That red thing they stuff in the mouth of a trumpet."

I am constantly humbled by the astounding accuracy of the man's descriptions. He's not called Science for nothing. Even if the flu has fogged up his voice a bit, his razor sharp analysis still functions. He took the time this week to explain to me why spiders have eight eyes.

"One for each foot," he said succinctly. And he proved it by going on to add, "You should know that. You've only got one and a half feet and you walk into the furniture all the time. Imagine the mess you'd be in if you had eight feet."

Next week we take off for the northern reaches of the lake, to look at Livingstonia at long last, and hopefully see the forest on Misuku Hills. Until then, keep your toes warm.

## Dinner with a Duiker
### 16th July

On the edge of the spill of light, a pair of eyes glittered greenly. The creature was crouched under the lip of a boulder. "Not very big," I thought.

Seconds later a small golden form flowed out of the shadow, moving like quick-silver, boldly flecked with russet and black. Soundless elegance, a forward urge unbroken by jut of shoulder or sway of haunch. The long tail echoed the boneless glide, tapering away to black.

It jinked across the open glare of spot-lit dust and vanished into the shadow behind the feeding platform. There was a momentary hush in the muted clatter of diners as a long cream snout eased nervously over the edge of the platform, sinuously followed by a long spotted neck. Between nose and neck there seemed little difference, just a pair of small rounded ears marked the transition.

"What is it?" I whispered.

"Genet," murmured Science, through a mouthful of beef cordon bleu. To the left of me the new manager of Kuti Wildlife Ranch swallowed a fork-full of schnitzel and added

"Large-spotted. See the black tip to the tail? That's diagnostic."

The appearance of the genet was the undisputed highlight of the evening, and I think all of us were far less concerned about the food than we were entranced by the wildlife. Before the genet appeared we had been entertained by a duiker and a young reedbuck who casually ambled out of the bushes and nosed around on the feeding area. The genet seemed a little ill-at-ease with them, and would start away at the stamp of a hoof. All of them ignored us completely.

The most remarkable thing about this very attractive wildlife haven, is that it just happed. The place is Safari Beach Lodge, an ex-Government Forest Lodge leased by Georg Kloeble and refurbished to include five permanent platform-mounted en-suite tents between the trees on a koppie overlooking Lake Malawi. Georg and his partner Suse began the Lodge as a way of raising money for the conservation of their great passion, Thuma Forest Reserve.

Wherever Georg is, animals seem to know they are safe. He puts out food regularly for them, and threatens guest with instant expulsion should they be caught feeding the animals themselves. Visitor to the lodge, both two legged and four, know the rules. This makes the whole thing work. Since the animals don't expect guests to provide food, there is none of the pestering that inevitably happens where wild animals are fed by the public.

So, the animals disregard the humans, leaving us free to watch interactions between normally shy creatures. Breakfast brought the baboons out to examine the early morning state of the feeding platform. Much to my surprise, they stayed clear of the tents, but lounged around utterly relaxed near the feeding area, in front of the restaurant.

"They're just so pleased to have a place where they can hang out," said Georg, making them sound like a bunch of misunderstood teenagers.

And it's quite true. You probably won't see baboons elsewhere around Senga Bay. Not because they're not there. The area is full of granite boulder koppies and the Senga Hills must be home to several troops. But they are deeply mistrustful of humans, and with good cause. Yet here, in a matter of two years, Georg and Suse have evolved a place where wildlife and people can live together with apparent impunity.

Just then Georg's dog came romping past, a young vervet monkey clinging to its back like a miniature jockey. The two are obviously good playfellows, and the dog seems content to be surrogate mother to the orphaned baby. Again, the monkey paid not the least attention to us, all its focus on the dog and the baboons. Most hand-reared monkeys are a real nuisance around people.

In case you're wondering about the name, there IS a beach—down a winding path to a sheltered little cove where Lake Malawi's golden and black sands blend. A grassy patch is shaded by a huge sausage tree, and—as Science describes it—"Dassies drop out of it like ripe pawpaws."

It's a remarkable place, and startling to see how much wildlife is still about, even along the densely populated southern lake shore. Interesting to speculate on how long the status quo can be maintained. Probably for as long as Georg is around, and certainly as long as he maintains his strict management of both wildlife and people.

While that happens, this is one of very few places one can visit and actually enjoy baboons with breakfast and genets with dinner.

## Glimpse of Spring
### 21ˢᵗ July

Suddenly the air smells like spring. There's an unaccustomed softness in the very feel of the air and one's spirits can't help but rise.

That we're off for a week to explore the north tomorrow hasn't got anything to do with it. Something has shifted, despite the fact that the combretums are still hanging onto their threadbare leaves like misers. We'll find new growth pushing though any day now. The acacias have been stark and skeletal for a while, so they'll be the first with a mist of tiny spring green flags.

John, the manager of Kuti, breezed in this afternoon with a baby Sharpe's grysbok. There is something particularly disarming about a big man carrying a tiny delicate creature. This little scrap of life seemed very comfortable in one broad hand, twig-like legs and tiny rubbery hooves no bigger than my finger-tips, dangling from between his fingers. A pair of children beside the road sold it to him. They knew enough English to state a price, but not enough to explain where and when the little creature was captured.

It'll be a day or so before it settles down, so we won't find out until we return next week if she survives or not. She's in good hands, since John has raised more baby antelope in a year than most people see in a lifetime, but it's always a little nerve-racking with a wild caught animal. I almost wish we were staying home to see how she does.

The week has escaped me again—I had wanted to get a story done for next week, but it hasn't happened. We're off with first light tomorrow, so you'll have to wait till we get back next week-end, when I should have got fired up by the fossils in Karonga and the bird-life in the Misuku Hills. Right now I'm off to throw my art materials into a bag, and myself into bed.

Till next week then, think gentle thoughts for all the world's defenceless young.

## Home from the Hill
### 31st July

Just when I'm getting a bit jaundiced about the Warm Heart of Africa tag, something happens to remind me of how warm the African heart really is.

We had a curate's egg of a trip, but the good parts were very good. Ironically, the highlight of the week was getting benighted in the Misuku Hills, a glorious if rather cold and nerve-stretching experience. It was here that we were reminded of the warm heartedness of the Malawians, who brought abundant muscle power along with good natured banter to lift us (on occasions physically!) from our predicament.

It was altogether a mammoth week—four days ago we left the little village of Nthalire heading homeward at 8.15 in the morning. We reached Vwaza Marsh Nature Reserve as the sun set that evening. Admittedly, we had an extended lunch break while Science explored the Chisanga Falls in Nyika, but we were on the road for a good seven hours. The distance we covered was a meagre 145 kilometres.

It's been bit like spending every day for a week in a dodgem car, bouncing over potholes and dodging rocks—lots of fun for half an hour, but a bit tiring after a while. Never the less, the scenery was fascinating. Northern Malawi is mountainous and has a shifting panorama of rugged beauty. Botanical wonders enlivened the close-up views, and often we saw the stub-tailed, elegant-winged bateleur eagle describing arabesques in the windswept skies.

As soon as I've got my mind aligned I'll tell you about our visit to the old mission station of Livingstonia, and a quaint little stop-over called the Lukwe Permaculure Camp. From there we dropped like an autumn leaf down the hair-pin pass to the Lake below. Then on up to Karonga to fossick for fossils, and inland to Misuku and our unexpected, intimate evening with a tropical montane forest. Then Nthalire, Vwaza Marsh, and home—one day late. Wonderful! Enough inspiration to keep me writing non-stop for a month!

Meanwhile, back on the Ranch... the diminutive grysbok is thriving under the tender ministrations of Kuti John. She seems just as tiny as before, but is suckling strongly, her entire little frame rocking to the power of each dragging swallow. John huddles down to feed her, his face close to the ground. She nuzzles her shiny nose into his hair and is gratified to find a plastic bottle-teat next to his forehead. It's as close as this big-framed man can come to being a 50 cm tall grysbok mother.

But weaning is not far away, and chopped apple, carrot and cabbage are all being devoured with growing enthusiasm. John will part with her soon. He says that he can't put her outside at Kuti, since the resident barn-owls would regard her as lunch, and keeping her indoors is not good for her. He plans to take her over to Georg Kloeble at Safari Beach, where she will have the companionship of other orphaned antelope, and Georg is geared to cater for a tiny creature like her fragile self.

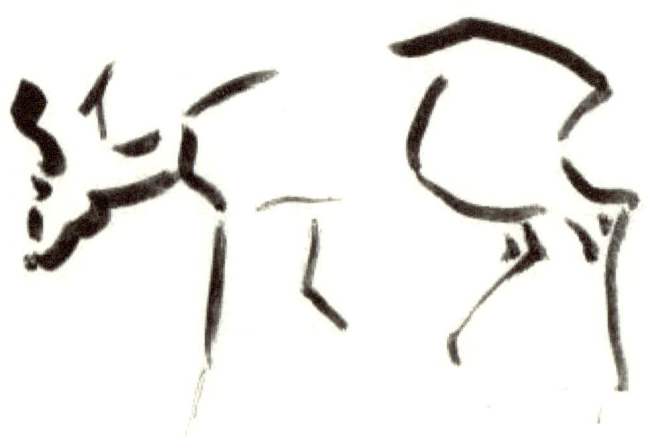

# August 2001

## Misuku Mistake—Getting in
### 1st August

My Scientific Advisor believes that the most important step in rescuing a damsel in distress is to manoeuvre her into the predicament in the first place. For me, the Misuku Mistake was his third and most satisfactory achievement in this regard. Having wished we could spend more time in the voluptuous extravagance of the Mughese Forest Reserve, I found we had the unavoidable privilege of spending the whole day and the entire night.

From the Smallholder Coffee Authority's guest house above the town of Misuku, we took a little used, rambling track along the spine of a rising ridge. Our gallant Japanese utility vehicle teetered between tiny agricultural plots of beans, maize and bananas and the occasional scraggy-looking rows of coffee bushes, into the misty dimness of the Mughese Forest. We had been assured that the road, though seldom used, was maintained by the little coffee pulping factory which it serves. And indeed, once into the forest, the road was beautifully tended. The vegetation had been slashed back to a neat lawn over the track, and hoe marks in the glistening red clay bank told of recent patching of the surface. Overhanging branches had been cleared, and the odd inappropriate sapling hacked down to keep a comfortable breadth to the roadway.

Buttressed and mossed, towering trunks of forest giants soared into the pale mist high above us. Clumps of red-ribbed wild banana, *Ensete ventricosum*, spread soft green fronds of so rich a colour that they seem to generate their own glowing light. There were football-sized melons lying in the road, hard as pumpkins and specked like marrows, and we searched for the creeper that produced them. We found instead an insignificant looking broad-leafed tree, fairly slender and nondescript, bearing these huge fruits on its unconcerned branches. Quite an event for us to find a tree unknown to Science.

So many things were new to us. I found a delicate pink flower, rather like the wild rhubarb, with deeply ornate, variegated spiky leaves, and ten minutes later saw the same flower on a bush with simple, entire leaves of one colour. An aspidistra-leafed ground orchid with a stem about a metre long had fresh disa-like flowers in purple and lilac and older blooms of wine red and pink. We heard the whistling call of blue monkeys[41], and the raucous braying of hornbills, but saw neither.

And still the rolling gentle road tugged us along. Breasting each new rise, we would sail effortlessly down the next steep grassy incline, bewitched by the green gloom and muffled distant echoes of falling water and hidden birds. Beguiled by ferns and enticed by the fluting call of the monkeys, we sank lower and lower through the roller-coaster rocky ridges and clay slicked slopes. All too soon we were out of the forest and looking down onto the roofs of the coffee pulping buildings, so we turned and started back.

---

[41] Also known as Samango monkeys; not to be confused with the southern African Vervet monkey, also called 'blue' in Afrikaans (i.e.Blou Aap) due to their brightly coloured scrotums. This Mughese group's colouring was subtly different to the group we saw in Lengwe.

Almost immediately we saw the monkeys. A troop of about twenty blue monkeys watched us with interest from the canopy. They are fat-faced little fellows with Victorian mutton-chop whiskers and fiercely jutting eyebrows, "Like little verandas," Science observed.

A tiny little chin belies all that podginess. They need a lot of fur to keep out the cold and the damp. Their faces are mist grey and their legs storm-cloud black, and the backs of the males are a glorious contrast. Dark brown on the spine, the long mantle grades through a russet band to hang in a silver fringe, marbled like the feathers of a pheasant. It's almost as if the males wear a circular cape from nape to tail. With their hind legs longer than their arms, they stand in a cheeky rump-up attitude. Some cuddled together like arboreal cherubs, solemn-faced beneath their outrageous eyebrows.

Grey mist still rolled overhead like cobwebs through the canopy, but here on the edge of the forest weak sunlight encouraged a pair of silvery cheeked hornbills to join the monkeys. Remarkable looking birds. Bigger than the trumpeter hornbill, the male has a huge creamy-pink casque above the bill. A most impressive structure, so delicate looking that it is translucent against the light. In contrast to this sculpted outcrop, the black feathers of the head seem a wild and unruly crest. Navigation in the wind beyond the  sheltering forest must be almost impossible with that bony superstructure. I pictured a turning circle proportionately equivalent to that of an ocean-going oil tanker.

We watched the birds and the monkeys without having to shift the binoculars for a good half hour. Then, with a sense of complete satisfaction, we started up the long slopes back into the dim forest. Within five minutes we found gravity and damp grass conspiring against our progress, and we slithered slowly to an ignominious halt with one back wheel teetering gently over the edge of the road.

Science turned and smiled at me. "This is where we get creative," he said.

## Looking back
### 6th August

Two years! Hard to believe we've been in this extraordinary country for two years. And where will we be next year at this time? That depends primarily on Science and where his particular expertise is required, it's pointless to even speculate right now.

I try to look at Lilongwe as I did two years ago, and find it impossible. Much is so familiar to me now that I've stopped seeing it; other things have changed subtly and I've become accustomed to those changes. But the indeterminate weather is very like it was when we got here in '99—a vague pewter but mainly cloudless sky, an irascible wind. Occasional overcast afternoons with a spatter of rain, just enough to make the dusty foliage mud coated.

It's a dry and brittle spring. But it is certainly spring. The parrots are back with their cheeky whistle, and the lilac-breasted rollers are growing noisier every day. Such brilliant plumage, and such a drab voice! We once found the wing of a roller that had perhaps been caught by a bird of prey. The dismembered wing lay in the cinnamon dust like a lost jewel. Turquoise and sky blue and iridescent purple, it was hard to believe so practical an instrument could be so exquisite. This, I thought, is what angels' wings look like, not the boring white we imagine, but this celebration of vision, variety and vitality. A dazzle of virtuoso artistry. And the bird has a voice that sounds like a thumbnail drawn over mosquito netting.

Out in the countryside the flame creepers are spreading a vermilion tinge over the bush and albizias are sending out clouds of white blossom that seem nothing but bunches of stamens. Driving home in the sunset we caught the wonderful warm smell of the potato bush[42]. Yes, it's definitely spring.

You couldn't tell at a glance, though. The veld is tall pale straw waiting tiredly for the dancing lines of fire to sweep through, or black dusty stubble where the flames have been. The sky is opaque with smoke, the sinking sun a wavering shocking pink in the lilac haze, almost swallowed by the smog before reaching the horizon.

In the Smallholder Coffee Authority's Guest House at Misuku I found a wonderful quote in the guest book, which perfectly encapsulates my feelings about Malawi after two years. It read, verbatim: "A wonderful place and provides a piece of mind. The scenery is beautiful and its weather very friendly and conducive. Its people are majestically hospitable."

That's Malawi!

# Misuku Mistake—Getting out
## 6th August

We found ourselves stranded where the thread of a jungle footpath joins the road. Though we had coped with the steepness of the incline to that point, a sharp bend to the right seemed to loosen what little grip our tyres had and we slid inexorably, if slowly, backward. Several attempts simply resulted in making us more deeply aware of our predicament. Ahead of us, the grassed and mossy road rose

---

[42] *Phyllanthus reticulatus.*

at what seemed a 45 degree angle, and on every other side the ground fell away steeply under tropical forest.

As the sound of the engine died away the forest seemed to become more attentive, as if waiting to see what we would do next. We waited too. The occasional tap of condensation dripping from the mist-vague leaves echoed the tick of cooling metal from our engine. The left rear wheel hung a little way over the lip of the road, and an adolescent sapling pressed itself against the rear window, as if to examine our camping gear.

Well, I thought, this is what I wanted. More time in the Mughese Forest. Looks like I've got it. So, while Science got creative about repairing our malfunctioning diff. lock, I set about staying out of his way and making the most of it.

Above us the trees towered fifty metres or more, and ferns flourished beneath them. Some were branched like a spread hand with stems as long as my arm, some were feathered like a carrot-leaf, and grew in fissures in the bark, tiny enough to be almost mistaken for moss. The gentle bird-like whistle of blue monkeys came fluting through the green and silver gloom, a sweet, companionable "Chip, chip."

Within an hour Science had got the diff. lock to engage, and we had lunch secure in the thought that we would be sailing up the slopes without a care in a few minutes. By three o'clock we admitted temporary defeat, and Science took off along the footpath to the White Father's Mughese Parish, promising to be back by dark.

He was back before I'd even had time to worry, accompanied by four young men whom he met along the path. With their strong-armed assistance we got a little further up the road. In fact, we were doing so well that they had fallen behind when a soft patch on the outside of a curve held us up. Rolling back to take another run at it set us once more a-slither, and again we fetched up poised on the lip with a wheel almost dangling. This time a ten metre sapling leaned against the driver's door, and Science had to commit dendrocide to get in and out.

We unloaded the pick-up and tried to lift her back onto the road, but the six of us couldn't budge her at all. We sent the tired lads home, and dug in for the night. Literally. It needed both of us on our knees to grub a level space into the road for our mattress. We had just succeeded in erecting our dome tent, which luckily doesn't need a level space to stay upright, when we heard a cheery "Herro!" ringing through the forest.

Out of the rapidly falling dusk strode a bright-faced Malawian, cheerfully swinging a pot of local beer in one hand and a battered knapsack in the other.

"Ah, pepani! Sorry, bwana, sorry!" he said as he took in our teetering little truck and belongings strewn all over the road. "I'm Burnet T. Mogha," he said, shaking hands warmly. He offered us a swig of his beer as compensation for our misfortune. This beer, he confided, he had bought to strengthen his legs. He had walked from Chitipa that morning, a distance of some thirty kilometres as the crow flies—and even a crow would have difficulty keeping to a straight line in this rugged country.

Nevertheless, he dumped his belongings, shoved up his sleeves, and proclaimed himself available for assistance. We squinted at him in the thickening mist and dark, and suggested he continue to his home, since attempting anything in the dark would be doomed to failure. Reluctantly he agreed that this was so, and wished us a peaceful night. As he left, four men from the coffee pulping factory arrived, and they too left reluctantly. Their voices echoed and grew fainter as they hurried back down the steep track.

What made the night not just tolerable, but downright enjoyable, was the fact that Science makes a habit of being fully equipped for any eventuality. It seems like a huge amount of clobber to lug around, but at times like this a gas cooker, fresh water and warm bedding makes a picnic out of a panic. We had a five-star meal and fell into bed hugely content and only slightly concerned about the morning.

To our bleary-eyed disbelief, Burnet T Mogha was back before dawn, his cheery "Herro!" startling us awake well before six. He brought his father with him, a stately elder who lent a dignified air of wisdom to the proceedings. With them came ten others, ranging in age from 12 to 60, and a yellow village dog. With the aid of the slaughtered sapling tied to the rear bumper, a huge rock behind the front wheel, and two dozen arms bunching and straining rhythmically, the stuck truck was inched back onto the road.

By nine o'clock, after a huge amount of cheerful banter, loud committee discussions, and silent intelligent interest from the dog, we sailed out of the forest. We were lucky indeed to have the help of so many willing hearts and hands, since we learned that neither the White Fathers nor the town of Misuku have a four-wheel drive vehicle or a tractor. Had we developed mechanical problems or actually tipped over the lip of the road, we would have been stranded for days.

Here we are, a full century and a half after Livingstone, and still utterly dependent on the good-natured willingness of the local African to physically carry the lunatic white-man out of his difficulties. Some things in Africa never change.

*Post Script:* There were two very entertaining occurrences during the mammoth job of getting a fully loaded pickup out of a position of extreme danger and then up the very steep grassy incline until we met friendlier gravity on the other side of the peak. These occurred during the re-loading of our bakkie; everything that could possibly be removed to lighten the vehicle for the physical lifting of it back onto the track had to be replaced, and Science has a particular way of packing stuff. So he stood at the rear of the vehicle and called for each item as he wanted them to be loaded.

It was his asking for the green bag that caused brief consternation. After a few moments of slightly anxious confusion, Science pointed out the bag he was referring to. With delighted amusement, our friend Burnet held up the brown bag and said, "This one?" The animated discussion that followed this discovery was in the language of the area, so all we know is that it both surprised and amused them.[43]

The second moment that really appealed to me was when Science, having been handed one of the beautiful Tanzanian hand-made clay pots I'd bought in Karonga, tossed it onto a pile of bedding in the repacking. The senior of the group was scandalised. He sucked in his breath, drew himself up to a full two-thirds of Science's height and gave him an emphatic piece of his mind, Burnet meekly translating as the tirade rolled. The essence was that an article that had required such loving attention in the making, and was such an object of usefulness and pride for both creator and owner, being fragile as well as beautiful and practical, should never be handled with such crass disrespect or thoughtless disregard. I still have one of those magnificent pots, and every time I look at it I think of that wonderful old man, the only person I've met who could give Science a dressing-down that he accepted.

## Meeting Mulanje
### 15th August

Herro from Marawi. Science went down again with malaria, but he's bounced back as usual. I am very glad we've been on Paludrine or the bout could have been really bad. We came back from a week-end jaunt to look at Mulanje; he went off to the office on Monday morning chirpy as a cricket, and by lunch time he was diagnosed with +2 malaria.

---

[43] Colour-blindness is almost exclusively found among Caucasian males, and generally unknown among Africans.

We had groped for Mulanje in air so thick that sunlight filtered though it in bars, the granite massif a murky blue against a dove-grey and platinum sky. Taking the back roads from Zomba, we jounced across the plains between Lake Chilwa and Mulanje, flinging a plume of dust into the almost saturated air. Bucketing through the village of Jali, we had just enough time to recognise this as the bicycle capital of Malawi. I've never before seen so many bikes in one place. Cyclists outnumbered pedestrians three to one, and the Saturday market stalls seemed predominantly bicycle sales, repairs or spares.

On through long-settled areas of sweeping flatness—not an indigenous tree in sight, only blue-gums, mangos and exotic cassias—and into Palombe, where we took the clock-wise route round the base of Mulanje's vague hulk, through the Fort Lister Gap. Not the recommended route. We had to turn back after about half an hour, since the anxiously jogging potential-porter at my window managed to gasp out that the road was impassable. A thick belt of porters surrounds Mulanje. Any driver who shows the slightest interest in the mountain is besieged by shouting men proclaiming their willingness, expertise and availability, and listing the sights and landmarks they can show.

"Bwana, bwana! When you have decided to climb remember my name, I'm Joseph... Matthew... James.... Godwin... Eliah..."

I find it particularly nerve-wracking, so we tend not to stop when a group of locals wave compelling arms. This particular fellow was remarkable. He trotted beside my window being the epitome of politeness.

"Good morning madam, (huff, puff).... how are you?.... (gasp, pant,)...... I am fine thank you... (pant, wheeze,)... You are going to Mulanje? (puff, gasp,).... ah, sorry, madam, but the bridge is down.... (huff, wheeze)...".

Vital and generous information. It's a difficult balancing act, being a mzungu in Malawi. If you protect yourself from the crush by just keeping going, you are inevitably humbled by one golden heart. If you open yourself to every person it feels like being steam-roller'd. I haven't got it right yet and am constantly grateful for Science's more socially graceful interactions.

The mountain is magnificent. Majestic, awe-inspiring and mystical in air thick as sea-water; secret green forests in folds and creases; waterfalls in delicate threads lacing sheer rock faces; soaring rock mossed over with grasses; groins and screes, chimneys and cols and peaks enough to engage mountaineers for years and years. One week-end is not enough.

On the southern side neat tea estates are quilted to the base of the mountain, manicured as Japanese gardens, fierce emerald and lime green against the non-committal pastel of the mountain. We drove right through one estate and out the other side, snuggling under the elbow of the massif and discovered what we think is the world's most beautiful power station. The little hydro-electric turbine was set on a leaping crystal cascade back in 1938. Over it hang giant forest trees decked in orchids and ferns, a carpet of moss and scarlet lilies among the boulders and between their buttressed trunks, tree ferns as tall as palm trees, and the high blue of Mulanje glimpsed between branches hung with lianas, graced with birds. Astounding—who would have thought one could fall in love with a power station!

## Livingstonia
### 15th August

I don't know what I expected of Livingstonia. A small plateau once heavily occupied and still imbued with a sense of power like Masada? Perhaps.

Trailing in the wake of that devout explorer and failed missionary, Dr David Livingstone, came a steady stream of God-fearing men, mainly Scotsmen, laymen, doctors and clergy, bringing "trade and religion" to save

Nyasaland from slavery and sin. Mostly they died of fever, but heat, exhaustion and frustration killed them too.

The Livingstonia Mission Station was established on the lake at Cape Maclear in 1875, but the low-lying land was really good for mosquitoes, and fever drove them out within six years. The second wave moved more than half-way up the long shoreline of Livingstone's "lake of stars" and set up shop in Bandawe, on a promontory with a view of the lake. It was still not high enough to escape the heat and the insects.

Thirteen years later, in 1894, the Livingstonia Institute was established above Kondowe. Set on a high plateau about ten kilometres inland from the lake shore, this soon became known as Livingstonia, and the high hilltop settlement still bears the name today. The word carries echoes of gentle heroes, wonders of co-operation between usually squabbling Churches, and selfless dedication to eradicating the harshness of local life that made Livingstone declare Central Africa "an open sore".

The echoes are only in the name; the place has lost them.

Africa doesn't have a lot of antiquities around. Somehow things don't last in Africa. Termites eat them, wood-borers tunnel through them, mice nibble them down and cockroaches take care of the paperwork. Things over a hundred years are amazingly old—for Africa. And they look it.

Just over a century old, Livingstonia is crumbling. Built of soft pink clay bricks and beige hand dressed sandstone, the heart of the Institute, the great Church, is fragile and powdery. Inside, the vast simple shape of the nave is starkly Presbyterian, the walls without ornament, the rafters purely functional. Only the repeating pattern of tall twin windows, crowned with vague trefoils and lead lighted, give a subdued sense of decoration.

The pale walls themselves are lovely, a subtle shifting of shades of brick-clay. The floor is paved with these same bricks, scuffed, cracked, lifting or worn into hollows. Termite channels criss-cross the ragged flooring and the long wooden bench-pews have been pushed awry. Channels are being gouged into the walls to take switches and plugs, and white pvc piping crawls across the brickwork leading electrical wiring to long neon tubes soon to be screwed to the candle-blackened wood of the rafters.

Over the main doors a badly repaired four-panel stained glass window depicts Livingstone conversing with a group of locals. Beyond him Lake Malawi is a glassy sea and the Livingstone Mountains in Tanzania are prettily blue across the still lake. The window was a gift to the church in the fifties. It does't look likely to last a full century itself.

All of the vast complex of buildings—schools, hospital, residences, halls—all have this air of neglect and dissolution. It's not a despairing poverty, though poverty is abundantly evident. It is an unseeing lack of interest in aesthetics and maintenance. If a window is broken by a casually tossed stone, well then, the window is broken. That's how it stays. If a pile of rubble has accumulated, then it simply stays where it is until rain and a growth of weeds make it perhaps less visible.

It's not that there is no-one there. The schools are crowded with children, the gap toothed mouldering museum has a lass who carries around the visitor's book and giggles helpfully, there are workmen in the church and repairing the roads... Livingstonia, like all of Malawi, is full of people. But no-one cares.

It couldn't possibly be anything like Masada. Masada was built by locals as a defence against the colonising Romans. Livingstonia was built as a toe-hold by well-meaning foreigners. Why should any modern Malawian care one jot if it all falls apart? Would Israel treasure Masada if it had been built by the Romans, regardless of their intentions? The great biotic mill of Africa will slowly grind Livingstonia to dust again, just as it should.
Dyingstonia.

## Crowing about summer
### 20<sup>th</sup> August

Herro from the warm heat of Africa, where things either move so slowly you could pop with frustration, or so swiftly you feel a little stunned.

Take the seasons for instance. Last week it was spring, with its gentle air soft as talcum powder and a new excitement to the day: birds a-quiver with thrilling songs of courtship. This week it is full-blown summer, the sun cranked up to maximum by nine in the morning and likely to set a new record by noon; Malawi women are wearing their cotton chitenjes with bare shoulders, and the birds are in full nesting frenzy.

A bunch of crows stopped by during one of their corvid conventions yesterday, about six of them ranged in two or three of the taller acacias. They shuffled up and down the branches, shrugging their shoulders at each other and shouting hoarsely. Occasionally they'd stop and beat fiercely at the branch with their beaks in a frankly aggressive manner. Now and then one would take off and zoom past an opposing cluster of shouters in a taunting manner, to be studiously ignored by the bunch.

Gradually they dispersed, having shouted each other down, until only a couple remained, and these set about pecking energetically at twigs, rather than the branches. A wrestling match between a twig and a crow developed. The crow hung upside down and heaved at the twig, finally losing his balance in the flapping struggle, but refused to release the twig. He dangled beneath it by his beak, flapping a little, and then resolutely folded his wings and just hung there, hoping to dislodge the twig by sheer impassive weight.

But the sap is rising, and the twig, like the lions in Liwonde, refused to extinct. The crow gave up, but it's the first time we've seen a bird put a "w" into "acrobatics". My

Scientific Advisor, restored to his razor sharp analytic state after his temporary lapse into malarial misery, commented.

"Competitive nest-building behaviour," he stated with authority. I picture the crows doing a little Better-Homes-and-Gardens judging: each entrant standing proudly but anxiously, spruced up in best black suit and white vest, voices reduced to purring caws, kicking a recalcitrant twig back into the nest and hoping the judges didn't spot it...

Suddenly it's summer, but there are still two full months before the rains begin, and that's going to feel like forever. The frogs have already started a few tentative choruses, poor things—such a long wait still.


## Beyond Livingstonia
### 21st August

The road that curls round Livingstonia and plunges over the edge of the escarpment in an exhilarating series of switchback drops has two pre-plunge points of interest. The first is a pair of spectacular waterfalls.

The 'darksome burn' of the Manchewe River streams off the Nyika Plateau and gallops to the lip of the Rift Escarpment beside Livingstonia, where it flings itself off a rock ledge in a glorious free-fall of some seventy metres. Paths lead from the road to the very edge of the falls. To our amazement no-one offered to accompany us, guide us, point out the route or otherwise be unwelcomely helpful with an eye to personal enrichment. We walked, un-accosted in the serenely careless bush, to the pool above the falls, and perched with our feet dangling over the blue-hazed drop.

In the circular lenses of my binoculars I watched pearls of spray float in a tropical blizzard, and was reminded of those plastic-dome snowfall toys we found in our Christmas stockings as children. Inviting vertigo we watched leaves spiralling down the sheer chasm and then up again, caught by the up-draft, and butterflies dancing erratically across the wind.

Way below, a msasa [44] tree had flame creeper sprawling over its blue-dark leaves, spreading tongues of brilliant orange flowers, exclamation points among the riverine green. On the ledge beside us, a stately quinine tree[45] spread long green fingers to the sun, and an orange and black Acrea butterfly landed on a spray-dewed clump of reed and got its wings soaked.

The butterflies were astounding. Flying fast and high, there were so many we could only fleetingly glimpse. Even the more sedate ones were mostly new to us. There was a huge white one with clubbed tail and a rusty black lace border on the lower wings, and a really big Acrea-look-alike with hind wings of a rich brick red. Our friend the golden-banded forester was there, iridescent lake-blue lower wings and body pearlescent as an opal in the sun, antennae and forewings tipped with yellow.

How blissful not to be harassed. The KC Lovers Nest Restaurant was open for business, and the proprietor called a cheery "Herro!" We waved and walked back to our car, leaving a donation towards the upkeep of the area at the Manchewe Grocery Store. It's good to see that someone has been taking an interest, maintaining the paths and planting what looks like vetiver[46] grass along the edges.

Further along the road is the second point of interest, a little lodging place called the Lukwe Permaculture Camp. (For those who don't know, Permaculture is a contraction of Permanent Agriculture, a method of sustainable multi-cropping and integrated land management advocated by Australian Bill Mollison. It's based on good common sense and the observation that monocultures tend to have mega

---

[44] *Brachystegia spiciformis*
[45] *Rauvolfia caffra;* latex once used as an ineffective treatment for malaria. Parts of the plant are highly toxic.
[46] *Chrysopogon zizanioides,* the main component of many vegetation-based bio-engineering and conservation programmes worldwide.

problems, and if we all grew what we needed the entire planet would be a healthier one.)

The Camp is an interesting blend of aspects that work wonderfully—like the open design of the kitchen-dining area and the little sleeping shelters—and some that fail significantly. For instance it seems a bit odd to put the chicken-house right next to the dining room and the composting bins beside the lounge. However, we stayed over for just one night, so neither of these features did more than get up our noses briefly.

The Camp is situated in a wild loquat[47] regrowth area. These adolescent trees form a rather dense thicket of spindly saplings, and could do with a bit of thinning out (perhaps not smiled upon by devout Permaculturalists) to expose the magnificent view.

And the view is magnificent. The little bamboo and grass cabins are perched privately on platforms overlooking a dramatically falling cleavage of the plateau and a distance glint of Lake Malawi. Each neat cabin has creamy tent-like flaps of wax-saturated cotton-drill to close out rain or too much wind, and there were ample blankets against the night's chill. As we watched the moon down (a simple orange segment of light) little kite spiders built suspension bridges from shrub-tops to the dark towering trunks of trees.

Morning through the drill flaps gave a view of distant smoke-saturated air, the solid sky banded in blue and pink and cream; a tangerine sunrise over the copper lake. A brief walk took us to the distant spectacle of Manchewe Falls, lit by the early light. In the forest canopy a sound of canaries, and hamerkops calling far below; a distant rooster crowed across the water-rushing chasm.

All this beauty is an excellent antidote to the sadness of Livingstonia itself. And still there's the delight of the seemingly sheer drop to the Lake. The earth road—freshly mended when we were there—takes you down in a glorious

---

[47] *Oxyanthus speciosus*

series of stomach floating swoops to loop yet another hair-pin bend. The superb views to Lake Malawi far below lift the spirit as the body tenses at the narrow road, tight bends, and steepness of the descent. And all the while the sense of plunging into the unknown—at least for us.

From here we would travel up the western flank of the lake to Malawi's far north, all of it terra incognito to us. Nothing enhances an already perfect view more than a sense of adventure.

## The lemon-grass dog
### 28th August

I've suddenly had to give quite intense thought to the problem of large mammal pressure on plant matter, and problems of overgrazing. See, it's like this:

When we moved into this spacious house there were only two things wrong with its glorious garden. It was just a tad too manicured, and it had no lemon-grass. We solved the first by almost forcibly restraining our ardent gardener, Hugely Happy Henderson, from cultivating the north eastern corner. Whenever he looked at this steadily declining (in his eyes) area of neglect his shining face lost its glow and his almost indestructible smile would falter and dim. After a few weeks of silent protest, he thought up a quiet coup. He asked for wellington boots, "to keep out the snakes".

Science and I thought that hilarious and awarded him the boots without a second thought. That unnerved him slightly, but he recovered and proceeded to register his silent antipathy by the simple expedient of ignoring it completely. The problem that the compost pit resides in that corner was clearly not of his making, and he proceeded to cart our lovingly collected kitchen waste out of the garden altogether and distributed it in the no-man's land that we slowly realised had become Henderson's Personal Maize Patch.

Obviously there are no snakes outside the garden. This simply proves what Science and I have always suspected. We are living in Eden.

The absence of lemon-grass was solved on one of our trans-Lilongwe cycle epics. Science and I and Bags, our tongue-lolling septuagenarian hound, pedalled steamily out of the riverine bush one day and started up the incline towards the suburban clutter of houses. As we paused beside a main road, as much to catch our breath as to check for the infrequent traffic, I noticed several shaggy clumps of slender grasses. They looked to me very like lemon-grass. Bags seemed to notice them at the same time. Both she and I broke off a few leaves. I crumpled mine and sniffed ecstatically. Bags chewed and swallowed. Science circled back to see what was delaying us, and I pointed out this wonderfully inviting, obviously ownerless and needful of nurturing, abundance of lemon-grass.

We rode home with a newly adopted clump of lemon-grass. No, we were not plundering the wild of its natural treasures. But yes, we were stealing a plant from the rather neglected relic of a once probably lovingly cared for municipal road verge garden. Lemon-grass is an exotic, but I don't suppose that reduces our guilt. Much.

I planted it tenderly outside our front door, where for a few months it rather failed to thrive. I noticed its leaves were hacked off into a sort of lanky brush-cut, so I asked Henderson not to trim it any more. He gave me his usual wide grin and agreed immediately that he would desist, though I noticed him gazing at the grass in a perplexed sort of way. Then came the rains, and everything flourished, as it always does.

I became so used to the rich spill of long fragrant leaves that perhaps I stopped actually noticing. Certainly I've not thought of lemon-grass tea for a while. But this evening, in celebration of the balmy spring air, Science and I took a slow turn around our satisfactorily shaggy and happily unkempt garden, ending at the front door.

"Look at that!" said Science. "Our lemon-grass has gone extinct."

I blinked. He was right. Where the bush had been, ground cover grew suavely. Nothing left... Wait! Yes, there it was! One single, brave, soft, green, supple stem thrusting through... Just then Bags shoved her nose over the flowerbed and neatly bit off the stalk.

"That's serious overgrazing," said Science thoughtfully. We watched Bags as she chewed with obvious relish and sniffed the bed for more. "Perhaps we'll have to cull."

On the other hand, maybe we'll just risk potential arrest by the municipal plant-police. Again.


# North to Karonga
## 29th August

In 1879, midway between their base in Blantyre and Ujiji, where the presumptuous Stanley met Livingstone on the shore of Lake Tanganyika, the African Lakes Corporation established a depot. Karonga. A town that has had to be moved three times in one century.

The road that sweeps up the northern narrowing tail of Lake Malawi is broad, curvaceous and alive with more than the usual Malawian pedestrian traffic. It's crawling with road-making equipment. That's good news, and bad news. The good news is that the road will be superb in a year or less, and will probably stay that way for a year or two more. The bad news is that right now, there's almost nowhere to stay along the route to Karonga. Certainly below Livingstonia almost every lodging house has been appropriated by the road-building team and sports a huge notice saying, "Beach XYZ Rest House is the private residence of ABC Road Building Company."

But this will change. Besides, the drive from Livingstonia to Karonga is easily done in one fairly lazy morning. Easy, but not lacking in interest.

The road meandered voluptuously over lake-side undulations, providing gorgeous sweeping views across serene beaches swathed in ample greenery, glinting blue water and the serried graph-line of the tall blue edge of the Rift Valley. Across the lake, the mountainous shore of Tanzania blended imperceptibly with the smoke laden air and the hazy water, as if we looked out upon the end of the world, sky and land and water all one nebulous, endless blue.

Peeling away from the road to the right is an outflung arm of muscular rocky peninsula, reaching longingly for hidden Tanzania just thirty odd kilometres away. On a whim we yielded to this stark appeal and drove up the gravelled detour road flanking the imposing raised bed of the New Improved Highway and headed for the town of Chilumba.

Chilumba is tiny. A random scatter of domestic and commercial buildings, a resigned sense that despite the impressive—for Malawi—cargo harbour donated by foreign aid in the last few years, nothing has changed, or is likely to. The harbour is geared to container loading. A gargantuan four-legged crane squats over a rail, immobile under its bright paint, waiting with infinite patience for a container-bearing vessel to dock beside it. There are none on Lake Malawi. One wonders what the thinking was behind this expensive and seemingly pointless expenditure of foreign money. Three people lounging on bollards stared idly at our car, perhaps the first non-local vehicle to pass in many days.

But the road continued across the track, and we followed it as it snaked its narrowing way to the ridge of the peninsula. The rough twiggy cover of miombo trees gave way to thickening patches of mango woodland shading small houses, with tiny swept squares of kitchen yard or neatly cultivated patches of garden. There is something charming about truly African roads. They are a product of the flow of people, not necessarily of wheeled traffic, and like those in mediaeval villages the routes have a spontaneous, logical-to-feet ease.

We edged delicately up this path, squeezing cautiously between mud-built walls, carefully tended mounds of lacy-leaved cassava and occasional hedges of euphorbia. Many homes show signs of considerable age. Dotted here and there are skeletons of long defunct but much loved trucks, luxurious weeds spilling from empty windows, not a trace of duco on the rich matt sides of softly rusting metal. Graveyards for their original owners drowsed in the dim green light beneath the trees, headstones proclaiming the final resting place of Mr Isiah Ndovi, Mrs Mary Ndovi, Henderson Ndovi...

Where the track finally became too narrow for us, we turned gingery among the cultivation and the golden shower creepers and started back. A gentle-faced man came sauntering up the side of a house, and raised an enquiring hand. Science stopped immediately, with I think a sense of relief that we had a reason to tarry a few minutes longer.

The gentle stranger greeted us politely and explained that we'd got off the main road. We smiled and nodded, and said we knew that, we were just interested in this attractive peninsula. His smile widened, and he said,

"You are South African! I spent many years there, working on the gold-mines in Germiston."

On learning that I had been born in a neighbouring town, he grasped my hand warmly and we spent several companionable minutes discussing the delights of those far distant mining days.

Then he shook our hands again, wished us a pleasant journey, and stepped back. Dismissed with great dignity we moved on, gently jolting over the unsurfaced pathway. I felt deeply moved, as if something of huge importance had occurred.

As we breasted a rise, the trees stood aside and we saw the bright crescent of an empty beach embracing the long sweep of Young's Bay, mirror smooth in the bright mid-morning light.

In no time we were back on the road to Karonga with the westerning sun warming our left cheeks. Karonga, the fourth largest town in Malawi, where a million years ago a dinosaur called Malawisaurus romped, and just over a century ago a slave trader called Mlozi held the town under siege.

# September 2001

September songs
3<sup>rd</sup> September

Dawn is palely beautiful, a glowing milky apricot in still, calm air. Bird song so thick in the early light it's like an audible aurora and a single toad rasping away like a snoring bulldog. We've tried to decide which bird is first to wake, but it's not easy.

Certainly the duelling Heuglin's[48] robins are among the first, shouting each other down with hysterical cries of "Mr. Phiri! Mr. Phiri!! Mr Phiri!!!" The coucal chortles away in the distance, and turtle doves, wood-doves and red-eyed doves all tailor their sounds to the dawn and the distance. The drongos saw and screech like amateur violinists, the oriole spins a swift phrase of liquid gold and a hoopoe sounds his single calm sweet note in a gentle triplet.

Breakfast on the khonde holds elements of uncertainty. If the clouds come up, it's uncharitably cold. If not, the sun peers rudely into our faces like a cheeky red

---

[48] White-browed Robin-Chat, *Cossypha heuglini*

monkey. But the tiny green blossoms on the combretum waft their delicate scent across our table, and we probably wouldn't bother with breakfast if we had to sit indoors.

By eight or nine it's wild exuberant weather and birds are flung about the sky by boisterous winds, the crows exulting in the rough air. Every surface feels faintly gritty with fine dust and black particles of burned grass.

Further out of town it is time for home repairs. Front yards are turned into mud bricks, all that top soil going into repairs or extensions, and the desolate resultant hollow will later be turned into hummocks for cassava plants. Fences of thatching grass are being made, the old grey ones, ragged and sagging untidily are replaced the new fences bright as gold and elegantly tall. The msasa[49] trees are beginning to show their spring colours, unfurling waxy fans of soft new leaves in shades of pink and red. It's a lovely time of the year. But then, perhaps one could say that of Malawi at any time of the year.

Not much has actually happened this week. We saw a crow chase a fruit bat who was trying to get an early start and nearly got eaten for his trouble; such a gripping display of flying skills! And later heard a long haunting ooooooop! repeated from the reeds beside the river; we think it could be one of the flufftails. But other than these moments of exclamation, nothing of remarkable significance has happened. Wonderful how life can be so satisfying without any excitement!

---

[49] Msasa refers either specifically to *Brachystegia spiciformis,* or generally, as here, to mixed brachystegia woodland.

# Karonga: Stevenson's Road
## 5th September

We stood, staring blankly out at the lake, on a featureless rise above a featureless beach. Our guide waved a languid hand.

"This," he said pleasantly, "is the start of Stevenson's Road."

"Where?" I asked bewilderedly.

"Here," and the guide swept his hand in a semi-circle towards the interior. I looked behind me at a wide swathe of obviously levelled ground heading towards a ridge of trees.

"This?" I asked.

"No, no. That's a drainage furrow, cut to stop the river from flooding Karonga." He didn't add "again".

I have no idea why Stevenson's Road appears to start in the place where the drainage furrow ends, nor how anyone can tell the place from anywhere else along that unremarkable beach. It reminded me clearly of Commissioner Johnston's[50] comment in 1879, "Karonga is an open roadstead, most dangerous for landing". In fact one is hard pressed to find any good reason for placing the little settlement of Karonga where it is.

The Moir brothers, John and Fred, had girded their loins in response to Livingstone's cry for Christianity and Commerce to cure Africa of her evils, particularly the slave trade. The brothers set out with zeal as unpaid volunteers in 1877, to establish the African Lakes Company in Blantyre. Lake Nyasa, as Lake Malawi was known then, was a focus of the central African slave trade, and the intention was to establish trade routes from the coast up rivers and lakes to Ujiji on Lake Tanganyika. Karonga is roughly mid-way

---

[50] British Central Africa, by Sir H H Johnston, KCB. Methuen & Co, London, 1897

between Blantyre and Ujiji, while across the lake to the east, roughly the same distance away, was the slavery capital of Zanzibar.

There seems little else to recommend Karonga, then or now. Low-lying and humid, it is plagued by fierce malaria and even fiercer floods. Between the rising of the lake water and the swift descent of the flooding North Rukuru River, the entire town was actually moved three times in less than a century. Perhaps it's not surprising that the first mile or so of Stevenson's Road seems a little vague.

This road, named for the Chairman of the African Lakes Company, James Stevenson, was to head overland to the southern end of Lake Tanganyika. Fred Moir wrote[51] "This was over two hundred miles north-west of Nyasa, and the intervening plateau was mountainous and unexplored, with no known direct route." Another steel-willed Scotsman, James Stewart, an engineer with experience of road building in India, took on the job of both surveying a possible route and actually building the road.

Picture the task in a land without rail, road or communications. All equipment was brought from the coast via the Shire river—lugged by hand up the rapids and hauled by oxen through the plains. Then brought by boat from Mongochi to Karonga, on that lake which Johnston warns us is "...as rough at times as the British Channel, with heavy breakers on unprotected shores." Once landed from this "dangerous open roadstead" at Karonga, the real work began, physically hacking a roadway from the hard-baked African earth. A hand-made road.

Fred Moir phlegmatically describes a few of the disadvantages: "Outdoor work on the dry, treeless plain is very trying during the heat of the day; mosquitoes, moths and flying ants are very annoying at night, whilst scorpions and snakes have also to be guarded against. There were many lions and hyenas..."

---

[51] After Livingstone, by Fred. L. M. Moir, Hodder and Stoughton Ltd, London 1923

Of the actual engineering he describes "...the ascent to the great inland tableland began.... The next fifty miles were very difficult, being steep and also so far from water... The steepest ascents were overcome by zigzags cut in the hillside, while rocks and boulders were removed to secure a good passage... Prospecting over these difficult hills to select the best contours was heavy work. ...turning up of soil in swamps and valleys was specially trying."

Harry Johnstone dismisses this heroic effort with a wave as languid as our guide's. "The Stevenson Road... was never completed... The engineers concerned in this work died of fever, and further operations were checked by the outbreak of the war with the Arabs."

We were shown the graves of the two engineers who gave their lives for Commerce and Christianity. At least, we think we saw their graves. The lake has been over the graveyard twice, and trees have grown up around them. The headstones are spilled and broken, the inscriptions are illegible. Like the start of Stevenson's Road, I know I've been there, but I'm not sure what I saw. Africa is careless of her history, and the land is not kind to her relics.

Fred Moir says that the road was completed by the British South Africa Company many years later. Today parts of the road are still in use in Karonga itself, and fragments of it can be traced through the rugged untamed hills. Periodically groups of energetic and adventurous hikers discuss walking the length of Stevenson's Road from Karonga to Lake Tanganyika, but so far we have no concrete evidence of anyone actually doing the walk.

## Summer lizards, some are not
### 9th September

It's always amazing how September seems to be pivotal. I have no idea what makes it so, but it seems to trigger something. Within the first few days of September the blue-headed tree agamas suddenly arrived. I looked up from my cornflakes, and there the old man was, sky-blue head and drab body, doing press-ups on the trunk of the combretum as if he's never been away.

He's a big lizard, about 40 cm from nose to tip of tail, and bulky. That head-bobbing display seems to go with wide shoulders. So where has he been all this time? Even Science is mystified. We've seen youngsters almost as long as my hand, patterned in beige and grey and chocolate, sunning themselves on the garden walls or peering down their noses at each other. But these big chaps were nowhere to be seen. Suddenly we've seen three in the last week, each with it's mating colours in varying stages of development—one with a pale misty blue head, our sky-blue fellow near the khonde, and the third near the front door beginning to show the sulphur yellow on his back. The year rolls inexorably on.

In the wake of the burning, fields are being prepared for the new crops. Our neighbouring dambo is gradually looking more and more agricultural, and the hacking of badzas[52] into the baked earth is easily mistaken for the sound of a chopper on wood. My heart shudders at each hollow thock. The summer leaves are not yet out, and the whole dambo looks denuded—the thought of losing yet another tree is hard to bear.

Perhaps this preparation of the fields is what has caused the wave of young fawns for sale. On the way home from Salima last week I saw a pair of little boys holding up a tiny brown bundle, and stopped to find it was another grysbok fawn. Its tiny front legs were grasped in a small right hand, the back legs, slender as straws, gripped in the left. The child was reluctant to let go until I had fished out the notes and paid his equally diminutive companion. I think the boys must have been about seven years old,

---

[52]Badza is a short-handled African hoe

certainly no older. They were not interested in attempting any conversation. All they wanted was the money.

And we are trapped. I know that to pay them what they ask means they will certainly go out and look for more of the tiny creatures who freeze so obligingly when afraid. They don't bite, they don't run. They are too feeble to kick. All you have to do is pick them up and walk to the main road where some daft mzungu will pay good money for them. And if that doesn't happen, well, the thing will die soon enough, so it might as well be eaten. I could refuse to pay the children, but I'd still not be helping the wildlife survive, and that one scrap of life would certainly be gone.

My heart breaks as much for the children as for the gysbok lamb. I wish they could understand they are selling their birth right, like Esau, for a mess of pottage. Like Esau their immediate need is too great to see beyond. All that can be done is to pay the asking price, raise the orphan as gently as possible and put it back in some protected area. With good luck and enough caring from someone, this frail little gift will produce descendants to stir wonder in the hearts of the offspring of those two boys.

In the meantime, we are filled with delight by the delicate perfection of this creature. She adores Bags, and is convinced there must be a source of succour somewhere on the lean old virgin form. Bags is vaguely embarrassed and stupidly pleased, and we fear her thrashing tail could break one of those pencil-thin legs.

We're on leave next week, and setting off to Liwonde National Park—a bit of a bus-man's holiday for Science, but we both look forward to it hugely. The little grysbok will be placed in the capable hands of Kuti John—it will be the third antelope orphan he's adopted in three months. Some men are just naturally better parents than women—perhaps it's because they panic less easily.

# Karonga: Strata of history
## 10th September

Way up north on Lake Malawi, the little settlement of Karonga has a stirring history. Set in the fertile plains of the Great Rift Valley where the North Rukuru spills down from the heights of Nyika and races into the sparkling water of Lake Malawi, Karonga is infinitely old.

This was the centre of the fierce war between the African Lakes Company and the Arab slave traders. A trade war. The Arabs came to buy ivory, and helped themselves to unwilling bearers to carry the loads overland to Zanzibar. Once at the coast, they simply sold both the ivory and the bearers, so doubling their profit. The African Lakes Company understood this well, and by offering just a little more for the ivory and transporting it by boat to the coast, caused serious disruption to Arab financial well-being. Siege and slaughter followed, attack and counter attack—stirring stuff to read.

But first there was the fertile plain, to attract the people. Driving towards Karonga I was surprised to find, not an increase in lushness, but a steadily growing aridity. I was reminded of the far north-eastern Transvaal in South Africa, or parts of Botswana—dry plains against a distant range of blue hills, a scattering of thorn trees, palms and baobabs. Dry hummocky ground and dusty scrub lay between the road and rising hills heaped like a rumpled blanket. Perhaps very old towns have a way of exhausting the surrounding land.

We drove into hot Karonga, baking under the midday heat, and threaded our way through the road-repair chaos towards the lake, looking for shade and perhaps a cooling breeze. We found the fabulously named Marina Beach Hotel, from whose gates one can just glimpse a flash of blue water 500 metres beyond a dense bed tall reeds. The hotel garden features variegated coleus bushes planted in big steel truck rims, and where the rims were not available the old tyres themselves form planters. We chose to have a picnic lunch between the hotel and the reeds, undisturbed in the shade of a wild fig tree.

Then we sought out the Cultural and Museum Centre where fifty percent of the white female population of this large, if remote, town turned up to welcome us. She is the public relations officer for the museum, a copper-curled grey-eyed Germanic sylph named Stephanie Müller. (The only other resident white woman in Karonga is a young Irish school teacher.)

After a brief introduction to the building site that will in time become the Museum, we were loaded into Stephie's car with her innocent, blond, flop-eared dog. This adolescent German shepherd has all the traits of a much-loved child who knows the universe to be unfailingly benign. Impossible to take his gangling, eager enthusiasm amiss as we jounced out towards those dusty rumpled-blanket scrublands, which on second thoughts looked very much like old prospecting sites, or old eroded mine dumps.

I was not entirely wrong. These are the Chiwondo fossil beds. Rolling shallow valleys of arid badlands, eroded by sudden rains of summers past, into miniature canyons and small crumbling earth cliffs, glaring yellowish in the afternoon light. Pale grass tufted the pale soil, and ivory white rocks gleamed like old bones through the flaking skin of dry earth. Old bones indeed, and old ivory, and millions of tiny fossilised shells. We found fragments of curved bony shell, fossil shards of prehistoric tortoises; clusters of compacted shells, coprolites excreted millennia ago by some long dead snail-munching, mud-wallowing dinosaurian whatsit.

So we strolled and scuffed at the pale dirt for the modern treasures of the distant past. Fossils found in the Chiwondo beds are said to be between five million and two million years old—relics of dinosaurs, early mammals, and hominid remains have been recovered. A lower jaw identified as *Homo rudolfensis* was found in this region;

dated at 2,5 million years old, it is said to be the earliest member of the genus Homo. The theory is that a corridor of pre-historic movement lies between the rich hominid sites in East Africa and those in South Africa. Perhaps like a migration route, I wondered? Science sees it more as a link in time, but my brain can't make that jump.

I sat on a crumbling ledge of dry earth, the flop-eared dog beside me, and tried to feel philosophical and 'alas-poor-Yorrick'y. Instead I felt profoundly grateful that the chalkiness of the Chiwondo beds makes them unappealing to livestock and unsuitable for cultivation. Not because it saves the fossils—I'm not nearly as concerned about our past as perhaps I could be. But because it was so serenely peaceful and unpopulated. The silence of the centuries rises from that old soil and presses on the ears.

## The Warm Heart Aches
### 18th September

Words, we know, are a frail shell that house our thoughts. In this changed world, where nothing will ever be quite the same again, words feel useless. There is nothing that can comfortably hold these tumultuous thoughts, nothing adequate to encompass the heights of horror, the depth of disbelief, the breadth of despair for all mankind. God bless America, God help us all.

We came in sunburned and dusty, a twig or two in our windswept hair, eyes still full of views of mopane galleries, the fragrance of fever-tree blossom lingering in our nostrils. The light had gone, and the warm glow of the fire welcomed us to the small cluster of dining tables under a great baobab tree. Science and I, with American relatives on a first visit to Malawi, were full of the quiet happy wonder of hours spent in the bush.

It was the 11th of September. The lodge manager at Mvuu Camp in Liwonde National Park broke the news to us. I would so love to find something profound to say, some word of hope or inspiration, but I find myself bankrupt.

All we know for sure is that the world that exists beyond our cities, beyond the torture of psychotic minds, beyond the reach of human terror given and taken—that world is whole and beautiful and complete. We watched the jewelled flight of bee-eaters; saw the voluptuous frozen writhing of heavy python vines embracing the stark unyielding trunks of tall trees. We stood in silence as a purple hippo, head down like a depressed Eeyore, shambled slowly to the waters' edge, an egret companionably on his back. We gazed into the open throats of pink and white impala lilies, and wondered at the sheer size of a single pug-mark of a lion, perfect as a plaster-cast in dried mud.

The wild world is real and whole. Hold onto it if you can. My love to you.

## Truncated Trunks
### 19th September

Across the pale shimmer of the Shire River tall reed beds were in bloom. Stems twice the height of an elephant were topped with soft dusky plumes like great ostrich feathers. Beyond them a frieze of lime-barked fever trees and shaggy-topped borassus palms fringed the huge dome of pearlescent, smoky sky.

The outboard motor idled gently as we nosed into a channel in the reeds. On either side the flood-plain was under water, and hippos waded shoulder deep through waterlogged grass. A pair of long-toed plovers clattered at us while African jacanas high-stepped meticulously across the half-submerged vegetation.

A bull elephant swung his huge grey bulk towards us. He eyed us calmly as he dragged runners of grass into his mouth with his trunk. He idly flapped his ears, tattered at the edges like old moth wings.

Science put his mouth close to my ear and said, "Notice his trunk."

I looked. It's hard to notice something carefully when it's in use, and the elephant was using his with busy deliberation. I noticed a growth over the right eye; I noticed a tusk missing on the left; I noticed the damp water-line up to his shoulders. But the trunk?

"What about it?" I asked quietly.

"The tip is missing."

So it was. The trunk ended in an abrupt flat edge, several inches shorter than it should be. The bull elephant seemed supremely unconcerned. He kept on dragging up strings of grass, giving them a brief sloosh in the water and trailing them into his contentedly chomping mouth.

The image troubled me a little, and back in Mvuu Camp I brought the subject up again. Losing that delicate tip of the trunk must be very like losing your thumb when you have only one hand. It must be a huge disadvantage. How could it have happened? Science got that far-away look in his eye, and I settled down for one of his rich reminiscences.

"Back in Zimbabwe's Gona Re Zhou when I was doing an elephant census in the late 60s, I found a young elephant bull with his entire trunk missing. He stood, oh, about seven foot at the shoulder, and seemed to be alone. He had tiny little stubby tusks, and his trunk barely extended beyond them. Where the trunk was severed it looked pink and septic and raw, and fluid was streaming from it. He was not in good condition.

"I decided he'd been caught in a snare. With just that stub of a trunk left, I couldn't see how he'd survive. How would he drink, for instance, or feed? I watched him awkwardly catching leaves between a tusk and the stump, stripping them straight into the side of his mouth, and browsing directly, like a rhino. Hard work, that. He appeared to be suffering, so I did what most biologists advise against. I shot him to put him out of his misery.

"On examination I found the wound had actually healed completely, though it looked awful, and the ooze was just clear sinus fluid. When I opened him up I found his belly was full, and there was sloppy stuff in his gut—he'd been coping very well indeed, far better than I thought possible. I had needlessly killed the little chap. It was an awful thing.

"Since then I've seen quite a few elephants with bits of their trunks missing. There was one the other side of the camp yesterday with about eleven inches gone. He looked as well-fed as our friend in the channel this morning."

"And it's all caused by poachers' snares?" I asked. Science shook his head.

"I've thought about it a lot of course, and though I've seen many animals with the ends of their trunks missing, I've never seen one with a snare actually on the trunk, and the end rotting away. Yet I've seen all sorts of animals with snares embedded in their legs. No, I don't think it's all snare damage. It could just as easily be predators. Hyenas could take on a baby elephant, or even a lion. These chaps here in Liwonde spend so much time in the water, I would guess it's mostly crocodile attacks."

I had a sudden vivid memory of the illustration in Kipling's "Just So Stories", the Elephants' Child bunched back on his haunches with the vast Nile crocodile clamped

to the end of his slowly stretching trunk. Somehow it's easier, now, to think of these mutilated creatures painfully adjusting to their handicap in the wild. One less burden of guilt for the family of man.

# October 2001



It's been a while, I know. Mostly it's due to a rash of computer related problems. My trusty laptop got a nasty infection which may or may not have caused the collapse of my hard-drive. I've been a full month without it, feeling like I've been robbed of my security blanket.

Science has loaned me his machine which I'm working from at the moment, but using some-one else's computer is only slightly less uncomfortable than using some-one else's toothbrush. Obviously it's not as intimate but it's almost as personal, and I'm constantly aware that he actually needs it himself.

Now his desk-top Main Machine has gone insane and is issuing random emails to any address it can lay it's demented virtual hands on, spewing out viruses attached to antique email messages dredged out of its cyber-subconscious. Some of these are fragments of emails sent more than two years ago and from a computer which was stolen before we even came to Malawi! Very spooky stuff.

And Malawi.net, server to the Warm Heart, has been engrossed in a series of "up-grades". This involves a slew of switches in log-on procedures, none apparently effective, and most people in Lilongwe seem to be reverting to snail-mail as quicker and more reliable. Internet access has been impossible for the last two weeks. The frustration is universal enough for it to be rumoured that the up-grade was designed by Bin Laden. It's a change from blaming our neighbour, Uncle Bob[53], for everything.

Talking of which, a friend returned from Zimbabwe last week, and announced that she had failed to bury her aunt. The aunt's wishes were to be cremated, and it seems that Zimbabwe has plumb run out of gas for its crematoriums. Who needs Bin Laden when you can trash your country single-handedly?

So the general state of the world has had a finger in my silence too. It's hard to keep seeing the pure and good when the corrupt and hateful seem predominant. But if we stop looking, the battle is lost. And there IS a lot to see and cherish.

A thrush has built her nest above our front door. Science dragged the ladder under it, and helped me teeter up to see three perfect eggs in heavenly turquoise, the colour of lake water around a tropical island. In the last couple of days we've seen Mama Thrush bustling round the garden doing serious grocery shopping, so the eggs have hatched. For some reason she likes to walk. She comes scurrying past our breakfast table with a beak full of wriggling worms, and stops to give us a slightly distracted stare before putting her head down for another little scurry.

I caught the russet flash of a female paradise fly-catcher's wings in the garden yesterday, and Science was all for rushing out to help her select a nesting site. The tree agamas are in their full blaze of mating glory, as gorgeous as birds in their kingfisher colours. I wish I knew where they will build their nursery.

---

[53] Robert Mugabe

The fact is that this is a pretty good place to escape the rest of the world, so last week-end we took it one step further and wandered off to visit Likoma Island.

Keep your eyes on the beautiful.

# St Peter's Cathedral, Likoma
## 16th October

If you look at the worm that is Lake Malawi on a map, head down and wriggling south, you'll see the island group of Likoma around about where you would expect to find its stomach if you didn't know much about worms—or stomachs, for that matter.

Chizumulu is the smaller, taller island to the west of long, flat Likoma, and both are almost against the Mozambique shore, well within that country's border. When the Lake was carved up for distribution by the colonial powers in the 1800s about a hundred kilometres of the eastern lake shore was handed to Portugal, much to the dismay of the Universities Mission, who had invested considerable effort in Likoma Island. To mollify them, the island group was exempt from the gift, and remained a satellite of the Nyasaland Protectorate. So it's not surprising that the island of Likoma still has a missionary focus.

The single most remarkable thing about Likoma is the Cathedral. Oliver Ransford, in his book *Livingstone's Lake*[54], describes it as being "like the figure of a knight in prayer beside the lake", and indeed there is something very Arthurian about this extraordinary building.

I strained to catch the first glimpse of it from our boat, and saw the white corrugated iron roof gleaming among trees as we rounded a rocky headland. The building seemed almost squat, more like a Greek church than an

---

[54] Published 1966 by John Murray, London.

English cathedral. The roof itself looked a little tired. Well, it was pointless to expect it not to be. Tropical Africa is a harsh environment. The Cathedral was built in the early 1890s, it would not be surprising if there was no roof at all.

We landed at the little cove at the foot of the town of Chipyela—or is it city, thanks to the cathedral? Small stone-built houses in beaten-earth yards, each marked by a perimeter line of round stones, were terraced up the slope and shaded by mango and pod-mahogany trees. My bicycle and I coped easily with the slightly rutted road, whose only two motorised vehicles are the glossy ambulance belonging to St Peter's Hospital, and the army's battered and camouflaged jeep.

Rounding a bend, the cathedral's red-brick cloisters lay before me, arched and cool in the scorching morning heat. Not squat, how could I have thought "squat"? If this joyful building were not an expression of worship, it would be a work of whimsy. There is certainly an inspiring serenity; soaring arches to lead the heart higher, stained-glass windows to provide immediate glory. But there is more. There is a delight in shape and space that is playful, a relishing of texture and pattern, a physical pleasure in the play of light and shadow. The building feels part legend, part hymn, and is utterly astounding here on a dusty and crowded African island.

The elderly verger welcomed us, and showed us round with pride. Reverently he opened the sacristy cupboard and brought out the crook of the first Bishop's crosier for us to admire—carved ivory with garnets set in silver, the Pascal Lamb crowned and triumphant. Hanging on pegs around the room the robes of the servers gleamed spotless in bright reflected light, threadbare and frayed, but pressed and ready for Sunday's mass.

In the red-brick barrel-vaults of the ceiling wire tailed swallows built heavenly stoops for visiting angels. The figure of Mary stands below the rood screen. She carries the Infant as local women do, in a sling of cloth. The young matron's face is turned right down to the child, her expression hidden, but there is intense motherly longing in the way her arms cradle and shield this chrysalis of salvation, her own flesh. He sprawls replete and froglike on her breast, vulnerable and disarming, his eyes unfocussed and half-closed. His powerlessness is astounding, an act of spiritual lunacy, like the building of this cathedral.

We came back for mass the next morning, and all of us—both worshippers and watchers—were deeply moved by the beauty of the service. There is little as stirring as full-throated African voices raised in harmony. The fragile shell of baked brick, shaped soap-stone and Victorian iron girders was fleshed out in vibrant sound; African rhythm and Anglican liturgy melding in a single joyous celebration.

## Likoma Island
### 22nd October

There is a great deal I don't know about Lake Malawi's Likoma Island. I don't know its latitude and longitude, its longness or flatitude, or even who its first inhabitants were. But I have visited the place, so all that I can tell you is gleaned from personal experience.

My island experiences are limited. I've visited South Africa's Robben Island, and Western Australia's Rottnest, the first an intensely emotional experience overlaid with a deep sense of oppression. Rottnest was more festive, but still holds overtones of its penal past; there is a rigidity of infrastructure that intimates tight control, but the island itself is large enough to shake off the claustrophobic anxiety that Robben Island engenders.

Likoma is perhaps even smaller than Robben Island, narrower certainly, but maybe longer. It feels utterly different, no penal past to sour its shadows. Likoma is an outcrop of ragged granite softened with shallow soil, and a fragile natural vegetation augmented through the ages with ubiquitous mango and gum trees. The soil was always sandy and poor, and tilled hummocks barely support scraggy tufts of cassava. Scrawny chickens peck at the ground dispiritedly. I saw no goats, no cattle.

Of my three islands, Likoma is the most densely populated. I'd guess it's about two kilometres long by about three-quarters wide, and it is home to around three thousand people. It's hard to know how they survive. Most of their food must be imported from the mainland—either nearby Mozambique or more distant Malawi. There are no industries; we saw piles of concrete blocks waiting to be shipped out, so perhaps they import cement and export the blocks—the one thing they have plenty of is beach sand. They can hardly rely on tourism.

There are three ways of reaching the island. No, that's not right, there is only one way to reach it—by water—but there are three possible means. The only commercial vessel is the Ilala, the elderly matron of Lake Malawi which does the aquatic equivalent of plodding up and down the length of the lake. There is the Department of Fisheries boat, which has been known to take visitors to Likoma in about six and a half hours. And there is the Bishop's boat. It's a semi-rigid inflatable with twin engines and plenty of power. Having a convenient link to the Bishop, we chose that option and slapped our way across faceted flint waves in a battering two hours, thinking all the while of the SS Viphya which sank here in a matter of minutes in 1946.

On any island, I think, there is a subtle shift in the dimension of time. The gearing down happens while negotiating gangplanks and piers, painters and bollards—as if the heart imperceptibly slows to a different rhythm. For once I found myself more in tune with the natural rhythm of Africa. We did a lot of sitting about and waiting on Likoma. Waiting for one of the two motorised vehicles to collect our luggage from the beach; waiting to hear if the village guest-house was available (it wasn't); waiting for our advance party to report back on the beach camp on the western side of the island; waiting for a boat to fetch us. Surprisingly none of it was tedious.

The beach camp, Mango Drift, is unimaginatively laid out—a straight line of bamboo shacks with saplings planted in straight lines in front of them. Somehow it doesn't matter. Baobab trees, the serene beach and the rocky heap of the island at their backs provides delight for the eye. The thatched shelter that serves as bar, dining-room and lounge is spread beneath a vast mango tree and has a charm of its own. Amenities are spartan but functional, geared for back-packers and priced appropriately. We loved it.

Further south is Kaya Mawa[55], an indulgent whimsy of stone-built cottages teetering on rocky outcrops above the water, split level buildings with an eye to excitement rather than practicality. It's unique, surprising, and aimed at the affluent younger set who will pay for adventure but don't like slumming it. Since it's only accessible on foot, I was unable to see it from the inside, and I'm told that it has a wonderful atmosphere, a cross between English fairy-tale and African legend.

From the sea, the grey undressed stone and silver weathered thatch on grey rock against silver baobabs has a sombre, almost sullen, look. Still romantic, though. I thought of crofters' cottages and Lorna Doone. Here one might meet a Heathcliffe on an African holiday. Science says the interior has a great quality of raw rock and hewn wood,

"Flooring of hand-cut hardwood planks, each smoothed with an adze. Unusual, that." Then he utters his final dictum on Kaya Mawa. "It works," he pronounced, "It works very well."

There is little of wilderness left on Likoma. Too many people for too long. A few pod-mahogany trees survive with the baobabs among the mangos and gums. I doubt if there is any wildlife left besides a few otters and a monitor lizard or two, and of course the crocodiles in the

---

[55] Kaya Mawa was acquired by Green Safaris in March 2018

lake. Islands usually have an exciting "special" because of their isolation—on Robben Island it's the Chukar partridge, on Rottnest it's the "rotts" that nest there, the tubby little marsupials called quokkas—looking like a cross between a rat and a miniature wallaby.

On Likoma it's the crimson-rumped waxbill. Like the rest of the island, it is singularly unprepossessing, but none the less special for that. I was pleased to have seen it, but wouldn't pine if I hadn't. Likoma, however, is worth pining for.

## Wilting in the heat
### 25ᵗʰ October

I had every intention of getting a letter out to you on Monday this week, but that fabulous female, Fate, had her finger in there somewhere. This week my excuse is a series of mishaps that didn't even happen to me. The celebrated East African bird specialists, Bob Dowsett and Françoise Dowsett-Lemaire, had a rather African experience with their hired transport and found themselves spending an unexpected amount of time with Science and me.

Needless to say we were delighted, and learned a great deal. In a welter of information transfer we discovered that the insensitive sparrow that has been waking us at first light is actually a cisticola, and that the only notable difference between the male and the female Kurrichane thrush is that the female's tummy is distinctly warmer in the breeding season. (All three of her chicks are practising branch-hopping prior to their first flying lessons.)

They—the Dowsetts—finally got away yesterday, having offered to show me the Angola pitta, perhaps even in my hand, if we visit them in Lengwe National Park in December. This richly enamelled but secretive bird only really advertises its presence in the breeding season, and

I've never seen it. It may be worth enduring the rain and the ravening hoards of insects for that pleasure.

Meanwhile, Lilongwe is bunching itself for the launch of the annual Art Fest, which happens to be a fund-raising event for the local branch of the Wildlife Society. Both Malawian artists and ex-pat wives work furiously toward this single celebration of fine art.

One Malawian artist has developed a collage technique using life sized paintings and actual clothing moulded to a three dimensional voluptuousness. It means there are literally outstanding elements in each painting. He sells well, though his first painting was rejected some four years ago. It seems that he had chosen a *Nyanga* as his subject, and had enlivened the vast painting with the actual trappings of the herbalist and diviner's trade—animal bones, the pelt of a spotted cat, various tails of indigenous creatures, and so on. It was decided that this display of unauthorised use of wildlife products might not be too comfortable for the conservation-hearted Wildlife Society, and he was asked to withdraw it. Ever since he gives an annual promise, with great amusement, that he will not exhibit any of his "animal paintings".

If you're having a bit of rain your side, please send it our way. The parched earth could do with a little damping down, and so could we. The brassy heat seems interminable.


## Dowsett and Dowsett-Lemaire
27th October

An elderly and subdued motorcar creaked to a halt in our driveway, bearing what I thought were two unknown men. Science and I glanced at each other in mild surprise. Who could this be? Science strode forward, hand outstretched in welcome as the doors opened arthritically.

"Hello," said the emerging driver cheerfully, "I'm Bob Dowsett." They shook hands as my eyes swivelled to the passenger.

Tall and slim, hair cropped like a man's and elegantly dressed in khaki cotton drawstring trousers bulging with pocket pouches, and shirt-sleeves rolled up above the elbow, Françoise Dowsett-Lemaire is perhaps even better known than her husband for her scientific publications on vegetation and birds of East Africa.

Of course we'd been expecting the Dowsetts, I just hadn't expected to be utterly overwhelmed by her presence.

"Um... how nice to meet at last... I hope the flight was smooth?" She gave me a sinuous hand and a pale smile. It had been a long flight and the ailing hire-car did not bode well for their continuing travel. We trooped indoors for a reviving cup of tea.

Within minutes they had introduced me to a couple of birds lurking in my shrubbery that I had never met before.

"Hah!" said Françoise, "Zat ees ze sing-ging cisticola!" And she looked at me as if expecting more than my rather blank "oh?"

Bob twinkled at me through his horn-rimmed glasses and said gently,

"Um... singing cisticolas don't exactly grow on trees, you know." A provocative comment that could have developed into a lively discussion if I had not been bewildered by the bird's name. I could hear no singing at all.

"Ah, non. It is a name, djust a name. The bird does not sing," Françoise explained patiently. "It goes 'tzeep-tzip' or sometimes 'pee-ooo', but singing? Non."

I looked at the unexceptional bird illustrated in my field-guide and had a sudden fellow feeling for the desperate ornithologist who named it. The bird has nothing to offer. There seems to be almost no distinguishing feature anywhere. The only exceptional thing is that such a pale little bird should make a brash noise like a rather large and boorish sparrow. So, okay, call it the singing cisticola and move on.

They found the redfaced cisticola too, in the dambo below our garden, singing much more fluently and attractively. I assume it was named by the same exasperated fellow, since the bird in my field-guide has only what could generously be called a cinnamon wash to the face. With no less than seventeen different cisticolas to identify, who can blame the taxonomists for moments of apparent desperation?

The common names may be a little confusing, but the Latin is wonderfully informative. Cisticola, I found, comes from "cistema"—a reservoir or water tank—and "incola" meaning an inhabitant. But there is another interpretation, which I think may be closer to the mark. A "cisti", Charles Clinning goes on to say in his invaluable little book *Southern African Bird Names Explained*, is Latin for a basket of woven twigs. These warblers, it transpires, are weavers.

But it gets even more interesting. My two specific cisticolas, the (non)singing and the (un)redfaced are tailor-birds! I didn't know Africa had any! Brought up on Kipling's stories of India, I remember with fondness the little tailor-bird who kept Rikki-tikki-tavi, the mongoose, informed about the movements of the cobras. Tailor-birds have been so far from my mind for so long that meeting two different ones right on my doorstep feels almost like stepping into a fairy-tale.

The birds use spider webs and fine threads from leaves or grass to tack the edges of leaves together, making a protective sheath for the nest. I'm told that the velvet bush-willow, *Combretum molle*, is a favourite, the leaves being broad and soft, and we have a couple of trees in the garden. Needless to say I wander around peering upward in the hope of spotting one, though I know it would be incredible luck if I did.

I'm incredibly lucky anyway—not only do I have tailor-birds at the bottom of my garden, but the odd itinerant biologist who wanders through and points them out to me. Bob and Françoise were a veritable cornucopia of interesting facts on just about everything.

They were off again, far too soon for me, to do a biological inventory of the National Parks and Wildlife Areas of the Lower Shire—an exercise like stock-taking, and then looking at the management and conservation issues of concern there, and drafting guidelines for ecological research and monitoring in Mwabvi, Lengwe and Majete. They have only four months in which to do this.

"And in between," said Bob serenely, "We'll fill in a few gaps we have in the Bird Atlas for Malawi."


## Giraffes and Katz' Jackals
### 29th October

October is the longest month. Still no rain and the very grass stems seem to sizzle in the heat. Hopeful green summer leaves hang limply in the restless hot breath of another panting day.

This is a daft time of the year to translocate game, but it seems that it's the only time various calendars agree—the schedule of the game capture specialist from Zimbabwe, the availability of game-moving trucks, approval from various Veterinary Departments, and so on. So, despite the heat, the first seminal breeding group has been moved into the very first commercial game breeding ranch in Malawi.

Stirring stuff indeed, for all its absence of hype. The first group of nyalas, eight females and three males, arrived at the Kuti Community Wildlife Ranch on Friday night and were released at first light on Saturday morning. According to Kuti John, all went flawlessly. One young male took exception to the handling and tried to poke his horn through John's ribs, but memory of previous similar surgical repairs lent John wings, and he avoided injury for both of them. Within seconds all eleven animals had quietly melted into the welcoming bush of the prepared paddock.

Today the giraffes are on the road, making their slow and stately passage in tall crates from Nyala Park in the lower Shire valley to Kuti, some 400 kilometres. They too will arrive around midnight, and Science and I will be there as they take their first look at their new home at dawn tomorrow.

In any other country this would be a great media event. Here in Malawi, no-one really knows about it, and perhaps even less care. Giraffes are virtually unknown here—one of the many surprising blanks that Malawi has. No-one can really explain why they seem not to occur here naturally; there is no record of them ever being here, but they are a favourite subject with the famous Malawian wood-carvers. For guys who have never laid eyes on a live giraffe, they create pretty good likenesses. Now, for the first time, Malawians will be able to see giraffes for themselves, within an hour of Lilongwe. It's a news item that is unlikely to make the local newspapers.

Birgitt, the surrogate-serval-cat-mother, came to lunch today, bringing with her an Oriental charmer named Katz (I really can't tell you what his full Japanese name is, but something that sounds like Katz is in it somewhere). Katz is the new volunteer research worker in Kasungu National Park, and Birgitt has convinced him that raising and releasing an orphaned animal is the best way to beat loneliness and evening ennui induced by the lack of electricity—no lights, no music, no television. Katz bought the story, and Birgitt traipsed him down to Mua Mission to adopt a little orphaned predator to raise.

Birgitt's car broke down on the way back, so we had the double pleasure of meeting Katz and his new charge. Charges, actually. All six of them. Not a cat this time, but an entire litter of side-striped jackals. I opened their cardboard travelling box and peered in.

Six pairs of anxious golden eyes followed my every move. Heads firmly down on their paws, brows wrinkled in puppy-worry, pale buff-brown bodies squeezing into the corners to hide in this stifling heat. I stretched out a tentative finger and scratched the nearest silky ear. A set of milk-teeth about as threatening as a blunt pencil challenged me. Poor little mites, they are so much less armed-and-dangerous than the cats are, as Birgitt's interesting array of scars prove.

We waved them good-bye, Katz looking like the traditional new father, one eighth delighted and the rest sheer terror. How they will cater for their new dependants is going to prove interesting. Seven growing carnivores (that includes Spots the Second Serval), eight if you count Katz himself, and not a working 'fridge within a fifty kilometre radius. One of the challenges of Africa.

Right, I'm off to create a portable supper and then we'll head for Kuti and the dawn giraffes.

# November & December 2001

## Rain!
### 9th November

It's almost two weeks since I wrote, and they have been pivotal in many ways. I don't remember the clouds coming over; it felt more like the heat and oppression grew thicker and thicker until it burst. From parched earth to glistening greenery and jubilant frogs in a matter of hours. We had around 100mm in two days. The night was full of the enveloping sound of falling water, and the frog chorus rose and fell like deep breathing, as though the earth were purring in its sleep. The next day the landscape was full of little knots of people hunched over termite holes as the first flying 'ants' made their appearance. Even in town, pedestrians will squat down to a crack in the paving and harvest the luckless alates as they emerge.

The wonderful drop in temperature, the rinsed freshness of the world and the notably clearer air inevitably lift the spirits and the flying ants lend a touch of festival. Drifts of their discarded wings gather like spent confetti under street lights and in the corners of verandas. Two days of delight, and a week of drought. Someone asked if the short rains were over. I hadn't thought of Malawi as having two rainy seasons, though I know Kenya does, perhaps Tanzania too. Science says that's East African, and we don't have the same pattern here—but certainly it seems as if the rains have gone again.

Gone, too, is Kuti John. He flew out yesterday, back to his base in South Africa. He ushered the giraffes, tall and elegant in caramel and honeycomb, into their new home together with a group of glossy blue wildebeest, the brindled gnu. These have a series of pale stripes that run vertically from the neck and shoulders, and I've always thought they make the poor beasts look thread-bare. These males were so bursting with good health that for the first time I saw the stripes as sheen and not hair-loss. The nyalas I didn't see released, they had come a few days earlier and melted into the welcoming bush like fish into a pond. So the first step in establishing Kuti as Malawi's only commercial game breeding ranch has been taken. We will miss John keenly.

And now we ourselves are off for just over fortnight—it's supposed to be a holiday, but we expect it to deteriorate to a wild scramble to fit everything in—visits to family and family doctors, re-establishing connections with colleagues, and scouting for a patch of land to establish our own base once we leave Malawi, for that day is looming too. So I'll be silent for the next two weeks. But there is a story for you—it's about a creature I met below Mount Mulanje.

## One Man's Vermin...
### 10<sup>th</sup> November

I find it extraordinary how accustomed we become to what is around us. We get so used to seeing what is on our own doorstep that we cease to wonder at it.

Recent discoveries of new mammals in Vietnam have had the zoological world agog. Who could have supposed that mammals never before recorded could come to light towards the end of the 20ᵗʰ century? With the earth showing signs of exhaustion, and man(un)kind proliferating as fast as cockroaches, it seems a miracle that any animal has managed to keep its existence a secret. Yet, for all of us, there are creatures we have never seen. I have been fortunate to meet one in the last few months.

I was staying as a guest at a tea estate below the eastern slopes of Mount Mulanje. The sprawling house was set into a knoll, with gardens dropping away before it, revealing a glorious serried view of emerald tea fields, lush riverine ribbons of jungle lining the valleys, and the rising mystical smoky blue of the eastern arm of the massif.

Behind the house the rising ground was a cheerful balance of neat lawns, rocky outcrops, rampant exotic shrubbery and natural wild bush. I meandered up along the steep path towards huge forest trees in the late afternoon. Science had said he caught a glimpse of a smallish monkey in the early morning, and I was curious to see if it was a samango or a vervet. What I saw was neither.

It was an extraordinary creature, long and lithe as a large mongoose, but russet red with a faintly banded shaggy tail. I wished it would slow down and let me look at it. It flowed like a rust-coloured streak along the topmost branches allowing me only flashes of its fluid shape as it crossed the gaps between the branches as if there were no gaps at all. It moved like a genet cat, quicksilver in a fur wrap; no jolt of foot or scurry of shoulder, just smooth grace and unhurried swiftness. Once or twice it stopped absolutely still. All motion one minute, rock still the next, moulded flat against the branch. A few sharp metallic whistles were accompanied by equally sharp tail flicks, and it would be off again like a brief russet river, an orange flash-flood as long as my arm.

The flicks of the tail gave it away. It's a squirrel, I thought, but far bigger than any squirrel I've ever seen before.

And far more arboreal. Cursing my lack of reference books, I sought someone to ask, and at length met exactly the right person. She was a young lass who grew up in the area, briefly back on leave from her zoological studies in England. Perfect! I asked what squirrels occur in the area.

She looked blank. I explained what I had seen, and she remarked that, yes, there were squirrels around but she hadn't really paid much attention to them. She supposed they might be bigger than those that occur at her family's lake cottage.

Obviously squirrels that one has grown up with don't classify as zoologically interesting creatures, they are just local rodents. I had to wait to get back to the library in Lilongwe to discover that what I had seen was probably a red-legged sun-squirrel. I found they are called sun squirrels for their apparent love of basking, though the only other example I saw was far too busy to bask. It seemed to be collecting leaves to line its nest, since it swept back and forth across the high branches on forays to neighbouring trees, returning with a good sized leafy twig each time, which, together with the long squirrel and its equally long tail, took some time to vanish into what I assume was a hole in the branch.

To my disappointment I seem to be the only one excited by the sun squirrel. Most books mention the creature in almost yawning terms, and even that inspired zoologist and artist, Jonathan Kingdon, only gets faintly animated when speculating about the evolution of these purely African squirrels. So I have no fascinating facts or quirky snippets of information to offer you about these beautiful beasts. I'm sure there are some; they are just waiting for someone to notice them.

A search should be established for a bored housewife with an all-consuming passion for arboreal rodents. That's not too wild a wish—after all, I personally know a vegan who is crazy about carnivores, so why not? We need a part-time Jane-Goodall-of-the-squirrels.

## Shrikes here and there
### 9th December

Malawi's rainy season seems to be having trouble getting started. After an enthusiastic burst in early November, it seems to have lost heart entirely. Summer is looking a little scorched and limp.

Our recent trip to the western part of the Eastern Cape—or perhaps it's the eastern part of the Western Cape—of South Africa was good, particularly rediscovering a couple of the old passes along the Garden Route that master-road-maker, Thomas Bains, laid out in the days of wagons and horses. Still in daily use, though in need of repair here and there, the old road through the Bloukrans and Grootrivier Passes is a delight. Where the Tsitsikamma toll road sweeps past what appears mostly pine plantations, the old road weaves through picturesque indigenous forest that one scarcely notices on the fast track. Tall yellowwoods hung with Spanish moss tower over fern-rich glades where wild violets, lobelias and impatiens brighten the shade with splashes of colour, and shy orchids glow like jewels. Out in the sun watsonias and irises blaze, and banks of heath soften the road verges. Old bridges of mellow stonework span streams of rich tea-dark water. We wished we'd allowed more time and packed a picnic basket.

In Plettenberg Bay I met an old acquaintance that I didn't recognise. Perched on a fairly exposed branch was a tubby little bird in shades of brown and cream. Soft brown barring across the chest and edging the tummy, a brown cap and deeper eye patch, reddish back and wings, with a single splash on white on the folded primaries. Here was a total stranger who had me charmed. I called Science excitedly.

"Oh, that," he said. "That's a Fiscal shrike chick[56]. There's another in the shrub behind him."

So there was. The parent bird in its more recognisable black and white flew in a moment later, to be greeted with much shuddering of wings and gaping of greedy mouths. We found their nest in the bougainvillea creeper just outside our window, and while the nestlings were nervously testing their independence a little further off, the female was producing a second batch of eggs.

A common bird throughout southern Africa, the Fiscal is regarded with some approbation by many bird-minded gardeners, so this week's story takes a closer look at the Fiscal shrike and our attitudes to it.

Here in Lilongwe we seldom see the Fiscal, but there are plenty of its relatives. The dapper little puff-back shrike[57] clicks and whistles among the combretums, and tropical boubous[58], also in full diner-dress though their linen looks a little creamier, forage low in the shrubbery. Grey-headed bush shrike stays in the shade and utters his long mournful cry. Occasionally orange-breasted shrikes do a noisy follow-the-leader dance through our trees, a joyful blaze of colour and sound.

I'm feeling as scorched and listless as the fading foliage. I'm off to hunt a bit of cool air.

---

[56] Now called Common Fiscal, *Lanius collaris*
[57] Black-backed Puffback *Dryoscopus cubla*
[58] *Laniarius major*

# Jackie Hangman and friends
## 10th December

It is said that a much-loved child has many names. Perhaps; but a despised bird has many names too, all of them unmistakably slighting. Jackie-hangman, butcherbird, even fiscal is an unflattering common name gleaned from the early Dutch East India Company in South Africa where one particular 'Fiskaal', a senior judicial officer in the distinctive black and white garb of office, was known to be merciless.

Another early name given to the bird was 'canary biter'. The Cape colonists claimed a shrike would bite the head off a canary if you left the cage unattended in the garden. I had a wire-haired dachshund who perfected that technique. He could suck a cockatiel clean through the bars in the blink of an eye, and even—we think, for we never found proof—ingested a sulphur-crested cockatoo without raising even a squawk. If a dog can do that, then why not a bird taking canaries through the bars?

My scepticism stems from the same rather unobservant early settlers calling vultures 'lamb catchers', despite the fact that vultures' feet are not designed to kill. Vultures have a pretty bad press anyway, but the 'lamb catcher' appellation has left them on the wrong side of farmers ever since. It's a hard job trying to clear the debris of years of misinformed prejudice, as South Africa's Vulture Study Group can tell you.

Perhaps fiscal shrikes are not equally maligned, but nobody seems very fond of them, all the same. They have a reputation for aggression—but so do the raptors, and no one thinks the less of them for that. I think it has to do with our perceptions (or preconceptions) of size. Lions, for instance, have always been regarded as noble predators. Wild dogs, on the other hand, were called merciless killers and shot as a matter of course by early preservationists. Is this because we expect dogs to be gentle, friendly and obedient? If so, then the acceptance of aggression in eagles is also associated with size—the diminutive fiscal shrike, by comparison, should be a cute little seedeater. The fact that it is a successful hunter rather offends our sense of what is fitting.

The second subliminal point against fiscal shrikes' popularity is their abundance. Fierce animals are supposed to be scarce. Someone wrote an entire book on the subject, I seem to remember. Certainly one does not expect to stumble over a proficient killer several times a day. And the Jackie-hangman is one of the commonest shrikes in the southern half of Africa. The Jackie has a rather gruesome trait which is the main root of the names 'hangman' and 'butcherbird'; a habit of periodically spiking its prey on a handy thorn bush or barbed-wire fence. Several of the shrikes do this, and I'm told it forms a larder when prey is scarce. What, I wonder, is the shelf-life of locust-biltong? Interestingly, the fiscal shrike does this less than other shrikes in the northern half of the continent. We are probably more aware of it simply because the fiscal is so commonplace.

Added to its reputation for ferocity, mercilessness and generally being a bully, the Jackie-hangman is seen as a con-man too. My grandmother held the opinion that the butcherbird copies the songs of other birds to lure them closer—just as the wolf mimicked Little Red Ridinghood's grandmother in the fairy story. What a low, sneaky trick! Actually the bird is not guilty of that either. No one seems very sure of the reason for mimicry, but lots of birds do it, including the innocent and lovable robin.

A really plausible explanation for vocal mimicry—at least from a human female's point of view—is mate attraction. It's thought that the bird with the wider range of mimicked sounds will be judged the more experienced bird, therefore the better mate. I can relate to that. A man with a wide conversational range is much better company in the long run that a single-topic fanatic.

However, my scientific advisor noted a fascinating event a day or so ago. A couple of juvenile African goshawks had settled in a tree in our garden, to the frantic despair of a forked-tailed drongo—the proud parent of two chicks. We could see two goshawks, one feeding on something—a drongo nestling, perhaps?—while the other kept up a monotonous high-pitched begging. Yet there seemed to be a third bird begging a little further off. On investigation, Science found it was the drongo mimicking the goshawk. Aping the predator, not the prey!

It brought to mind a story told by Konrad Lorentz in his initial book on animal behaviour[59], where he describes a parrot repeating the loud yell, "I've got him!" uttered by the chap responsible for the parrot's capture. Lorenz ascribed that mimicry to what today is called a post-traumatic stress response. Could that explain the drongo's echo of the goshawk's cry, especially if it was a drongo nestling being eaten?

Interesting thought, but it gets us no further towards understanding the fiscal shrike's use of mimicry. I think we should stick to the sex-appeal theory, that it shows the bird to be a man-of-the-world, so to speak. After all, when it comes to vocabulary, size really does count.

# Year's End, 2001
## 16th December

Season's Greetings from the Warm Heart. Two weeks to the end of the year. Hard to come to grips with it. Time speeding up as we grow older is one thing, but each year seems to cost us more energy in keeping up. So where is this serenity I've been told comes with age? Or is it simply exhaustion?

It's been quite a year. Yet looking back is like gazing into the distance in Malawi in late winter. I can see very little, and that only hazily.

---

[59] *King Solomon's Ring* 1961

"What," I asked Science, "Has the world done for itself this year?" His reply was immediate.

"It has lowered the mean altitude of Manhattan Island," he said, "And made travel more expensive."

I suppose that about sums it up. That's the fog I can't see through—as if the year didn't exist before September 11. What a victory for evil that is, beyond the actual event. Of course the year was there! It was rich and full, corrugated with emotions and tinted with the multitudinous shades of meaning that our fellow creatures show us. It tasted of new bread and cold coffee, smelt of mown grass and snow and engine oil. It was the year of the total eclipse for many of us; of first anniversaries, birthdays, family visits and job promotions. The year we fell in love, or got divorced, or went to school, or graduated. All that treasure we seem to have lost in the billowing smoke of New York.

For many of us, clearing away that cloud of dust and destruction will be as difficult as the actual clean-up was. But it has to be done. We must reclaim what is rightfully ours—our delight in life, our trust in humanity, our faith in good. I don't know how; I only know we have to do it.

I saw a baby donkey this week. Donkey carts are not common in Malawi; ox carts are more frequently used, so this was a surprise, and the slender high-stepping colt a pace or two ahead of the harnessed pair is the first I've seen in Lilongwe in two and a half years.

The donkey-child was glowing with youthful energy. Its ears were alert and its eyes alight. Its feet seemed too light and sprang up on their own, the slender fetlocks coming almost as high as the perky little chin. I have seldom seen any creature more alive, more thrilled to be alive or more beautifully complete.

It broke my heart. To be born a donkey in Africa is the ultimate misfortune. That this exquisite young creature should be so brimming with joy and utterly unaware of all the potential misery of its life seemed unbearable. Is that the shadow of September 11? Why didn't I notice the condition of the pair drawing the cart? I think they looked well cared for; I know donkeys are not often seen, perhaps this little fellow will be cherished as unusual, as useful, as valuable. What's happened to my unsinkable optimism? The young, innocent and beautiful should move us to delight as an unending affirmation of innate purity and goodness, not to despair.

Christmas is a week away. For those of us who believe in it, this should be the resurgence of our faith in the future. At a time when mankind was sliding out of God's reach, he put out His hand to us—His chubby, defenceless little hand. How much worse than the donkey, to have been born Christ to a Jewish family two thousand years ago! What if God had looked at the script and said, "No thanks, it's going to be too painful"?

Please have a wonderful holiday season. May it be a time of healing and regrowth for you, a time of peace and joy. I'm going to stop writing for a while, to do a bit of my own rubble-shifting. By the end of January I'll probably find I desperately need to write again, and I'll be in touch then.

Meanwhile, take good care of you.

# The Year 2002

## Back in the Saddle
### 20th February

Hello, at last, from the Warm green Heart of Africa. It's been a while. Like a sleeper still heavy with dreams, I find it hard to begin. Perhaps it's best to pick up where I left off—the rubble clearing.

The sad truth of Ground Zero is that even when the rubble has been moved, the towers are still irrevocably gone. I think I've got most of my rubble shifted, but the open space that's left is intimidating. Perhaps that's the place to plant a Peace Garden and learn to let the towers go. Thank you for all your letters of concern and appreciation; each one is a little green slip, a seed, a pair of folded leaves like wings, a reminder that life is insistent.

Malawi itself is like a wildly overgrown garden right now. Green as Ireland and warm as a glasshouse, foliage cascades down from a moisture laden sky and grasses gush up in fountains of electric green. Maize plants stand head-high, tobacco spreads its broad blades in astounding generosity. Creepers festoon everything—yellow flannel loofah flowers punctuate the green curtains that swathe hut roofs—and every spare inch of ground is ridged and hoed and bursting with neatly planted rows of rich greenery.

"All this juice and all this joy," poet Hopkins once called it, and the heart can't help but rise on the crest of this wave of lushness. Yet this is when the call goes out to donor countries that Africa is starving. It's another of those hard-to-grasp apparent Africa lunacies.

"Malawians are dying from hunger related diseases," our esteemed vice-President announced last week. Despite the phraseology, the predicament is all too real. You can't eat maize until it's grown. Pumpkins need to ripen, though the leaves make a good relish, if you have a little maize to accompany it. Last year's maize has either been eaten or planted, and the storage bins are empty. This is always a desperate time of the year, and this year is worse than most. The fact that the National Grain Reserve turned up missing doesn't help. Ah, it must have gotten sold; pepani! Sorry for that.

It's hard to fathom the reasons behind so much apparent idiocy, like why a building erected within five steps of Lake Malawi should have a diesel powered water pump. Simple, really—because it was donated by a first world country. Naturally the building has no water, since no-one has money for fuel.

Talking of fuel brings up another mind-jolt, the sudden rash of Petroda Petrol stations around the country. There are more than a dozen in various stages of construction around Lilongwe alone. Why? The vast majority of Malawians do not own motorised vehicles. Who on earth is going to buy all that fuel? Who is paying for the building? Why is there so much money available for building fuel stations and none for food?

Tourism is recognised as important to the country's economy, yet lake Malawi National Park, the only World Heritage Site in Malawi—and a mere few hours from Lilongwe—is virtually cut off by the state of the roads. This is not the result of a sudden flood; the roads have been steadily deteriorating over the last three years. But why worry about the roads if we have a million petrol stations, right?

A huge bill-board has suddenly appeared outside the Capital City Hotel. It reads:

"As A Former Fetus, I Oppose Abortion."

I wonder who paid for that. And why? In a country where a woman is not really regarded as being worthy of marriage until she has proved her child-bearing abilities, abortion is not exactly an issue.

Yet, here I sit, gazing across the shot-silk surface of the Shire River, its banks fringed with palms and fever trees, the mist-blue wall of the Great Rift Valley merging into the cloud-ornate sky. Bee-eaters sweep and dart in the shade of a baobab and weavers golden wings flash like feathered flame in the creeper-hung shrubs. Hippos splash and grunt downstream, and the serried calls of birds echo down the corridors of sun-dappled distance—coucal, wood-dove, palm thrush, oriole and tropical boubou.

Africa is sinking. The Congo is starving, scorched by sudden volcano and steady war. Zimbabwe is starving, emaciated by personal greed and political stupidity. Malawi is starving for so many reasons it's hard to explain—all in the heart of this wonderland, this glory, this green and gorgeous garden.

I think it's all a matter of learning to let go. Letting the towers go. Letting Africa go. I'm not very good at it yet, but I suspect I'm going to get a lot of practice.

## The Coming of MacCat
### 9th March

It all began last Saturday afternoon as the late sun raked our snake pasture with claws of yellow light. Science and I were admiring our rumbustious clump of guinea grass, self-seeded and at least twelve foot high, the leaves a constant shimmer with bird traffic.

Thinly among the flutes and warbles I head a plaintive "Yow". Drongo? The second time it came, Science glanced at me and without a word we walked right to the edge of the wild patch and craned our necks into the thicket of grass stalks and tangled flame lilies. The calling stopped when we moved, and we stood quietly a while to see what happened.

Nothing happened. Perhaps a kitten was being carried by someone walking the path beside the dambo. And we forgot about it.

At two in the morning I was reminded. The thin complaint came squeezing though the darkness to prod insistently at my ear. "Eeow. Ow. Ow. Ow. Yeeeeowww." Gradually the voice got slower and more ragged and stopped. I sighed, shut my eyes and rolled over. A pearl-spotted owl called in the distance, the falling tailnotes a distant "ow. ow. ow. ow." The kitten responded desperately. This went on till dawn. No sooner would the kitten run out of steam when some night sound would set it off again.

By five it was light enough to see, and I roused our gently snoring old dog and together we braved the drizzle-dewed jungle of the snake pasture. Bags dived through the long grass like a submarine and pounced over open patches with terrier-like abandon. I followed more cautiously, trying hard to sound like an anxious but reassuring mother cat. I had a clear picture of the kitten in my mind. It would be golden and stripy, half African wildcat half domestic moggy, fluffy and charming despite the ready claws.

Suddenly Bags quivered and froze like a pointer, and there it was. A scrawny black kitten with khaki eyes. We took it back to the house and fed it small chunks of meat and diluted milk. It ate voraciously and hid. When it wasn't eating it yelled. We named it Macbeth since it, too, had murdered sleep.

But Big Mac has settled down, shaken off his agoraphobia and developed a passion for Bags which the old virgin spinster is deeply embarrassed by. He has a throaty purr that can melt the coldest heart, and all the playful enchantment of any kitten.

Life can be pretty sneaky, sometimes. Here we are, within ten weeks of leaving Malawi, and we have inherited a new dependant. Apart from that, Science and I derive such pleasure from the birds that owning a cat has not really been much of an option. Nature has no respect for human preferences. We should be deeply grateful.


## The Scent of Honey
### 18th March

Mary put her dark head around the door and said in her gentle way,

"Medem, there is a bed in the dining room."

I glanced up from the keyboard and said blankly, "A bed?"

"A bed," Mary confirmed serenely. I blinked.

"In the dining room?!"

"Yes, Medem. In the dining room." She looked at my expression of exasperated disbelief and said,

"Better you come and look, Medem."

Of course she was right, I was just not listening properly.

"Oh, a bird!" I exclaimed, as it fluttered against the window, olive grey head tapping at the pane in fright. Mary gave me an amused look and tactfully withdrew, leaving me alone with the "bed".

What on earth was it? I had very little trouble closing my hand round the thudding breast, and stood for a while staring at the bird. I'd never seen one like this before, and I looked at it closely. It was perhaps a little smaller than a grey headed sparrow. The head and tail protruded from my fingers, and were not entirely featureless. The outer tail feathers were white—a honeyguide perhaps?

Drab coloured, more olive than grey, lighter on the underside, wings washed with gold, eyes dark. The bill was dark at the tip paling to pink towards the head and embellished with tiny tubes on the nostrils. Tubes! On a bed, I ask you?! What on earth for?

By this time my little captive was looking at me in a plainly beseeching fashion, so I took it to the front door an opened my hand. The swift neat swoop up into the trees belied all its trauma of the previous five minutes. I raced for the bird books.

It was a honeyguide, an immature Lesser[60], to judge from the size and colour, and our location. But what of the nostril tubes? Well, *Roberts' Birds* does say "nostrils open as short tubes on bill" as a family feature for all the honeyguides, but remains infuriatingly mum about the purpose. Great. They've all got them, and no-one will tell me why!

Maybe, I thought, maybe the birds need a little wall to stop the honey running up their noses when they feed on beeswax? Then again, the books all say their voices are often ventriloquial and make the bird hard to find. Perhaps it has something to do with deflecting the direction of the call? Then again, it may be more physiologically obscure, like something to do with conditioning the air it breathes, some thermoregulatory device?

Dr Alan Kemp, naturalist and nomad, who had been head of the bird department at the Transvaal Museum for years, came to my rescue.

"The one thing you do not suggest," he said in reply to my wild scrabbling for logic, "is that the special tubular nostrils are for smelling! Which seems a sensible place to start as noses go," he adds, unkindly.

New data on honeyguides from field work in Kenya, Alan tells me, seems to show that they have a good sense of smell. Apparently there are records of honeyguides visiting bush churches using beeswax candles!

"Most honeyguides have them, so probably all have better than average odour detection abilities," Alan concludes.

---

[60] *Indicator minor*

That makes sense of the comment in the *Complete Book of Southern African Birds*,[61] where there is some deliberation over whether the Greater honeyguide, *Indicator indicator*, looks for honey first and then finds someone to guide to it, or vice versa.

"On one occasion," writes Carl Vernon, "I was led directly over half a kilometre to a hive; on another occasion a honeguide took me along a most erratic, circuitous route." The birds were following their noses, and the wind was in the right direction for the first bird, while the second had to cast about a bit.

So the minor mystery of the nose-tubes is explained. Perhaps there is no mystery at all in why I had never seen this bird who is so *au fait* with my habitat that it saunters into the dining room unannounced. Although fairly widespread, it's not common, and the bird books tell me it can be easily overlooked. So much so that for years it was thought to be a silent bird; now it is known to call almost incessantly throughout the year. That is a bigger mystery to me—I've not heard its characteristic and monotonous "frip - frip - frip- frip" call at all, even now that I know there is one in my garden and I'm listening for him.

While I sit with one ear tuned to catch the "frip" I know should be there, I have yet another mystery to ponder. It seems that besides the albatrosses and petrels, which also have nose-tubes to sniff out fish oils across the ocean, there is another group of birds with nostril tubes. This I learned from a post-script email Alan sent the following day. It said:

---

[61] Ginn, Mcilleron and Milstein 1997

"In my dreams I remembered that nightjars also have odd rather-tubular nostrils. Maybe they are smelly because they can smell?"[62]

# Farewell, Snake Pasture
## 26th March

I write to the sound of slashing, and the scent of cut grass drifts in through the window. Henderson of the Huge Smile, armed with a stick in one hand and a *bemba* in the other, is cutting our snake pasture down to size. Perhaps the stick is to ward off snakes, perhaps to ward off larger surprises.

We have had a series of break-ins in the last few months. It's taken Science and me a while to work out that it is not that we really have anything worthwhile to steal— it's just that we are such an easy target. We have no desire to live in a prison, and could see no good reason for keeping doors locked and windows clamped up in the sultry air.

Besides, the last fellow who broke in very kindly left everything he'd stolen carefully packed and placed at the laundry door. Why he didn't unlock the door with the key we left in the lock and totter off with his loot, we cannot guess. But he left everything there, and presumably went out the way he came in.

There was something even stranger. He very kindly left behind the old hunting knife which he had stolen from Science the time before. He apparently used it to prize open the window, and thoughtfully left it on the bed below. It reminded me of the silly story about the manocleptiac who walked into shops backwards and left things there.

However, this time someone wandered in just after lunch, having no doubt seen Science and myself leave in

---

[62] In fact, all birds can smell. Look at this article on the subject:
https://www.audubon.org/magazine/january-february-2014/birds-can-smell-and-one-scientist

both cars. Sweet-faced Mary, our chocolate-skinned pocket-Venus house-maid, wandered up the passage waving a duster and found a burly fellow in my study.

"*Muli bwanje?*" she enquired politely. "*Ndile bwino,*" he replied equally politely, though in retrospect Mary insists that he was glaring at her threateningly and waving a knife of terrifying proportions. Never the less, she calmly walked out the back door to ask Henderson who this big chap was. On Henderson's denial of all knowledge of the visitor, Mary's composure vanished and she rushed to call the neighbours, moving just slightly slower than her scream.

By the time the neighbours had rallied to her call, the polite fellow had scarpered, taking with him my computer mouse, the remote to our CD player and—apparently—half a dozen hot cross buns.

Science and I came home to find the garden full of people. The neighbours are extending their home and the entire crew of builders came to Mary's rescue, armed with a deadly array of spades, spirit levels, rocks and assorted bits of plumbing.

Once the hue and cry had died down to a gentle roar, we gave the matter serious thought and recognised that the fault is primarily our own. We should never calmly wander off and leave the entire house open to the breeze, even with Mary and Henderson there. And mostly we should not have such an enticing thicket of long grass between the perimeter wall and the open screen door on the veranda. It's just too succulent an opportunity to resist. Mary deserves better from us, she was plainly terrified.

So, goodbye, snake pasture. I'm very sad to see it go. In its wake will come more boring old mown lawn, and the seed-eaters, blind snakes, dwarf shrews and occasional visiting mongoose will have to find another home-from-home. We will re-discover the compost heap, and the second guard-hut will once more spring into view. But with luck—and a bit of diligence on our behalf—it will keep the burglar from the door.

I've learned a few more fascinating facts about honeyguides on the one hand, and recently visited the ghost town of Chiromo on the other. I have no idea which will make it onto my keyboard first. It'll be a surprise to all of us.

Till then, carry a big stick and watch out for anything larger than a snake in the grass.

## More of Honeyguides
### 8th April

It seems that I've only scratched the surface of what is interesting about those species of birds called *Indicator*, the honeyguides. The dauntless Dowsetts, back for another bash at documenting Africa—or at least getting an accurate inventory for Malawi's Lower Shire Parks—stopped by, and I told them the story of the lesser honeyguide I caught in our dining room.

They looked mutually amazed that I'd not seen the bird before, since its presence was no surprise to them.

"It's probably here for the barbet's nest," they observed.

"What barbet's nest?"

Bob kindly smothered his expression of pity, took two steps outside and pointed.

"That one," he said.

Screwing up my eyes to see the faint outline of a hole in a neighbouring acacia, I gradually learned that honeyguides are like cuckoos, sneaking into another bird's nest to leave an egg, and the resultant problem child, with an unsuspecting avian surrogate mother. The lesser honeyguide likes black collared and acacia pied barbets, the scaleythroated likes woodpeckers, and the greater honeyguide goes for anything other than those already mentioned, as long as it nests in holes, like hoopoes and bee-eaters.

Françoise recalled seeing a pair of woodpeckers desperately trying to make their honeyguide fledgling behave like a woodpecker. It's the done thing for a young woodpecker to follow its father to learn the art of scuttling up bark, listening, tapping and probing. To the parents' distress, the fat little honeyguide was simply not interested. They called and encouraged and kept coming back to get him to follow. He just sat there like a surly delinquent, yelling for more food. At the end of a hugely frustrating day for the parents, they tried to encourage the chick back to the breeding hole for the night, as all good woodpeckers do. Again, the chick refused to budge.

At last the exasperated parents gave up in disgust and retired to their individual roosts, avoiding the brood nest altogether.

"I suspect that most honeyguide chicks are abandoned like that," Françoise concluded, "It would account for the fact that all of them have a lot of fat for fledglings. I think they have to cope alone for three or four days before instinct really takes over and they pick up the scent of a bee hive."

More surprises were in store. There is the matter of the honeyguides' call. Ever heard of a lek? It's a word thought to be taken from the Swedish "leka" meaning "to play". It's a term applied to a sort of avian display ground, or stage, where the male struts his stuff, and Scottish grouse are the best known of the lekking birds. Well, honeyguides have leks, too, but not on the ground.

The dominant male has a calling-perch lek, a place from which he proclaims his general availability. The lek seems to be one specific and traditional site, since Carl Vernon remarks having visited a honeyguide lek 74 years after it was first recorded. That's an impressive legacy for birds with an individual lifespan of maybe five years.

The lek takes a load off the lady honeyguide's mind, since all the girls know exactly where to go to get their eggs fertilised. It makes it a pretty busy place. As Carl says:

"The other males hang about the lek aiming to become dominants or hi-jack the incoming females. No *Indicator* male with balls would stay away from such a market place."

But the female has other problems to overcome. Like how to get her egg into a host's nest. For *Indicator indicator*, the greater honeyguide, this is particularly problematic, since many of the host species are communal breeders, like bee-eaters, and that makes the nesting site pretty well sewn up from a security point of view.

"Thus," says Carl, "female *Indicators* have to be cunning and use their feminine wiles. It is my impression that they gang up together to form cohorts of females. These females plague the breeding hosts by using the subordinate females to act noisily and display conspicuously around the host nest. This enrages the hosts and lures them from the nest, providing the opportunity for the dominant female, who has been siting unobtrusively and silently nearby, to slip in and lay her eggs."

This sort of group co-operation is astounding, especially in birds. Somehow one expects it from creatures like suricates and mongooses, but a bunch of feather-brains?

"For such a system to work," Carl continues, "the female honeyguides must own a communal territory in which they monitor several host nests. The advantage to the subordinate females is that they get to inherit the territory. This on the principle that it is better to wait for a good existing territory than to go out and try to find one on your own."

Carl points out that no studies have been done with marked birds, so a lot of this is speculation. But it does seem to be another example of male competition and female cooperation, which many of us would recognise as basic to plenty of mammalian species. It also seems to lend weight to my impression that the drabber the bird, the more colourful its life-style.

## One month to go...
## 28th April

Herro from the Warm Heart of Africa.

I was getting fearfully tired of that opening line, but now, with less than a handful of weeks before we leave, I'm already feeling nostalgic about it. It's the perfect appellation for this country, no matter how jaundiced I get.

Here's an example from when I went to report Yet Another Burglary (he came back for the CD player to go with the remote he took last time) to the police. I was waiting, sullen-faced and irritable, on a crowded and grubby bench in the crowded grubby charge office, until called to step up and explain why I was there. It was a long wait. No sooner had I been called to the counter when the large police lady on duty inexplicably thrust her finger up her nostril, gazed at the ceiling, and wandered slowly out of the room.

On the point of exploding, I suddenly heard a soft voice at my shoulder.

"Excuse me, please, Madam?" it said. I turned to see a glossy-faced youth one pace behind me, a lovely smile gleaming shyly at me.

"Excuse me," he repeated, "But you have been leaning against the ants." And he gently and carefully picked them all off.

So, you see, I don't know how I feel about leaving. I do know that the timing is bad. At last the various threads that make up a book have come together, and I need to have the text complete before we leave, so I'm head-down over a steaming keyboard when I want to be ankle deep in packing boxes. It shouldn't be too much of a magnum opus, since the book is predominantly a photographic essay on Malawi—I'm simply doing evocative areas of printed stuff to give the eye a break from the riot of images. But it's my first Real Book[63], and I'm in a froth of panic and delight.

So here I am, on a glorious Sunday, rattling away at the keys when the sky is china blue and the late summer grasses are nodding heavy heads in a small cool breeze. I should be lying on the lawn watching Schalow's louries[64] scuttling around in the still dense foliage of the combretum, or trying to decide if that busy tapping is a golden-tailed or a cardinal woodpecker. I need to allow time for a long and loving farewell to all this beauty.

We said good bye to young Macbeth last week. The skinny catlet with khaki eyes has turned into a svelte charmer of wildly extravagant humour. He would greet us in the mornings with a spread-eagled hopping dance; front paws extended, claws sheathed, four or five back-leg bounds and a small furry body suddenly clamped to your ankle.

He's the only cat I've known to really take to a stuffed toy. I gave him a little WWF panda-bear, and he's killed it over four hundred times by now. Such ferocity and violence! Such focussed terrorism, such lunatic comedy. There seems to be nothing so light-hearted and playful as a golden-eyed kitten, and MacCat even lured dear old Baggs into wild games of pounce and romp.

But we can't take him with us when we don't even know where we'll go, and we were very grateful when dear friends of ours fell as much in love with Macbeth as we had. In a way, Mac is repeating history. A few years ago we released a wild serval cat at Namitete, on the same farm that is now Macbeth's home.

I can't tell when I'll get another newsletter out, but I promise there will be at least one more from Malawi before we set off into the unknown future. There is a very vague possibility we may wind up in North Africa, but wherever we go, I'll be writing about it.

---

[63] *Malawi:The Warm Heart of Africa,* Johnstone and Ferrar, Central Africana Ltd 2002. Reprinted by Struik 2006
[64] *Tauraco schalowi*

# Elephant Marsh
1ˢᵗ May

In 1883 the private secretary to the first British Consul for Nyasa, Mr D Rankin, described his view of the renowned Elephant Marsh:

"As far as the eye could see, to the base of the highlands, stretched out a vast plain, covered with low sedge grass and reeds... From the paddle-box we could see innumerable herds of animals—gazelles, antelopes, buffaloes and elephants ... one of the finest hunting-grounds in the world, and well worthy of a visit from European sportsmen."

European "sportsmen" were already well acquainted with Elephant Marsh. The opinionated and egocentric Faulkner, almost twenty years earlier, apparently joined the search for Livingstone as an excuse to take pot-shots at anything that moved in this paradise, counting the number of animals he wounded with as much pride as those he killed. He so enjoyed himself that he came back for more wholesale slaughter in 1876.

Already the numbers of game had dropped alarmingly since Livingstone first set eyes on it some forty years before, and despite the protection of being proclaimed a Government Game Reserve in 1897, the last elephant was shot in 1901. It was de-proclaimed ten years later.

A century on, Elephant Marsh is still a place of wonder. Seen from the top of the Thyolo escarpment, it's a flat blue-green expanse of reeds, threaded with glinting water and dotted with nebulous shapes of palm clusters. It looks deserted, as uninhabited and mysterious as the dim bed of the sea.

Once in the valley we found that it is certainly not uninhabited. The gentle, mushroom-coloured Malawian thatching blends perfectly with the landscape and entire villages vanish easily from sight. The view too, vanishes behind a wall of tall grass and thin, scattered woodland, allowing only distant views of the hazy escarpment.

The place to hire boats, we had been told, is James' Landing. After a few fruitless enquiries, we found a young man whose face suddenly lit up and he exclaimed,

"Ah! *Nchacha Jemus!*" And he directed us on a slow meander through muddy dambos, patches of cultivation and innumerable clusters of houses. The road is little more than a track, but it led us to the water's edge where thirty or so dugout canoes were drawn up. Some good humoured, if vociferous, deliberation over the price of an excursion into the marsh took place while I drank in the view.

The boats themselves are a delight to the eye. Beached neatly side by side, each dugout is as individual as a fingerprint. The wood is dark and very old. All signs of the adze have worn away; the surface is polished smooth by

hands and water and weeds, and the ridges and whorls of the grain exposed. In the scooped lip of the prow the central vortex of the heart-wood shows, and the narrow sides have knife-thin edges worn down in eccentric, almost rococo, curves and waves. Not a single boat is dry inside. One contains a bottle of grey wriggling leeches, freshly caught for bait.

Gingerly we step into these elderly relics of once great trees, and are pushed off. A few seconds of uncertainty as we adjust to the boat's narrowness and the shifting weight of the poler behind, and suddenly we're free to become absorbed in Elephant Marsh.

There is a gentle splash and hiss of the pole, a clonk as it connects with the boat, a few drops scatter as it lifts, and another soft gurgling splash. The water is peat-dark and clear; a submerged lily leaf gleams amber and cornelian red through the topaz water, and mats of lime green water-cabbage bob on the surface, stiffly crimped velveteen leaves bunched in whorls. Beyond are tall sedges, then darker *phragmites* reed beds, and beyond again, romantic lilac hills.

Dragonflies play aerial skipping games above the water grass, and a squacco heron[65] does a cloak-and-dagger stalk across the weeds. A pelican, pink and pale as frog's legs, nestles hugely among water lilies, jacanas pertly skitter across lily pads on spread clown's feet. A pair of fulvous ducks float stem to stern, looking gilded as Cleopatra's barge. An anxious trio of black-and-white long-toed plovers[66] chivvy and scold each other. An open-billed stork stands demure in black, a sparkle of iridescence around the throat like a sequined collar. With a sudden lurch he hunches into flight, trailing long toes like lightening conductors behind him.

A tern spins and dives with glorious agility, sweep-stall-dip on wings bright as sickles. A pelican circles like a Sunderland, and against the blue-green backdrop of the escarpment are dark palms in silhouette against tumbling billows of smoke. Glossy ibises probe delicately under lily pads. Between these dish-like leaves, the perfect reflection of a blue and cloud-puffed sky makes you feel you're drifting through a Monet painting. A fisherman bends a polished back, dark and lustrous as wet wood, over the hollow centre of a distant dugout. Another swings out his net like a filamented lasso, the circular splash of sound carried over open water like a special gift.

There is a hush of lily pads against the hull, and foam froths from feathery weed compacted by the prow. Our poler points out pretty rosettes of scalloped, diamond shaped leaves, each with a small basal float on the stem.

---

[65] *Ardeola ralloides*, though the Dowsetts, viewing our photographs, proclaimed it to be the rarely seen Madagascan Squacco, *Ardeola idae*.
[66] Long-toed lapwing, *Vanellus crassirostris*

"Water chestnuts," he tells us, and drags a dripping, fiercely barbed seed from beneath, which he cracks with his teeth. The little nugget of fibrous white pith that he offers tastes faintly of coconut. This is pigmy goose food, and we strain our eyes, but don't catch a glimpse of the diminutive beauty.

The ghost town of Chiromo marks the end of Elephant Marsh. Once the major gateway to the country, home to some 300 traders and settlers, the income it generated from transport, excise and postal charges was a high proportion of the total for the entire Protectorate. It was also, of course, the base for ivory hunters. In fact the first policeman and customs officer, collector of revenue and postmaster, one Hugh Charlie Marshall, was himself a former hunter. There is a photograph taken in 1891 outside the Chiromo Post Office of himself, slung nonchalantly in a *machila*[67] while his gun-bearers support tusks and horns and other manly spoils from his war on wildlife.

## Goodbye to the Warm Heart
### 12th June

Herro for the last time from this almost-home, Malawi. It's impossible to believe that we are actually leaving, but the container has been loaded, the house emptied, and Bags taken to her new home. There's nothing here but ghosts, now. We have to move on.

I'm writing from the sanctuary of a friend's home in Namitete, surrounded by the gentle sounds of farm life and a peaceful timelessness. Science is in Ghana briefly, exploring Mole National Park and considering a possibility for employment. When he gets back we'll take off for northern Mozambique for a much needed holiday before

---

[67] A hammock on a pole for the use of sick, lame or lazy intrepid European explorers

fixing our attention firmly on the next step of the adventure. While he's away, I'm adsorbing as much serenity as possible and trying not to be impatient for his return.

The move went as smoothly as moves ever do. Packing up was compounded by the need to keep out camping equipment for Mozambique, and warm clothing for our return to South Africa in the dead of winter, and anything else we might conceivably need in the next three to six months. If Ghana likes Science and the feeling is reciprocated, we may head straight for Accra. Our container may take a couple of months to reach SA, and then be routed on to Mole, which could take several more months... I may not see what we packed until Christmas. By then I will have not the foggiest idea where I packed the kettle.

The worst, of course, has been parting with Bags. She suffered our steady packing with a pained depression that plainly said she had seen it all before. I couldn't bear the thought of her watching all our belongings being carted away, so two days before the move I took her to her temporary home. She was wildly excited. She romped and danced, and invited Science to play grab-my-tennis-ball. It was her second visit, and she looked comfortable and at ease in the surroundings. When we came to leave I told her to stay and she did, mouth full of tennis-ball, her tail slowly drooping as we drove away without her.

I know she will be fine. She's being adopted by Dr Martin Ott, who is taking over our house, too, so she will be going home. Martin is a devoted dog-man. He has had the goodness to suggest that if we find a dog-friendly home he will put her on the plane for us, a wonderfully generous gesture. He is as besotted with Bags as I was when I

met her, and I know that he will take loving care of her. This is her fourth new home, she HAS seen it all before, and I think she will adapt easily and well. More easily that I am right now.

The pain of parting is always as great as the joy experienced, and we have been very blessed here. The warmth of the Heart is the people, and we have made wonderful friends, the sort of friendships that will easily survive shifts in geography. Malawi has been very good to us, and we will always have a warmth in the heart for this green and rumpled landscape and its lovely lake.

I'll try to get this off before we head for Mozambique, but communications are more difficult when one is essentially homeless. After that there will be a gap for some time while we settle somewhere, but I'll let you know what's happening as soon as I can—and where the Next Step will take us.

## Heartily cold
### 14th July

Five thousand kilometres later, and we are in a different world. The South African highveld is tawny brown beneath a sapphire sky. Science and I are staggered at the opulence everywhere—superbly surfaced roads with clean verges carrying an endless stream of glistening traffic. Streetlights with globes, telephone poles carrying wires, bridges with the metal railings still in place, street signs!

One days' gawping, and we are already back into the flow, whizzing along the highway serenely with more traffic in our rear-view mirror than could be seen in Lilongwe's entire City Centre at rush hour. A few delirious moments in the food shop as I wrestled with the concept of getting everything I need—and a heap of things I don't—all in one place, and here I am, bored to death and longing to get back to the REAL world.

The most unnerving thing is that we have no idea when that will be. Or where for that matter. It won't be Ghana—luckily Science didn't have to make a decision on that; the job at Mole went to a friend of his who is less ambivalent about the position. We are relieved and a little sad—I hunger for the chance to live in a conservation area and experience the full sense of isolation, but perhaps that will still come.

In the interim we will prowl around South Africa, searching for a place to call home and a job to take us back into the bush. Having just written that sentence, I suddenly realise why we feel a little confused. But it's only temporary—one or the other will crop up first and simplify things. Till then our only fixed address is my email one. And our only real aggravation is the cold.

To mark our arrival, Pretoria had its first frost. A particularly malevolent thing to do, especially since my sandals aren't built to withstand plunging temperatures, and I've forgotten how to wear closed shoes comfortably. Actually the sandals do pretty well, as long as I refrain from accidentally dropping frozen peas into them, an experience I don't recommend.

I began this letter more than a week ago. The distractions of attempting to make head or tail of whirling urban complexities seem endless. We had hoped to have settled all our personal admin stuff by now—replacing my stolen passport, and so on—but those sorts of bureaucratic services bear a strong resemblance to the mills of God[68], and here we are still, rediscovering wide screen movies and the occasional superlative restaurant. But at least we have located a temporary home, down in the eastern part of the Western Cape... or is it the western part of the... Whatever, as soon as we have all our ducks in a row, we'll be off.

I had forgotten how bitter winter can be, and how dry. The very air seems to fragment into a sifting powder that coats everything. Sunbeams through the window are

---

[68] ...grind slow, but very fine.

thick as honey, laden with dust. An olive thrush[69] outside has his feathers puffed out against the cold, looking almost like a robin. The sound of turtledoves and hadedas[70] filter through bare suburban gardens, and high overhead a pair of crowned plovers [71] scold as they wing across the crystalline bowl of sky.

## Hello at long last!
### 23rd December

The New Year is racing up to meet us, and I feel I can't see the old year out without wishing you all the joy and peace of this season and letting you know where we are and what has been happening, or is likely to happen, in our neck of the woods.

Between my last letter in July and this last day before Christmas, Science and I have been across the northern end of South Africa to Augrabies Falls National Park, where the Orange River hurls itself over a granite drop of nearly 140 metres into a water-worn canyon. It's surrounded by a fawn coloured semi-desert landscape picked out with spiky topped quiver trees, often holding a miniature haystack in their succulent branches. These are the communal nests of sociable weavers, who could have been driven to this habit by the relative absence of trees generally. The rare pygmy falcon sometimes joins them, and we were delighted to see one of these charming little raptors perched on top of a shaggy muffin-shaped nest lodged in the cross bars of a telephone pole.

From Augrabies we wandered across to the West Coast, and meandered through the wonderland of early spring flowers. Arid, over-grazed land gets its first taste of

---

[69] *Turdus olivaceus*
[70] Onomatopoeic name for the Hadedah Ibis, *Bostrychia hagedash*
[71] Lapwing, *Vanellus coronatus,*

rain, and bursts into exuberant blossom, tinting the undulating red earth yellow, pink and mauve against the rim of distant purple mountains. Bars of rich sunlight shafting between purple storm clouds illuminate a section of tender green fields, and project a delicate tint of rainbow against the rain sheathed backdrop. Harsh, beautiful, dramatic landscapes.

We stayed briefly in Cape Town, cramming in a few visits to old friends and drinking in the jaw-slacking magnificence of Table Mountain. Kirstenbosch, the world renowned botanical garden and the headquarters of the Botanical Research Institute[72], was our home for three magical days. We would wake to the piccolo trill of sunbirds, and the sight of bald oaks sunning their gnarled limbs below the buttressed crags of the mountain. The velvet green scrub in granite groins showed thin wisps of waterfalls like delicate silk scarves. Residents say the mountain talks to you in the winter, when rainfall gathers in runnels to whisper and chuckle down the dizzying sheets of rock.

Leaving Cape Town far too soon—even people who leave after four or five years feel it's far too soon—we headed up the eastern curve of coast to Plettenberg Bay, our interim home. Tucked into a tiny cottage, we have our backs resolutely to the sea and our faces to the mountains— hidden from us, alas, by a deep green barricade of tall pines and black-woods. But Science and I settled almost immediately, soothed by the sight of a pair of ichneumon, the large grey mongoose, silently scouting through the relic fynbos on the edge of our mown patch of grass. A few days later a noble bushbuck ram appeared beneath the trees, so richly dark he seemed almost black. Since then we've seen two female bushbucks and a couple of solo grysboks picking their delicate way over fallen logs in the plantation.

We were actually flagged down one night, on our way to dinner at the main farmhouse, by a bird. It was a spotted

---

[72] Now SANBI, the *South African National Botanical Institute*

dikkop[73], and he raised himself on his long legs to look as tall as he could, and opened his wings wide and high, showing us the white under-feathers as clear as a flag. He stood there with his wings raised, his big yellow eyes fixed on our headlights, unblinking. He waited a second or three to make sure we had stopped, and slowly furled his wings. Suddenly two little fluff balls behind him caught the glare of our lights—two tiny chicks! We were delighted.

He held us at bay for fifteen minutes or more. Each time we turned on the engine, his wings would shoot up, a silent shout of "Stop! Stop!" It was utterly enchanting. However, dinner was undoubtedly waiting for our arrival, and we eventually had to edge our way off the road and creep as carefully as possible past the little family group as they searched the dark veld for their supper.

And since it's close to Christmas, I thought of Joseph and his loving protection of the baby he knew was not his own. No-one recorded what he felt when that same child came to a bad end, publically executed as a criminal.

Somehow fathers, and surrogate fathers like Joseph especially, get a pretty poor press. Being a male parent is not politically fashionable these days, we women get all the glory. It's a pity. A good woman, it's said, is priced above rubies. But a good father is to be treasured above all things. Hang in there, Dikkop!

Here's wishing you all the warmth of a father's love this Christmas, and a blissful New Year.

Science and I are off to Zambia's Kafue National Park early in January—I hope to be able to send occasional e-mails, but there is little infrastructure in Kafue, and we are likely to be camping. I'll tell you more about that just before we leave.

Till then, much love.

---

[73] *Burhinus capensis,* now called Spotted or Cape thick-knee. *Dikkop* means 'thick headed' though the Latin name suggests it's the nose that's large.

# *The Year 2003*

## The first step to Zambia—Mount Melsetter
### 10th January

We left Plettenberg Bay in misty rain, the roads flanked by wild watsonias in massed banks of pinks and oranges. Here and there agapanthus held up balls of blue flowers between rambling grey honey-scented shrubs with blossoms like a spatter of clotted cream. The majestic Cape scenery was reduced to a ghostly wash of trees and mountains fading into the immediate mist and drizzle. Car lights shone buttercup yellow in the gloom, and reflected wetly on the blue grey tar.

The rain stayed with us for most of the day, reluctantly breaking up into scattered cloud over the vast bowl of the Great Karoo. It's a landscape I've always loved—vast and somehow expectant, like a stage set, as if it's been put there to focus your attention on something of epic significance. Even in the 21st century, this feels like pioneering country. In the distance a single vehicle on a dirt road threw up a plume of dust, like a lonely horseman galloping in with exciting news. The tinge of expectancy spreads the lungs a little wider and makes the blood sing.

We stopped overnight half way to Pretoria, five minutes from the twin mesas of Teebus and Koffiebus, in the shadow of gentle Mount Melsetter. This is a family home dating back to the early Karoo settlers, the first thoroughbred stud in the country. There are horses still, now kept for outrides into the sweeping distance of lilac and blue. Here Candy, descendant of the pioneering Southeys, and her husband Mike Ferrar, run Great Karoo Safaris.

Dinner was superb—antique mahogany and willow-pattern; candlelight gilding the silver; smoky white wine and fragrant dishes of home grown vegetables. On a corner table stood a vast epergne, African antelope cavorting eternally beneath a tree-fern, transfixed in Cape silver. Mike and Candy are as smiling as the silver, as warm as candlelight. The old house breathes an essence of generations of comfortable family laughter.

In the hushed Karoo midnight, lightening played across the window of our bedroom like the headlights of a ghostly passing car.

Early morning was heralded by the chink of blacksmith plovers[74] and tea in bed. We set out to view the farm as the rising sun wrestled with the clouds and lost. A rim of ragged hills dissolved gently into purple misted sky. Blond grass and the scent of new rain, with a dust-cloud of springbok scudding through the olive scrub. And everything has babies! Christmas season in the Karoo is decidedly a family affair.

Black wildebeest cantered in elegant circles through a spatter of rain, looking ridiculously noble, like punch-drunk knights in armour. It's my first view these hugely heraldic creatures with their drifting blond tails; they are so exaggeratedly elegant and sexy, they could be the Barbie dolls of the animal kingdom.

---

[74] Named for their call, a metallic "tink-tink", now a lapwing, *Vanellus armatus*

A bat-eared fox stared quizzically at us over its shoulder before jogging off down the rutted track. Against the ancient rock strewn hillside a serene group of mountain reedbuck picked a deliberate path. Delicate ochre heads and stone grey bodies, they seem outlined in white as they move, animated rock-paintings beautifully camouflaged among the boulders.

Then the mystery of gemsbok, their dawn-coloured blend of lilac and pink embellished with black and white, like mother of pearl set in onyx and bone. They skimmed up the arid scree slope like a shoal of languid silvery fish.

The air was haunted by clapper lark's thin nostalgic whistle[75], and the rhythmic creaking of black korhaan.[76] Among the scattered boulders rosettes of jade green aloes showed thornless leaves edged with a blush of apricot. Mountains rimmed the horizon in softly shifting tones of purple and rose. Such a clarity of light, and such clean air. Each breath was full of the scent of new rain and wild herbs, and towards the house a fragrant trace of petunias reached out to greet us.

We left reluctantly, promising to return. It was far too short a visit, but Zambia calls—and we need time to kit ourselves for four months under canvas in Kafue National Park. Our trip has to do with research into elephant meta-populations, a project headed by Professor Rudi van Aarde, now (at the time of writing) head of Pretoria University's Conservation Ecology Research Unit. Way back last century I wrote about Rudi's elephant work, you'll find "When the Culls Stopped" in Volume 1, page 9; that gives a bit of background. This trip of ours is a tiny part of Rudi's ongoing project into the problems associated with elephant populations in conservation areas.

I still don't know if we will have access to email while we're there—I hope so, since some good stories are bound

---

[75] *Mirafra apiata*
[76] *Eupodotis afraoides*

to come from these four months. All I can say is I'll be in touch as soon as I can.

## "The Real Africa"
31ˢᵗ January

That's how Zambia markets itself. Unlike Malawi's "Warm Heart", this is a little harder to accept. All of Africa is real, even the unbelievable bits. But let's not quibble over marketing strategies, when there is real Africa to discover and discuss.

Kafue National Park is due north of Victoria Falls and west of Zambia's capital, Lusaka. Said to be the third largest park in the world, Kafue remains relatively unknown. And it's easy to see why. Firstly, the terrain is not kindly. The area is an uneven patchwork of mainly low-nutrient miombo woodland (beautiful, but endlessly monotonous, and not good for game) and rich, open grassy dambos (also beautiful, very good for game but often on black-cotton soil—hard as rock in the dry and rapacious, sucking mud in the wet.)

Then, the distances seem vast. Between Livingstone, the Zambian town on the lip of the Victoria Falls, and the southern entrance to Kafue at Dumdumwese are some 230 kilometres. It took us four hours of steady driving. Another 129 kilometres lie between Dumdumwese and the central scout camp of Ngoma. That took another three hours. It is all hard driving, mostly on dirt roads which are often little more than tracks. We eventually arrived feeling thoroughly jolted and jarred, and coated with sweat, grass-seeds and muddy grime.

But it was beautiful. Zambia has roughly the same population as Malawi, though the country is nearly nine times bigger. The result is a landscape noticeably less stressed. The trees grow thick and tall, and though in the grip of a two-year drought, the bush looks glowingly green and lush. I had forgotten Zambia's magnificent skies. These are tall skies, piled high with voluptuous clouds of cream and pearl and silver, or weighted down with swollen angry thunder-heads that let down veils of rain like a bolt of cloth unrolling.

As we drove we watched purple sheets of rain envelop the distance, and grasslands toss like choppy seas. The wind stirred up dust wraiths in the road, which scurried ahead of us like startled animals. We saw very little game, but then miombo is notorious for that. We did have to do a thousand diversions to circumnavigate trees pushed over by elephants—a good sign, we felt. The elephants are why we are here. There are various attempts being made at finding a solution to elephant over-population in conservation areas, and our task is to establish a research camp at Ngoma to track the movements of elephants in this region, in the hope of finding the age-old elephant routes that have been severed by human intervention.

Everything has been tried, from culling to contraceptives to translocations, and they are all stressful for the elephants. Prof. Rudi van Aarde has been wrestling with the problem for years. The current research is an indication of a steadily widening vision, initially seeing elephants as the problem, to recognising that limited space is the problem. With the advent of the "Peace Parks" thrust, which aims to link adjacent conservation areas in neighbouring countries, there is a hope that the ancient elephant migration routes across southern Africa can be re-opened.

But where are these elephant paths? Do today's elephants remember them? There is still considerable travelling done by elephants, but without tracking individuals, there is no way of knowing where they go, or when. Rudi's project is an ambitious one, covering five countries, and supported by NGO's like International Fund for Animal Welfare (IFAW) and Conservation International (CI). Funding is crucial. A single radio-satellite collar for an elephant costs around US $ 6000[77], and that's a crumb compared to the costs of putting it on the elephant. Capture involves helicopters, a bevy of wildlife veterinary specialists, mobile ground crew, expensive drugs, and a base camp. Rudi plans to put radio collars onto twelve elephants in Kafue, six matriarchs and six bulls.

This is where Science and I come in. We're the advance troops to set up camp in Kafue, and then do the basic ground work—finding where the elephants are, and identifying a dozen likely animals for collaring. Neither of these tasks is easy in the wet season, but Science is so delighted to be out of a mainly cerebral advisory role and back into hands-on conservation, that he's breaking all his own rules about not going camping in the rains.

But so far, so good. We've had a couple of wet days, and our own little tropical-igloo tent has stayed dry and standing. Right now we're visiting Lusaka to load up with materials to build the base camp, so have brief access to e-mail. We head back to Kafue tomorrow at daybreak.

I've already had a glorious private viewing of a cheetah, and a startling face to face encounter with a young elephant bull which I'll tell you about in dribs and drabs, whenever I get access to power and telephone lines.

I'm revelling in running hot water and sleeping in a real bed—that's after just one week of roughing it in the bush. I wonder how I'll feel by the end of February when we come back to Lusaka for supplies. Till then, admire your clean fingernails, you have no idea how hard they are to achieve in Real Africa!

## Kafue National Park, Zambia
23rd February

We have set up our temporary camp in the lee of a termitarium thicket, overlooking a few last pools in the

---

[77] In 2003.

Nkala River. The water is the colour of milky coffee and is as warm as old bath water, but on the very first day we saw two of groups of elephants come to drink.

The first was a family of females with young, and later a band of five males arrived. These seemed intent on crossing below the pools, a course which would bring them right into our camp. Aware that we were hidden in the foliage, Science stepped out into the open to show himself. I remembered elephant researcher, Marion Gerai, saying that she sang to elephants, just so they would know where she was. So I sang.

They clearly didn't much care for the tune. They mulled about in group confusion. There was an uneasy flapping of ears and surreptitious curling of trunks to get a sniff of whatever was making this awful noise. They decided not to cross after all, and set off along the north bank, unhurried, but looking mildly miffed.

Perhaps the fellow who visited me in camp the next day was one of those five. He was a youngster, I guessed, and came scrounging the mango peels and tomato skins I'd stupidly tossed into the bushes. Biodegradable, no harm to the environment, I thought. I had even been careful not to toss any seeds into the scrub. Of course I had never for a moment thought of possible harm to me!

I was sitting in the shade of a bush washing clothes. I thought I heard an almost-noise behind me, and turned to peer over my shoulder. It took some seconds to see him. He was too close, too tall and too utterly astonishing. My mind refused to register him at all. Once I recognised that there was indeed an entire elephant within five metres of me, I did what we had done the day before. I walked out from behind the bush so that he could see me, greeted him politely and sang him a verse of my favourite hymn. Perhaps he recognised the tune from the day before, and found it less off-putting on a second hearing.

He eyed my quizzically, and came a step closer. I took a big step backwards and held out my arms.

"Thank you, brother, for the visit," I said, nervously, "And now, you must go," I concluded hopefully, and clapped my hands at him.

He was obviously offended at being shooed like a chicken, and shook his head at me, unfurling his ears and doing a little shuffling mock charge.

I had no confidence in the mock-ness of it at all. Those huge ears looked like the spread wings of the angel of death. I launched into the second verse with more fervour while taking refuge behind a Natal mahogany.

When I peeped out, he had come almost to the edge of our ground-sheet. He was watching me closely, absentmindedly pulling bunches of leaves off a *Peltophorum africanum* and putting them in his mouth. It reminded me of the way researchers pretend to be feeding to put gorillas at their ease.

Not being a gorilla, it didn't work for me. I stopped singing long enough to point out to him that there were hundreds of *Peltophorum* trees around, and to ask if he wouldn't please go and eat a little farther off.

He moved around my tree to keep me in sight, and idly munched a bunch of combretum leaves a mere trunk reach from me. By now I was standing on the top of our cold-box, wondering how to clear the gap between my head and the lowest branches.

I told him honestly that I was very small and he was very big and that the thudding he was listening to was simply my heart, and that it meant him no harm.

He leaned closer.

I abandoned the idea of climbing and scuttled round the tree like a bark spider. I peeped back to see him cautiously examining my bicycle.

While I told him what it was, and extolled its docile nature, he whiffled his trunk over the handle bars and the front wheel. For the first time since I saw him, he took his eyes off me.

The bike seemed to satisfy his curiosity completely. Slowly he turned his back and sauntered off. My voice wavered after him, saying thank you, and goodbye. I felt like a five-year-old waking from a bad dream, relieved, but still shaken by the inner blackness of fear.

It's been two weeks since that encounter. Despite having heard that a twelve-year-old boy was killed here by a lone elephant five months ago, I'm becoming a little less fearful. My large visitor is often seen among the parks' staff housing, and is ignored as the bushbuck are, tolerated like the ubiquitous vervet monkeys. In a month or two I might even feel very foolish about my fright. Yet, the Kafue elephants have a reputation for being a little irascible. And who can blame them? Last week, we are told, an employee of the local electricity provider was arrested, carrying an AK47 and a number of tusks. A load of Zambian ivory was discovered being smuggled through Malawi just before we left there last year.

Meanwhile, life under canvas is settling into a pleasant form of vague order. As Science says, our camp is more or less goat-shape. That's like sheep-shape but more intelligent. The rains are intermittent, without much dedication or drive, and serve to cool things off and damp-down the dust without being too much of a nuisance. We are more or less tethered to the site while the larger research camp is being erected, and most of the elephants have moved off after a couple of good showers. Once Science has the main camp sheep-shape, we start finding out where the elephants are.

I'm looking forward to exploring Kafue a little more. I have no way of knowing if my last newsletter got to you, or even if this one will. It's like sending a message in a bottle.

## Herro from Kafue.
### 28th February

It's a grey, miserable day. The magnificent Zambian sky, usually indigo with extravagant sculpted clouds, is a dull uniform pewter. Drifting across the dambo with the drizzle is a soft concurrence of doves, spiced with the brusk "aw-right!" of bee eaters. The squirrels, who entertained me so last week, nibbling grass seeds while hanging from a branch by their back feet, are nowhere to be seen. I picture them curled into a warm little knot, like kittens, eyes closed and paws folded against the grey damp.

I'm sitting in the Research Laboratory at Ngoma Camp. The paint is a mottled sunshine yellow, riven by cracked plaster and studded with gecko droppings and spider webs. Where the ceiling has pulled away from the walls a cascade of bat and rat droppings sift down to a dusty work surface. But beyond the cracked and grimy window a male bushbuck has just danced across the grass, sending up a scatter of small birds—two paradise widow birds and their retinues, the males flying like unsuccessful paper darts.

I don't think the lab has been used for actual research for an awfully long time. On a couple of shelves behind me, a dusty collection of specimen jars hold a depressing range of elderly bleached looking relics. A few snakes, an embryonic Lichtenstein's Hartebeest, a very large scorpion, others I can't identify from a distance. Beside a stained sink are the badly cleaned skulls of a young hippo and a large sable antelope. It's a fairly depressing place to be. But it's dry and there is power, so it suits me very well just now. Camping has its limitations in continuing wet.

Ngoma, once the best of Zambia's National Park rest camps, is little more than a clutter of dilapidated buildings. The old lodge stands empty, much of the roof missing, windows broken, the ornamental gates rusted and askew. The chalets form part of the staff housing now, and we're told that close on five hundred people live here, all park staff and their families. There is a primary school crammed with joyously noisy children, and an assortment of broken metal desks scattered around the grounds. The roads are muddy tracks that meander between buildings, and scattered throughout what is now called "the compound" are contented groups of bushbuck, the occasional elephant, and insolent hoards of vervet monkeys.

The atmosphere of grinding poverty and neglect are symptoms of all Africa's struggle for equilibrium. There is no money. No money to pay the staff, to keep the vehicles repaired and running, to equip the guards for effective anti-poaching patrols. Certainly no money to fix the roads and maintain the buildings. Even so, a patrol made contact with a group of poachers last week, and managed to arrest one and confiscated three weapons. I'm not prepared to scratch through the eternal depressing theories and gloomy predictions of wildlife's future in Africa—there is far more of interest to look at.

For instance, this problem of the monkeys. The vervets own Ngoma. They obviously know it, for they loll indolently wherever they please: on the hood of the geriatric tractor, on the door-steps of houses, in the road. You can see children playing and monkeys cavorting in the same bare patch of earth. Mostly the inhabitants have learned not to leave anything where the monkeys can get it, but that doesn't stop the monkeys from looking. They are wonderfully adept at raising pot-lids, opening boxes and unscrewing bottle tops.

They are as quick as lightening and utterly unafraid. A monkey will tolerate being chased, but only for a short distance. Then it will turn and chase the chaser, a sight which always provides the onlookers a great deal of merriment. For all its apparent innocence and fun, this interaction between monkeys and people has sinister undertones.

There are thought to be instances of diseases passed between wild monkeys and humans. The ebola virus, green monkey disease, and of course, AIDS. What troubles me more is the possibility of the reverse flow. I have been subjected to a couple of raids from the monkeys, and in the wild skirmishes that followed—me armed to the teeth with a hand-made wooden catapult and a small heap of stones—I noticed at least two monkeys with really nasty coughs. A lot of them have rough, staring coats, which seem to indicate ill-health. People should know better, but monkeys cannot possibly guard against human diseases.

So I arm my catty with a will—I'd much rather cause a few smarting bruises and have the monkeys give our camp a wide berth, than be subjected to their insistent, unwelcome presence. For their own good as much as mine. However, the last battle was won by the vervets. The piece old rubber tubing snapped and left me unarmed. Within seconds the monkeys realised their advantage and swarmed all over camp, fishing in our picnic basket, peering into pots, snatching at anything that might be munchable, and scuttling back up the trees to enjoy my frustrated rage.

In the end I retired to the tent, muttering darkly MacArthurish phrases, and buried myself in a book. No point in getting worked up about something you can do nothing about. When we get to Lusaka, I'm going to invest in some toy snakes. That may put them off until I can get my catty repaired.

Later:

These Lusaka trips happen once a month to replenish our supplies, and log on to our own email. Such a delight to find I am still in touch, and my letters have been going out—thank you for the reassurance. That pleasure is marginally eclipsed by the voluptuous indulgence of a hot bath.

Much to our profound surprise, the manager of the Lusaka Holiday Inn is a wildlife enthusiast, and he has made a room available for us with his compliments. Having never been much of a Holiday Inn fan, I have changed my mind entirely. This is the epitome of luxury, I cannot recommend it too highly. It even has a few young crocodiles in the fish-pond—just to add a bit of local colour.

It's still raining, though. The amazing thing about being under a roof is that you can stay dry and you don't track mud across everything!

I'll be firing off the odd blind missive into the ether from Kafue in a day or so, I hope. For all the glorious luxuries of urban living, Science and I can't wait to get back out to the peace and quiet of the gently dripping bush.

## Elephant Death
### 9ᵗʰ March

We returned to Kafue's Ngoma camp on Sunday, arms still smarting from anti-tetanus shots and dosed to the eyebrows with antibiotics. Both of us had succumbed to a degree of septicaemia in the heat and the damp, even the smallest scratch flaring up into an angry oozing wound. But in Lusaka, housed among friends, we rested, stayed dry, indulged in automated laundry, and set out for the damp outdoors refreshed and cheerful.

The day was beautiful. The sky rich with its towering burden of spectacular clouds, the breeze fresh and smelling like corn-silk, the green world rinsed and vivid with recent rain. The earth road glowing ruddy as sunburned skin, the flush reflected in the feathery tops of grasses on either side. We stopped once to check the tyre pressure. In the sudden silence bird song came pressing in, and the gentle clonking of wooden cow bells. This is Africa at her most disarming, when you're glad to be alive and aware of the unique privilege of being witness to all this wonder.

It is wise never to forget that Africa is a land of extremes. Between Musa Gate and Ngoma camp is a rutted winding road of some fifteen kilometres. Roughly half way between the two lay the corpse of an African grandmother.

We heard the story with growing horror. She and her granddaughter had been out gathering roots the previous afternoon, and had lost their way. After dark they stumbled onto the road and were making their way along it when they met an elephant. The grandchild fled back into the bush, but the old woman was not as agile.

I find it as hard to bring my mind to bear on this, as it was to force myself to look at that sad, slight mound. Her huddled remains had been covered by an earth coloured chitenge, transforming her into just another hummock in the haphazard surface of the road. From one end her slender feet protruded, folded together as if in sleep. A cloud of flies rose and fell above her. Two game guards waited with her for the police to come.

Yet the glimpse of her hidden remains was not the main horror for me. The real shock, the deep seething inner morass, centres on a kind of betrayal.

I must have been told as a child, for certainly I have known all my life, that wild creatures are not vindictive. Even spiders, despite my continuing mistrust, are not out to get me. Snakes I know are more fearful than fierce. Most wild animals would rather be unthreatened than attack.

Of course some animals will kill you. An old, toothless lion knows humans are easy prey. A leopard may kill because you're there and the opportunity presents itself. Hyenas will take a sleeping man without question. Crocodiles will grab at anything in the water on the off chance of a meal.

But cheetahs, like wolves, have never deliberately harmed a human. Neither have gorillas. And elephants, those huge, shambling, wise old pinnacles of motherly caring and family unity? Surely not! It can't have been just any elephant—which one was it that she met? In the brief half-light when colour bleeds from the landscape and suffuses the sky, when all the world is grey, how soon—or late—did she recognise that vaster, too-solid grey?

Was it that lone adolescent male who scared me in camp, outcast and angry? Or was it one of the anxious females that move in tight groups, protective of their little ones? How much threat can an elephant read in the short-sighted blundering of an old woman?

Just enough, it would seem, to lash out in fear, a quick swipe and a trample, just as I would react to a spider. Black fear cannot be made reasonable by daylight analysis. All the same, in the week it has taken me to worry my way through writing this down, I have come to realise that there is no betrayal. No matter how highly we regard creatures of the bush, they remain wild, and every wild animal knows that the most ruthless predator is man.

It doesn't matter which elephant it was. Viewed against the world's concern as we teeter on the brink of yet another cataclysmic war, what is the death of one barefooted old lady? Who was it who said, "One man's death diminishes us all"[78]? I can't remember. All I know is that this death has dimmed the veldt for me. It stands behind the graceful clumps of trees, and moves in the shudder of reeds in the rain-swollen river. It keens through the cry of hornbills and the moaning of doves.

And it is no help at all to recognise that it is not the death of this particular woman that haunts me, but my own. This is the reality I glimpsed a few weeks ago, this is my inner spinning vacuum made manifest.

Yet, nothing has changed. Ground-hornbills still usher in the new day with contemplative organ notes, rain still strings pearls onto the arched necks of tall grass stems, impala still stand to see us pass with daisy petal ears, or flash the little black hearts on their heels in their arabesques to safety. And I am privileged to be here.

## Anouska's charms
### 17th March

One of the unexpected pleasures of being on the edge of beyond is meeting the most unusual people. Here at Ngoma there is a group called Greenforce. No, they are not a bristle of angry eco-terrorists, but an effervescent cluster of gentle British enthusiasts, each of whom has paid a considerable amount of money to come out here, live like the locals, and

---

[78] John Donne, No Man is an Island, Meditation XVII

do some semi-scientific research for the sake of conservation.

The group's scientific advisor is a fragile looking Irish lass called Anouska. How did an Irish girl get a name that whispers of Siberian blizzards, troika bells and Cossack sword fights?

"Ah, well, me mother just liked the sound of it, is all," she throws over a nonchalant shoulder as she manhandles the elderly jeep through a brimming pot-hole big enough to be a swimming pool.

Dr Anouska Kinahan is fine boned, with an Irish lilt in her step and eyes that change from grey to khaki, depending on what she's wearing. And what she wears can be quite eye catching, in an off-hand, bush-bashing sort of way. Once she was having some difficulty with the police in the nearest town over regulations concerning the jeep. The police were simply trying to follow the President's dictum that all government departments must generate their own funds. Naturally, a mzungu has more free wealth to expend than the local watu, so it's politic to dream up a few extraneous fines.

Anouska was outraged. She complained at length to Science, who stood patiently hearing her out. When she finally ran out of steam, he commended her on her patience and unflappability, and ended by saying,

"Of course, it might help if you dressed more aggressively."

"Meaning what?" Anouska demanded.

"Well," said Science, running a critical eye over her shoe-string top, short bush shorts and sandaled feet, "Perhaps a little less like a teenager at a beach party?"

Anouska's glance followed his own. Then she looked up and beamed.

"Got ya! Fatigues and boots ya mean!"

All the same, she's enough her own woman to have tossed Science's advice into the out-basket together with her annoyance at the police.

Greenforce are the owners of the only satellite telephone in Ngoma. It's essentially for emergencies, but the volunteers need to have some contact with their families, and once a week a batch of e-mails go out, my newsletter with them. As I handed the disc with last week's letter to Anouska, I couldn't help noticing the leather thong around her neck. From it hung a large and rather tasteless charm, a mass-produced impression of an ornate hand-gun.

"A strange choice of jewellery for a conservationist," I remarked. Anouska laughed and explained that it was a gift from Gift, the young lad the Greenforce volunteers have sponsored through school this year.

"Sure and he bought it in Itezhi-tezhi yesterday," she sang, pronouncing the town's name the local way, Ee-tesh-tesh. "And I'm only glad he chose this one. The other is Osama Bin Laden. I'd rather put up with a gun than have Bin Laden around my neck!"

All of Anouska's dealings seem to have this balance of empathy tinged with amused resignation. A few days ago, one of Greenforce's Zambian counterparts, a shy, sensitive young man named Levy, ran foul of the compound's grouch. The grouch cursed him loudly, and declared that if Levy didn't leave Ngoma immediately, he and his family would suffer terribly. Levy rushed to Anouska, gabbling incoherently about a curse, and needing help to get himself and his belongings away, fast-fast.

Once she established what the problem was, Anouska calmly sat the distraught Levy down, and fetched a tiny teddy-bear from her room.

"Now, Levy," she instructed, "Do ya see this symbol here?" pointing to a shamrock on the bear's chest. Levy nodded.

"And do ya see it on the door to my room?" Again Levy nodded.

"Well," she continued comfortably, "That symbol is a charm my Grandmother gave me before I left Ireland. It is very, very powerful. And it is to keep away all the curses of Africa. So you just hang onto that," she said, pressing the pocket teddy into his hands, "and you'll never have to fear another curse, ever."

"Did it work?" I asked her. She replied with a twinkle, "Like a charm!"

## Another death
### 25th March

I've just come in from staring at the sky and my eyes are still dazzled by the bright clouds. It looks dim and gloomy in this roomy mess-tent that is now our general living area.

We moved from our lovable but damp bush camp into the two-tent splendour of the new research camp on Wednesday. It was a hard day, made harder by the stresses of the previous night.

Tuesday saw us lugging bits of kit from one site to the other, like a very small colony of ants with a large family of grubs. Science and I were standing admiring his handiwork at the new site, when Prince, his foreman, appeared.

"Suh," he called with a wide grin, "You have a visitor to the old camp. A little elephant."

"How little?" asked Science, while I pictured my huge friend of some weeks before. Prince patted the empty air beside his hip.

"About so big," he announced.

"And the mother?" asked Science.

"No mother. He is alone."

By the time we had covered the odd 200 metres between the camps, the elephant had vanished into the bush. Prince insisted that it was alone, and Greenforce had seen a very small elephant the previous day that appeared to be alone. But since tampering with little elephants is a sure-fire way of annoying some large elephant probably close by, they were sensible enough to leave it well alone.

We didn't. All six of us—Science, me, Prince and his three labourers—combed the scrub until we found it, a scrawny dust-grey shape plodding doggedly through the bush. He was still young enough to have a lot of hair on his forehead and back, looking rusty red in the mid-morning sun. It reminded me of children with kwashiorkor. He would stop every few steps, tug at anything with his trunk, and push it into his mouth, but it seemed to fall out at once, as if he was too tired to chew, or even close his mouth.

There is no way of knowing what tragedy separated him from his mother, but it was obvious he'd been alone for some time, three or four days, Science guessed. He estimated its age to be around nine months to a year, and not fully weaned. Its hip bones jutted, and each rib and knot of its spinal ridge was painfully clear.

The thing one should do, in a case like this, is nothing at all. There are always many infant mortalities in the wild, and to a great extent the cycle of life depends on it. The weak, the sick, and the babies are the fuel that keeps lions and wild dogs alive and well, and all the other wonderfully romantic predators that earn tourist dollars for Africa. One creature's death is a means of another creature's survival. The supreme rule is "Do Not Interfere."

But this desolate little creature was within earshot of a village of 500 people, all of them well aware of the lethal potential of elephants. His last minutes would be filled with noise and terror. So we broke the rule. Two of the labourers were assigned to quietly stay with him, and make sure he stayed out of trouble.

Greenforce have an ex-member running a wildlife orphanage called Munda Wanga, near Lusaka, and wheels were set in motion. But Lusaka is eight hours away from Kafue, and by mid-afternoon the little calf was weakening. We stayed with him, rigging up a makeshift shelter to keep the sun off him when he finally collapsed.

Poor helpless one. He went through phases of blessed unconsciousness, when his eyes closed and his breathing was slow and steady. Then he'd wake, and his wide frightened eye would blink with difficulty. There were seizures of some kind, stretching his back, arching his neck, making his legs rigid. Then he'd gasp for breath, a heaving wet sound. And he'd call, that deep rumbling flutter like a sub-sonic purr.

Science murmured, "We'll be in real trouble if he manages to call that aberrant mother of his."

All the same, I wished she would come. I tried answering his call with a purr of my own, and gentled him as best I could. I like to think it helped, but of course I can't know. He was too ill to do more than lie there, drifting between sleep and pain.

By nine thirty the Munda Wanga fellow arrived, with two assistants and a para-medic. In the moonlight they set up an intravenous drip, and turned the little fellow over to make him more comfortable. We worked past midnight, but at last the effort of breathing was just too much. As the elephant child slipped away, he took our energy with him. For each of us was left with an emptiness and deep fatigue that felt like failure.

So he gained his freedom. It's not life that is precious, but freedom from pain, freedom from fear. If he had lived, he would be in captivity all his life. If really fortunate, he'd be domesticated, valued and useful, and pampered as an asset. But the fact is that he would be raised by a series of alien foster parents in what used to be a Zambian Zoo. He would have concrete under his feet and noisy children being carelessly brutal as children are everywhere.

While we moved the last of our kit the next morning, Science and a couple of game guards took the little body out beyond the village area, and left it where it should be, in beautiful unspoilt bush and available to scavengers. So I've been watching the sky, waiting for the vultures.

And they've come, just as they should. They are wheeling in a high graceful arc, turning like corn husks in a dust devil. Lappetfaced, white backed, and even hooded vultures, I've not seen them before. It's good to see the majesty of so many vultures wheeling in the tall sky, it's a sight that has become increasingly rare in southern Africa. I watched as the spiral gradually slipped away, one bird after another hunching its wings for the rapid descent. And it's good to know the little one has gone home as he should.

So I'm sitting in the new spacious camp, with the laptop running on electricity, blinking in the dim light and puzzling about something Science told me. He went back at first light to the spot below the tall terminalia tree where the elephant calf died, and found that the corpse had been visited in the night. There were elephant tracks over our own, and scuff marks made by elephant feet, trying to nudge the little fellow into getting up. Blown sand had been scattered over the little body.

It's pointless trying to speculate. We make so many mistakes about wildlife by giving them motives that are entirely human, as if we are the ultimate touchstone of wisdom and understanding. We know as little about the minds of the wild as we know of the mind of God. Perhaps that's as it should be. Life without mystery would not be worth examining.

## Farewell to Zambia
### 8th April

Hello from Ngoma, for the last time.

Time, they say, flies when you're having fun. If that is so, then we must have a whole lot more fun as adults than as children. I can remember when a month was an eternity. Now it's over before it has even begun, and three have been swallowed up in what seems a single gulp.

Our phase of the project is over, and it's time to leave Ngoma. Science and I both have very mixed feelings. Yes, we're torn at having to leave this glorious tract of vast wild space, there is still so much to explore and experience. But it has been a hard time, both physically and emotionally.

The new research camp stands ready for use, the mess-tent as monkey proof as we can get it, which is "not very"; two working bathrooms with open-air showers and long-drop loos, electricity and a fridge (staggering advance, that; can't believe camping could be so stress-free!) And even piped water—if the Parks' authority manages to get the bore-hole pump going again, it's been out of action for more than a month.

Watching this camp going up has made me a little possessive of it, and it's hard to have to leave it to others, even though that was always the object. But I've learned that advances in living standards are not without a cost. The mess-tent provides an all-weather shelter, with electricity for kettles, freezers, toasters, laptops... but you are cut off from the gorgeous view of the elephants' favourite bathing pool, and the leafy canopy above, with its constant traffic of glossy starlings, bee-eaters, hornbills, and the occasional yellow-fronted tinker barbet. You can't feel the soft touch of a breeze stir your hair, or see butterflies flicker among the shadows like multi-coloured flames.

I once spent a lot of time worrying about what was "good" art, and what was simply a matter of taste. I finally came to the conclusion that really great art is what you carry away with you in your mind's eye. It's as if an outstanding work leaves an imprint in the mind, as the sun does on the retina. Magnificent places are like that, too. Science and I will carry Kafue away with us, tied to our minds eye by our heart-strings.

The dazzling green of a grassy dambo as we walked slowly behind a group of ground hornbills, feeling our very insides shimmer to their booming call, like being in the organ loft of a great cathedral.

The massive ant-hill like an ancient temple, overgrown with vast combretums, knotted fig trees and a single soaring apple-leaf with a ghostly pale trunk. Beneath their gnarled roots is a worn cave, carved from the ant-heap by elephants. Drawn by the mineral-rich clay brought to the surface by the termites decades or even centuries ago, generations of elephants have come to this spot, scuffing with their blunt feet, scooping with soft trunks, prying with tusks; now the roots that are too solid to tear away have been polished to a high gloss by hundreds of elephants rubbing against them as they lean in to reach the receding clay wall.

Sitting on the roof-rack to see over the shoulder-high grass, watching a pair of saddle-billed storks pick their stately way around a pan, their lunatic bills marked in scarlet and yellow and black, and delighting in the whimsy of the wild.

The constant running battles with the vervet monkeys, and the repeated hurried repairs to our hand-made catty. Science saying,

"When they're not thieving, they are so entertaining. Only a few are thugs, the rest are just hanging out. I feel like a lout taking pot-shots at them."

The sight of close on a hundred elephants, moving across a vista of marshy grassland rimmed by miombo, their grey backs like the slowly heaving hulls of boats, upside down on a sea of golden green.

The night sounds—a desultory tinkle of frogs, like bamboo wind chimes; the gut shuddering call of lions through the starlit bush; a bushbuck's single dog-like bark; the splash and burble of a midnight elephant bathing party; a lone hyena's distant whoop; the mad distorted elephant yell, distressing in its strangeness. The nights were velvety, even in the rain, and full of inexplicable grunts, squeaks and small furry sounds. Sometimes there would be the hysterical call of a pearl-spotted owlet, or the subdued "krupp" of Scops owl; almost always the nervous puffing of impala, and far away the fiery-necked nightjar repeating his litany, "Good Lord, deliver us."

We'll remember, too, the serene patch of bush enclosed by stands of stately trees, backed by a rising termite mound and graced with a small pool, that Science chose as the elephants' child's final resting place.

As much as we take Kafue away with us, we'll be leaving part of ourselves here. Not in the physical relic of the research camp, but in our continuing wonder at the landscape and all things that shape it, from weeds to weather, from termites to elephants. But it's time to leave, and endings are only beginnings seen from the other side. We need to get home.

# A Story for Carol
## February 04

*Ageing is an irksome thing. Especially for us women. Along with the knees that stiffen a little, the hands that gradually loose a bit of grip, and the back that will neither bend nor unbend as it used to, there is the whole gamut of visual pleasures that fade, chiefly our pleasure in our view of self. Standing before a mirror eyeing skin once satin now more like crépe, and hair no longer rich and full but heading towards being fine and colourless, one can't help thinking: is this all? Is this a worthy final metamorphosis? What happened to my energy and drive? Life's marks are clear on me. Have I left marks on Life?*

We came back from a frustrating afternoon in Itechitechi. The little sawmill was closed, the hardwood planks needed for the camp we were building were simply not available. The electricity had been down, so no ice could be bought to replenish our cold box. Few fresh vegetables were on sale, a few wilted onions, a couple of over-ripe tomatoes, and not a single banana for love nor money. No eggs? Ah no, sorry for that. Maybe tomorrow.

The road back into Kafue National Park seemed longer and more potholed than ever. Even with the windows wide open our clothes stuck to our skin in the heat. Tsetse flies swarmed in, seeming more persistent and fiercer than usual. Jolting over ruts and lurching through mud puddles, hair glued to our foreheads, we saw the unexpected hunched shapes of vultures in the road ahead. Crops distended, they lurched awkwardly into the air at our approach. One was so over-stuffed it just kept staggering on down the road, wings hopefully extended, but not a chance of getting air-borne.

As we stopped the sickening stench of death filled the cab. Science walked into the thicket beside the road, sending up another scatter of vultures and marabou storks. He came back with a face soured by the sight of an elephant carcass, tusks hacked off, not ten metres from the road. And this within five kilometres of Ngoma Camp—the Southern Headquarters for Zambia's Kafue National Park.

We drove into Ngoma in a silence as thick as the heat. Anger at a slip-shod management system that could allow poaching within earshot of the camp choked us. Ngoma itself is like a slum. The once graceful lodge is a roofless, derelict shell. Every chalet is occupied by staff, or family of staff. Almost every window is broken, some have sheets of beaten tin to keep out the rain and the monkeys. Where a road has become impassable, a new track simply goes around it. Paint work is peeling; power lines hang askew, the poles leaning drunkenly. The camp water-tank leaks, but only when there is water. That hasn't been for a few weeks, since the bore-hole pump broke down. The camp houses some five hundred souls, and there is no running water. Frustration at Africa's inability to cope with simple maintenance enfolded us in a cloying depression.

No sooner had we stopped than a voice hailed us.

"Herro!" called the assistant warden.

"We have been watching for you. Please, there is a woman, she is sick. She must go to Itechitechi hospital, and we have no vehicle."

"You have vehicles," Science objected, "Why don't you use one of the Park's land cruisers?"

"Ah, no. One is out taking a patrol to the drop-off point, the other is broken. This is the only vehicle available."

Science and I looked at each other, our eyes full of resentment and helpless annoyance. Resignedly I refilled our water bottles as Science asked about the woman. She had been delivered of a healthy baby early in the morning, he was told, but the after-birth refused to come free. With sunset on its way, she needed to be seen by a doctor, and soon.

We emptied the back of the pick-up, and laid down a couple of camping matresses and a few blankets, a futile attempt to make the trip comfortable for her. And in silence we drove round to the little clinic.

Ngoma clinic is a surprise. It is the one building that has a fresh coat of paint. The windows have been cleaned, and curtains hang behind the glass. The assistant warden had walked ahead of us, and stood with a little knot of women at the door. An older woman from the group came towards us with a smile. She took my hands and squeezed them.

"Thank you," she said, "Thank you for coming. There is no need. The mother is fine."

"The placenta...?"

"It has come away," She smiled again, and with pride.

"The mother is resting well."

Our selfish relief was obvious, and mistaken by the midwife as concern for her patient.

"Wait," she instructed, and bustled indoors, reappearing with a tiny bundle in her arms. As I moved a fold of cloth aside to peer into the clenched little face, puckered and pouched and utterly beautiful, she asked,

"What is your name?" I answered automatically, lost in contemplation of that small, entire world in her arms.

"Zendi," she repeated after me. "Her name will be Zendi."

We drove away in a different silence. Carol, I thought. I should have said "Carol".

Carol, a trained nurse, was the girl who started that clinic, back in the 1960s. Her husband was the biologist at Ngoma, John Hanks. John's research laboratory is still there. The sink is full of bat droppings, the plug-hole housing a large skink, like a miniature crocodile. The floor and walls are veined with termite runnels, and a few dusty shelves support a ragged collection of bottles: a tangle of pale snakes, a bleached-looking scorpion, a hartebeest embryo suspended in cloudy fluid.

John has made quite a mark in conservation circles in southern Africa, and indeed around the world. Carol brought up their children, ran a beautiful home, stayed behind while John toured the world to meet with princes and presidents. Most people involved in conservation know the name Dr John Hanks.

But there is a girl child growing up in Zambia's largest wildlife park who goes by the name of Zendi. She, like many others, owes her life and the life of her mother, to Carol Hanks. Very few know her name, but the clinic Carol built is still there, clean and fully functional in the tropical mud.

*Happy birthday, Carol. You have left your mark on Life, and it is wonderful.*


## Hello from the Wild Frontier
### 13th August 2003

There have been the odd mutters from around and about, suggesting that there's been very little news from me of late. Sorry for that, as the Malawians taught me to say. It's been a fairly eventful time inwardly, the kind of internal adventure which seems fairly dull when written out. But it went something like this...

Our brief stay in Zambia's Kafue National Park was a fairly potent catalyst in our lives. I knew it would be pivotal in some way, but—as is my dramatic wont—I saw it in terms of life and death. Reality intended something far less extreme, but almost as fundamental. It brought home to Science and I that really roughing it in the bush is no longer the easy adventure it would have been ten years ago. This has nothing to do with the bush, or with the level of ruggedness, we revelled in both. It has everything to do with our own physical resilience.

For me, this has been particularly hard to accept. Like training for the ballet all one's life, landing a leading role at the Bolshoi, and then discovering that your toes won't take it. Not much you can do about it, except find a way to keep dancing that doesn't feel like second best. That takes lots of mental spade work.

One of the shards of comfort unearthed in the shovelling was the realization that we are at last ready to find a home of our own. Great. But where? We compiled list after list of our requirements, personal and joint, and reviewed and eliminated town after town. This sounds very logical and easy, but it's remarkably hard to select where you want to live. It's easy to make your home where your employment dictates, but to "find a place that feels like home" is unnervingly tough. What happens if you make a choice, and find you don't like it? Who do you blame when things go wrong?

Besides, employment is still essential. So, where do we want to live that provides opportunities for both a wordsmith and a consultant wildlife ecologist? Somewhere out in the bush that's still close to town, obviously.

If you're determined enough, you can actually find what you're looking for. Science and I packed up our stuff yet again, and headed north-east towards the Mozambique border. Tucked under the northern mountains of Swaziland is a small town called Barberton. It looks out over a sweet green valley seemingly enclosed by serried ranks of rocky hills and rising mountains which enfold the newer city of Nelspruit, the gateway to the Kruger National Park. Barberton is an old mining town with a small community, about an hour from an international airport, and three to four hours from Pretoria and Johannesburg.

We arrived in Barberton, and moved into rented lodgings in the middle of July. Practice doesn't make moving any easier. I still don't know where we packed the kettle, and am still irritated at being separated from my reference books. Close to, the little town of Barberton is shabby and sad. A new shopping centre with all the desired amenities like chain stores and supermarkets opened recently, effectively killing off the little businesses in the main street, so urban rot is setting in. Our spirits sank as we scratched among numerous boxes for our essentials—the chopping knife, the bread recipe, the medicine box. House hunt? I don't think so!

Then Science met a fellow called Nico Oosthuizen, who offered to show us around the Mountainlands Nature Reserve. Within twenty minutes we were in country that seemed a million miles from anyone. Mountains crowd around, sheltering rich green kloofs echoing the whisper of water, and rustling with wings. Rolling hills provide grasslands for zebra and eland, mountain reedbuck and perhaps even oribi. Tall aloes blaze with flowers, coral trees scatter scarlet embers among the white dombeyas. It's a wonderland of rugged terrain, changing scenery and diverse vegetation. It's the second most important plant biodiversity area after the Cape Fynbos.

Ironically, the joy of it is that it's not pristine. The gold rush that established Barberton in the 1880s has left a spider web of tracks across these almost impassable hills—roads cut across frighteningly steep inclines, wide enough to take a pair of donkeys or a couple of oxen. Roads that today would be prohibitively expensive to build—besides, no-one in their right mind would allow that much disturbance to the area today. These old roads make it accessible to hikers, horses and four-wheel drive. It's earmarked for adventure tourism, and is still in the opening phases of development. This is, we are told, Mpumalanga Province's Wild Frontier for ecotourism.

Driving back after a blissful afternoon, our hair stiff with dust and our eyes shining, we found Barberton at its charming best. A scatter of houses under tall trees backed by steeply rising ground, all tinted golden in the sinking light. Across the valley the evening thickened to smoke blue and the far mountains rose like fragments of gauze below a heavy orange sun. Flat topped thorn trees and occasional palms framed the view.

Yes, we thought. We've found it. This is home.

I think there is some kind of universal law, like gravity, that ensures that nothing much happens until the human heart is committed. Within two days of recognizing that we have made the right choice, I have been inundated with work. So this is snatched between more weighty stuff, but there is so much to tell you about the quaint little town, its rich past and astounding natural assets. I will try to put it down in digestible bites, and at least this is a beginning.

# Acknowledgments

Astonishing to realize that Science and I have been in Barberton now for sixteen years, it's the longest period either of us have spent in one place.

The reasons are multiple. For a start the morning bird calls are familiar, though the local Heuglin's robin doesn't demand the attention of Mr Piri, but calls instead for Mrs. Sip Sissy, adding random syllables in a fading and uncertain way. Our garden trees still have visiting turacos, mostly the purple crested, with a call that's growlier than Schallow's. Forked-tailed drongo is here, and though we don't have the pearl-spotted owlet, we do have woodland and brown hooded kingfishers, and when we're really lucky we spot the tiny African pygmy kingfisher or the elusive Narina trogon. The fierey-necked nightjar blesses us with his litany through the dark hours, and I have the added delight of evesdropping on the midnight conversations of fruit-bats, who have delightfully expressive and varied communication. In the last week I've been thrilled to find not only trumpeter hornbills, but also—for the first time—green pigeons in our wild-fig tree.

The rumpled beauty of this all but enclosed bowl of isolated lowveld is a blessing in its own right, and the continual pleasure of lifting ones eyes to the hills unfailingly lifts the heart also. Added to the beauty of the landscape is the suppressed excitement of the stories contained within the the rocks of these ancient hills. They have bewitched Science completely. He is no longer a wildlife ecologist, but a wildly excited and utterly dedicated student of the ecology of the early-earth; on the brink of retirement, he has a new career, a new depth of delighted discovery. Suddenly, I'm married to a geologist, and I'm finding the transition a little difficult. We visualise things in different time-dimensions now; I lack both a scientific background and a comfortable relationship with numbers, so I cannot fathom chemical analysis nor mega-millenia. The rocks that fill his mind with delight and wonder offer me a closed door. Perhaps in time I will discover a key. Or at least an open window.

So firstly, thanks to Barberton, which has supplied us with all that we need to keep us usefully busy and intellectually engaged. Pivotal has been the friendship of Nico and Delia Oosthuizen of Mountainlands, who gave us the freedom to roam their own patch of paradise; thank you to you both.

Thanks to Dr Alan Kemp, who at the time these stories were written was head curator of the Bird Department of the Transvaal Museum (now Ditsong Museum of Natural History) for his generally amused advice, and to Dr Carl J Vernon, ornithologist and naturalist of East London, both of whom generously spent time answering my questions.

Thanks again to my family for hoarding my blogs as they came out, and special thanks to Shelagh Nation and Craig Inch, my editors. Finally, to Science, who, despite having rocks in his head, is still my starting point and my completion.

*Soli Deo Gloria*